no words for this

Ali Mau

no words for this

A memoir

HarperCollinsPublishers

If this book raises any issues for you or someone you love, you can contact the Lifeline helpline (0800 543 354), Need to Talk? (1737) or visit www.outline.org.nz or www.iamhope.org.nz.

HarperCollins*Publishers*
Australia • Brazil • Canada • France • Germany • Holland • India
Italy • Japan • Mexico • New Zealand • Poland • Spain • Sweden
Switzerland • United Kingdom • United States of America

First published in 2025
by HarperCollins*Publishers* (New Zealand) Limited
Unit D1, 63 Apollo Drive, Rosedale, Auckland 0632, New Zealand
harpercollins.co.nz

Copyright © Alison Mau 2025

Alison Mau asserts the moral right to be identified as the author of this work. This work is copyright. All rights reserved. No part of this publication may be reproduced, copied, scanned, stored in a retrieval system, recorded, or transmitted, in any form or by any means, without the prior written permission of the publisher. Without limiting the author's and publisher's exclusive rights, any unauthorised use of this publication to train generative artificial intelligence (AI) technologies is expressly prohibited. HarperCollins also exercises its rights under Article 4(3) of the Digital Single Market Directive 2019/790 and expressly reserves this publication from the text and data-mining exception.

A catalogue record for this book is available from the National Library of New Zealand

ISBN 978 1 7755 4253 7 (paperback)
ISBN 978 1 7754 9284 9 (ebook)
ISBN 978 1 4607 3005 8 (audiobook)

Cover design by Michelle Zaiter, HarperCollins Design Studio
Cover image © Stuff Limited
Printed and bound in Australia by McPherson's Printing Group

For the survivors

Prologue

In my family, we never talked about the past. Through all the years of raucous compulsory Sunday dinners, there were no retellings of family history and no colourful descriptions of our grandparents or their parents. There were only snippets of insight into our parents' lives before we three sisters were old enough to form our own memories. I have sat with other clans while they reminisce about family celebrations and what an aunty did that one Christmas, and I've done my best to contribute – to feel the warmth of memories plucked from their treasury, held up to the light and cherished. But in those moments I've felt disoriented and out of place. Perhaps my family are not so unusual, though; perhaps there are plenty of others that have only fleeting impressions of the past.

The family photo albums, filled with images of us as children in the 1960s, 70s and 80s, have helped me piece together some of the fragments over the years. When I was eighteen months old and my sister Lisa was three, our mother took us, alone, back to England for a holiday with her parents. In the mid-1960s there was no jet travel for people of extremely modest means, so we went by sea. For six rolling weeks my mother wrangled two toddlers on her own. She dealt with Lisa's freakouts at the toilet water that sloshed almost up to the rim, and she hauled us to the ship's surgeon when, a day out from the first stop in Auckland, we both stopped eating altogether. He advised Mum not to worry too much: Vegemite toast would get us through.

In photos from our stay at Mum's parents' home in rural Somerset, Lisa and I are dressed like the young Princess Anne in A-line buttoned woollen coats and white ankle socks, our hands held firmly by our grandmother Alice. There is a striking dissimilitude between those perfectly dressed little girls and their slightly wild selves in shorts and T-shirts back at home in Melbourne. We stayed for nine months.

On a visit to Melbourne thirty years later, I was sitting with Mum on the faux-leather couch in the living room, leafing through her photo albums, when I came across those small square black-and-white snaps. An epiphany: why would a young mother take two tiny children on such a voyage on her own and stay such a long time if it was simply a holiday?

'Mum,' I said, turning to her, 'you were leaving him, weren't you?'

Her expression was unreadable. She sighed and said, 'Oh, Alison,' her go-to response when I ask awkward questions. There was a long pause while she searched for the words. 'My mother told me I had made the decision to marry your father, so that was what I was saddled with. She told me I had no choice but to go back.'

I struggled to understand this. It didn't match the image of

Nanny Alice I'd been spoon-fed all my life: a cuddly, unthreatening Mother Christmas of a woman who loved her daughter above all else. Mum adored her back. She must have been crushed. But then that compliant good girl she'd always been took over, and she quietly accepted the inevitable – with one final card to play. Refusing even to contemplate another sea voyage, she insisted we would only return by plane. The nine months of the visit elapsed while my father saved the money for our fares.

So, not a holiday, but a failed escape attempt. The happy story I'd believed all my life was a family legend with just enough detail changed to protect me from exposure to the truth.

I shook my head at myself, astounded I hadn't worked it out earlier – but that's the thing with family lore, isn't it? The things you're told when very young become part of your belief system; you don't ever think to challenge them.

Then I looked up at her face, without a line even in her sixties and so, so desperately dear. I thought of the powerlessness she must have felt, supplicant in front of her own mother, begging for help. It took my breath away.

No, my family never really talked about the past, but it reverberated between us. And when another truth finally did come out, there was chaos.

1.

For most of my life, I believed my first memory was of watching the Apollo 11 astronauts land on the moon. I was four in 1969, so my belief was feasible, and there's no doubt I saw the grainy black-and-white footage of Neil Armstrong stepping onto the lunar surface at the same moment the rest of Australia did. The living room was packed with adults marvelling at the extraordinary sight, nudging us kids and saying, 'Well, will you look at that?'

Only, this is not *my* memory. I worked that out absurdly late, just a decade or so ago, when out of boredom or curiosity I googled 'moon landing au'. I found that Armstrong had stepped out at 12.56 pm AEST. My memory is of being woken up to see the previously unthinkable moment, but I was only months from my fifth birthday, so I would have been way too old for naps. The interior of the house where the memory takes place is also wrong: my family moved in two years later.

My childhood is a sea fog punctuated by beacons of memory. Everything in and around those moments is brightly lit and heavy with sound, smell, taste and feeling, and everything else is mist.

My real first memory is of stumping along behind my father in another sort of lunar landscape, one of dust and boulders and stubby bushes. I was five, gum-booted and wrapped in corduroy and Shetland wool, with no hat despite the cold of the early morning. A line of men in drab clothing, ammunition belts slung around their waists, moved across the landscape in loose formation. The dogs were out in front, crisscrossing the volcanic rock and tufts of grass, weaving tracks in the dirt that looked like stretched hourglasses. Dad's long limbs ate up the ground much faster than mine, so I had to half walk, half jog on stiff legs to keep up. He had his shotgun in the crook of his arm as he directed our German shorthaired pointer, Schultz, sometimes in German and sometimes in English, to seek, sit or fetch.

Every few minutes, as they appeared and disappeared through the wisps of mist that clung to the scrub, our prey would break from behind the outcrops of pocked volcanic rock, racing for safety. With smooth, practised ease, the hunter closest would raise his rifle and aim. To me, there was never any discernible time between aim and echoing boom.

I had a victim grasped in each inadequate fist, the rabbits almost longer than I was tall. After a while I noticed one of them was, unfortunately, not yet deceased. I gripped tighter, worrying the animal would get away and lower the count.

I wasn't supposed to go anywhere even close to the line, and Dad was focused on the mounds of rock ahead, any of which might be hiding bunnies – but if I lost one he'd shot …

I caught up to him and tapped awkwardly on his leg. 'Daddy.'

'What?' He kept his eyes up, still scanning the rise for movement.

'This one's not dead.' I raised my left hand a few inches to show him the heavy rabbit.

He stopped then and gave the squirming creature his full attention. There was a pause as he looked down at me, his face briefly blocking out the watery sunlight. 'Well, bash its head against a rock.' His tone was dismissive, and he turned back to the horizon.

Chastened but obedient, I did as I was told. The task was grisly, and it wasn't easy given my size, but I didn't ask twice.

Sometime later – it might have been the same day – Dad taught me how to skin and gut the rabbits, guiding my hands on a huge hunting knife. 'There ya go, just like a zip,' he said with satisfaction, while I tried not to vomit. Its skin came off with difficulty, the sclera hanging on at the tricky bits, and the flesh was shockingly pink and slick; there wasn't much blood, though, for which I was grateful. The rabbit seemed much smaller without its mottled grey-and-brown covering, skinny and sinewy. The worst part was the removal of its innards – Dad was stern about the possibility of ruining the animal for eating if I nicked the bladder or intestine. Once the incision was made, I turned my head away as he flicked the disgusting, foul-smelling contents out onto the dirt.

Dad wiped a blood-covered thumb across my forehead, a ritual showing I'd achieved the first step in my outdoor education. The other hunters laughed and congratulated me.

Rabbit-hunting trips with Dad and his mates were semi-regular outings for Lisa and me, summer and winter. The drive to the Western District took a dog's age. From Geelong we'd travel west to

Colac, then on and on towards Warrnambool, a breezy two-hour trip these days but twice that back then. Often the journey would break at homesteads where the wife of the household would fix us toast and jam for breakfast; once, Lisa was so cold from the trip she was given a sheepskin coat to wear, and she paraded round like a queen all weekend.

Accommodations at our destination were basic, usually in the shearing shed of whichever landowner had allowed the shooting crew to help get their rabbit plague under control. 'You girls sleep there.' Dad would point to the skirtings bay, a pen of feet-deep shearing offcuts that acted as a bouncy mattress if you could stand the smell of lanolin and dung. We'd climb in, a coat thrown over us for warmth, and listen to the men spinning yarns into the night, our vocabulary of swear words expanding with each trip.

Out in the field, the task of hauling some of the loot fell to me and Lisa. There were sometimes other children with us at the hunts, trailing the men at a respectful distance, but no women. If the trip was a weekend stay, and if the wives were permitted to come, they would be back at the campsite setting up the grill and the sleeping quarters.

The rules around guns were drummed into us sisters. At home, the weapons were locked away in a Dad-made gun cabinet mounted on the living-room wall. Every time they were brought out for cleaning, he would repeat a story that began to haunt my dreams, one of a sports-shooting friend who had blown his head off with a rifle he hadn't checked for ammo before beginning the breakdown process. Suitably freaked out but still wanting in on the action, I nagged Dad for years before he finally allowed me to handle one.

Although Lisa and I went on quite a few of Dad's hunting trips over the years, they sometimes had a haphazard feel, as if we had been included at the last minute and not without an argument. I suspect they were an opportunity for Mum to have a couple of days free from domestic slavery; I picture her settling back into bed with a grateful sigh after our 4 am departure, the instant the tail-lights of the Holden Kingswood disappeared in the pre-dawn gloom. Revelling in the quiet, she probably spent the whole next day with her feet up on the patchwork leather pouf in the living room, a book, a cup of tea and a shortbread biscuit at hand.

***

Our mother seems as close as you'll get to sainthood, a dedicated maternal figure who cared for us and loved us to bits (and still does). But, but – despite the love and advice, the cooking, sewing and sacrifices, our mother did not protect me and Lisa. I've long wondered whether that was a choice she had to make at some crucial moment: turn her life upside down to save her two eldest daughters, or stay quiet. Perhaps it wasn't that she wouldn't, but that she couldn't.

By the time Lisa and I came along in the mid-1960s, this loveliest of English roses had experienced a harrowing, lonely and confusing few years in a country she loathed, a long, long way from home.

Maureen Prosser was born in the Somerset market village of Frome in 1936. Five years after her older brother Derek was born, her parents Alice and Reginald Prosser had a girl to make a matched pair. She was given no middle name at all because her mother, Alice Matilda Burbage Buddon Prosser, so loathed her unwieldy handle that she refused to saddle her daughter with anything like it.

My mother's first memories were of Luftwaffe bombers screaming overhead as they tore towards targets in Bristol and South Wales in the Blitz. Photos from her youth show her as an exquisitely pretty, pale, hazel-eyed child with thick dark hair styled in the fashionable finger waves of the time. A shy smile hid somewhat crooked teeth. At age eleven, she was packed off to elocution lessons to banish her West Country burr and replace it with the received pronunciation of the English toff. Derek, because he was a boy, was not required to make the same change; from then on, family dinners had an oddness about them, with an adolescent Maureen speaking like the princesses and everyone else at the table purring their 'ooh-errs' and 'me 'andsomes'. It marked her out as different within her own family, but even after sixty years in Australia that accent remains unsullied.

She went to Sunny Hill School for Girls in nearby Bruton, then moved up to London in her early twenties to work at a bank in the heart of Marylebone. When I was young, Dad liked to tell us she was the first-ever female bank teller at the Westminster Bank in Harley Street. I was enormously proud – what a pioneer for equality she'd been!

Not so many years ago, I brought it up at a family dinner. 'You were a trailblazer, Mum.'

'Oh, I don't know about that. What do you mean?'

'You know, the first woman teller to work at the bank!'

Mum shot Dad a pointed look across the table – no one delivers a look like that quite like my mother. She turned back to me, stifling a laugh. 'No, darling. I was the first teller on the right as you came in the door.'

I was floored, thinking of all the people I'd told, how I'd believed my mother was at the vanguard of women's liberation in the 1960s, pushing boundaries left and right. 'Dad! How could you?'

He was completely unrepentant, laughing like a kookaburra at how well he'd pulled off his bit of mischief.

Mum has always said she was born just a few years too soon to suit the times. However beautiful, when she reached her teens the iconic female form in popular culture was that of Marilyn Monroe, curve-hipped and busty in pointy brassieres. My mother was the opposite: rail thin, flat-chested, pearl-skinned and delicate. By the time Twiggy and Jean Shrimpton seized the zeitgeist in swinging 60s London, Mum had missed the style train and was heading down the aisle.

In 1961, a friend – a dashing cruise line captain – had invited her to a flat party in Kensington with matchmaking in mind. 'Maureen, I'd like to introduce you to Leigh. He's a journalist from Melbourne, working on Fleet Street.'

She'd clocked him already. There was no missing his otherness among the smart London crowd in the room; he was hugely tall and lanky, sandy-haired with a sharp-angled face, pale-eyed and jug-eared, and his accent was overpowering along with his risqué humour and brash Antipodean opinions. 'Gidday,' he said. 'Mornie, was it?'

'It's Maureen.' Firmly.

Whatever connection their host might have been imagining, Mum was having none of it. An Australian? And worse, a journalist? After a few polite exchanges, she smoothed her skirt, made her excuses and moved on.

My father was not one to be put off. He was two years younger than Maureen, just twenty-two at the time of the party, and had recently arrived in London to work on Fleet Street as a photojournalist. An only child, he had a complicated relationship with his parents back in Melbourne. He shared a name, D'Arcy Leigh, with his father and had followed him into journalism, but the closeness ended there. He saw London as an escape, the big adventure.

An hour or so after the introduction, Maureen found Leigh following her up the stairs. 'You've got great legs,' he told her. It wasn't much, but it did the trick: no one had ever paid her such a compliment before.

They were married at the grey-stone Parish Church of St John the Baptist in Frome, in January 1962. Maureen was wasp-waisted in a full-skirted brocade gown with a high scalloped neckline and a tiara fashioned from tiny pearl flowers to hold her veil; Leigh wore a dark suit, a pale tie, and a white carnation boutonniere. They toasted their union with champagne in coupe glasses. I'm sure my grandmother Alice cried – not with joy, rather with anguish at where love had led her previously quiet and compliant daughter. But my mother had no qualms and no plans to leave England; she believed they'd be setting up house in London, and there they would stay.

Not long afterwards, a letter came from Melbourne with news that Dad's father D'Arcy Leigh Mau had keeled over from a heart attack and was in hospital, apparently near death. The newlyweds boarded a plane in a rush, at huge expense, and headed to Melbourne. It was Mum's first time on a plane, a 36-hour flight.

When she stepped off into the airport, she was a dead-set stranger in a strange land. Melbourne in the early 60s was still British to the core in its social mores, but it was also hot, flyblown and beset by drunks pouring out of the public bars every night at six. Just a couple of years before, the Hollywood star Ava Gardner had spent three months there filming *On the Beach*, a movie about the end of the world; she'd told the press – or so the legend goes – she felt she was in absolutely the right place for the job. For Maureen, that was spot on.

D'Arcy Leigh Sr had survived his cardiac scare, but the welcome was not warm. If Maureen had expected to walk into the arms of a surrogate to replace the mother weeping for her ten thousand miles away, she soon became friends with disappointment. My grandmother, Dulcie, greeted her daughter-in-law with a cold lack of interest. It wasn't that Dulcie thought Leigh was somehow too good for his bride; by all accounts – mainly his – she loathed her only child. Perhaps she loathed everyone. (She's certainly still, sixty years later, the only person I've ever heard my mother – who usually despises swearing – call a bitch.)

I'm not sure why they stayed. My best guess is that Mum, ever the stoic, refused to let on how unhappy she was; and if she had, it might have made no difference at all. She was a wife now, and pregnant within a month of their arrival. The choices for a woman in her situation, in the 1960s, were limited.

The newlyweds stayed with D'Arcy Leigh and Dulcie Mau, Dad's parents, for a matter of weeks before finding a tiny walk-up flat on Caroline Street in South Yarra, a pretty tree-lined suburb. Leigh photographed Maureen sitting framed by white-bloomed vines in the street-facing window: a serene black-and-white portrait of 60s womanhood. Green-and-yellow trams with their slatted wood seats rattled past the end of the road.

A few streets over from the flat were the Royal Botanic Gardens, where the swathes of lawn and exotics from the Mother Country would have been a comforting reminder of home – had it not been for the creatures. Warbling magpies are unrelated to their English counterparts and are vicious in the swooping season; they'll take your eye out if they get close, and they remember your face – they make you run in zigzagging terror as they divebomb to keep you clear of their nests. Rainbow lorikeets screech like banshees, and the black swans, just as noisy, are film-negative images of the birds Maureen was accustomed to.

While she set up house with Dulcie and D'Arcy's cast-off furniture, my father went back to what he knew best: chiefly, convening with his journo mates at various pubs after a hard day at the typewriter. There was no question of his bride joining him on these outings – until the mid-1970s, women were banned from public bars, and the blokes liked it that way. Maureen knew a handful of other couples, introduced by my dad, but saw them only at infrequent dinner parties – raucous events where both men and women drank and swore. She could not have hoped to find work with a baby due within months. She'd never learnt to drive – anyhow, there was no car for her – and it must have been hard to use public transport alone while pregnant and then with a baby. Most days there was no one but the cat to have a conversation with.

Maureen would dress her pretty baby daughter in a home-knitted outfit and wrestle the huge English-style pram onto the street for the twenty-minute walk to the Prahran Market. At least there she was among a crowd, able to eavesdrop on snatches of conversation and imagine having a friend to talk to. Over the months, a fleeting ritual became her lifeline: each week the same stallholder, an older woman, would step in front of the pram to coo over Lisa, distracting Mum with questions about her gorgeous baby. Some weeks, this was the only connection she had with anyone outside of the flat.

It was a punishingly lonely existence, but Maureen had been raised with *appearances* as the paramount rule of life – there was no chance she'd break in front of anyone. At rock bottom, she drew the pram into a local Anglican church on a spring day, found a pew and, sitting alone in the silence, finally let the tears fall. Watching in the shadows at the back of the church, the vicar's wife made a decision. Moments later, Mum was startled by the woman's soft voice at her elbow. 'Hi there. You look like you might need a mate. Would you be interested in joining the church wives club?'

The connections Mum made at the church slowly began to draw her out and give her a community, which survived her and Dad's move to a brick semidetached right on the tramline in Camberwell, a few suburbs to the east.

At some point in the two and a half years between Lisa's birth in 1962 and mine in 1965, she convinced Dad to allow her to take on work as a waitress at a seafood restaurant, La Bouillabaisse, a couple of nights a week while a babysitter minded Lisa. The opportunity to work was the truly transformative development in her lonely life, and although she never stopped pining for her West Country home, I suppose she decided to just get on with things – a phrase that very much fitted her attitude to life in general.

We were still in Camberwell when Lisa and I started school, but within a couple of years Mum and Dad had saved enough to buy their first home in Surrey Hills, a few stops on the tramline to the east.

2.

Surrey Hills is quite the desirable place to live these days. The brick and weatherboard bungalows built during the suburban expansion of the 1930s and 40s have been gutted and refitted one by one, to meet the needs of wealthy couples and their broods. But in my day, to a young person's eyes, it was a wasteland: a retirement zone packed with the old, a hilly fifteen-minute walk from the tramline and with little to interest children.

In 1971, my parents bought a house in one of those deathly quiet, tree-lined streets, bidding $12,000 at auction for a modest wooden three-bedder. It was no period beauty – in fact, it had a slumped, defeated look. A concrete path led from the street to a decrepit porch flanked by dirty weatherboards. Whoever had lived there before us had given up and let nature take over: the yards were choked with weeds and overgrown shrubs. And the interior was no great shakes either. The first time I saw it, which was probably on moving day, even I was dismayed – and at seven I certainly didn't have any grand concepts of luxury.

But my parents were excited as first-home buyers are. Mum was pregnant again, and Samantha, who we've always called Sam, was born in September of the year we moved in. My father fancied himself a skilled handyman with a shed full of power tools, and he was certain he could rebuild the place to glory. The road to glory was a long one. 'Whoever lived here must have just chucked their empties from the back steps,' Dad grumbled as he dug mountains of brown Vic Bitter beer bottle shards from the backyard. When Dad started digging at the front of the house, he found an entire car, dissected into bits, buried under my parents' bedroom window.

Dad did eventually rebuild the house, mostly on his own, and in the process lost the tip of his finger in a fight with the table saw. ('Maureen, I think I'm in trouble,' he muttered with classic Aussie understatement as blood spurted in crimson fountains from his hand.) Almost single-handedly, Dad turned the one-level cottage into a four-bedroom, split-level home, everything painted Dulux Mission Brown. This was the 70s, after all.

Lisa and I were sometimes allowed to help – or, more likely, ordered to help – bucketing rainwater from post holes so concrete could be poured, handing over hammers and pliers on Dad's barked orders, or fetching him another beer when it got hot out. I doubt any of these 'improvements' were council-approved – toeing the line with authorities just wasn't Dad's style – and in the end we had a bigger house but with few doors and windows that would shut or lock properly.

* * *

Lisa, Sam and I did what kids had to do back then: we made our own fun, and for a long time, when Sam was still a baby, it was just Lisa and me. On weekdays, our fun started early, often before dawn.

In 70s Melbourne, believe it or not, some suburbs still had their milk delivered by horse and cart, and ours came via Horrie Breeden's dairy (est. 1919) one street away. Behind the ordinary house there were red-brick stables, and inside were two magnificent Clydesdale horses, rich bays with black manes and feathery white legs. The rubber-wheeled wooden milk cart they pulled would reach our street at around five every weekday morning. We had no such mechanical fandangle as an alarm clock, so we'd bank on being woken by the metallic clop of hooves on tarmac – just a faint *tick-tick* as they left the stables, then ringing louder in time to properly rouse us. We'd race to dress and get outside in time to run alongside the moving cart and jump on the backboard. The driver was okay with us riding along but was certainly not going to stop and wait, so if my sleepyhead sister was slow out of bed and we missed the cart, I would be in a spitting rage at her.

Once we'd proved our worth by running the milk bottles from cart to doorstep – free child labour! – we were allowed to visit the stables after school while the horses were resting. I would run down our street, ducking neighbours' hellos, around the corner and down the driveway, then tug on the heavy doors until the rusted wheel in the overheard track shifted and I could muscle my way in.

The contrast between everything on the other side of those doors – mainly people, who I had already learnt could be confusing or cruel – and the time-slowed tempo of the horses' domain made me think of the place as my own private Narnia. (I kept that to myself, as enough people thought me an odd child.) In summer, stepping into the dark and cool of the high-ceilinged stable block was an escape from the relentless heat; in the worst of a Melbourne winter, the warmth of the horses raised the temperature by a few degrees. In any season, it was the ideal place to curl up on a pile of clean straw with a 2B pencil and one of the blue-lined exercise books I carried everywhere for my relentless scribbles.

I wasn't brave enough to touch the Clydies or climb into their stalls – they were huge, and I was a tiny, weedy child. But their gentle snorts and even the smell-blasts of their urine and manure were part of the magic, deepening an obsession with horses I'd already – even at the age of seven – had for at least a couple of years. On every outing in the car I stared until my eyes watered from the window, scanning the roadsides for a glimpse of a horse; whenever I saw one, I would crane my neck to keep it in view for as long as possible. I spent hours at the dairy stables every week, and I suppose Mum knew where I was as she'd send Lisa down to fetch me for dinner or homework or chores.

Our other chief amusement was roaming the streets until we were due back in for dinner. We did most of our exploring by scooter: painted green tin versions brought by Father Christmas (no 'Santa' in our Anglophile household). The scooters were handy for adventures, and we considered ourselves expert riders.

One blistering Christmas Day, the jolly man in red brought us a basketball: a new Spalding one, nubbly orange rubber with black stripes, not a hand-me-down. After the Christmas lunch table – stuffed roast chicken, fruit trifle, and brandied pudding set alight – had been razed as if by locusts, we lit out to the street to play for the rest of the afternoon.

The heat mirage glimmered and flared inches above the blacktop road as we stood apart on the yellowing grass verge, dying blades crunching under our bare feet. We passed our new treasure back and forth, back and forth. The exertion in the sunshine beat us after a while, and we trailed indoors, pink with heat, to find all the adults flat out and snoring. Never mind – there was a small assortment of other new toys to explore, and we quickly forgot about the ball game. We left the basketball out that night, on the nature strip by the road. In the morning it was gone.

I was terrified of any outburst of anger from Dad. He was a giant, and if we displeased him enough back then, it was down with our shorts and underwear for a proper bare-bum belting. I'm not sure why smacking required bare skin – I assume it was for maximum sting, but given Dad's height and weight that was unnecessary. He always held us tightly by one arm, too, although there was no chance we'd try to run off; pure terror shot its roots into the ground and kept us anchored until it was over.

That Boxing Day morning, Dad's fury was off the charts. At the end of the barrage, we were told the ball must have rolled away and ordered to scour the neighbourhood for our lost treasure. As short on logic as this theory was, we didn't question it. Lisa and I have always been epic with the tears, and I was already crying as we started the search. We were scouting every street in about a kilometre radius, stopping house by house to peer into front yards and down driveways. At the end of each street we paused to confer, like Diggers waiting for orders in the trenches.

At the bottom of the hill, where the tramline dissected the suburb and Wattle Park stretched for miles on the other side, a new slice of quarter-acre paradise was under construction. Half-built houses slumbered in the beating sun on bare clay lots, their labourers no doubt sleeping off Christmas Day excesses like every other Aussie worker on 26 December. Culs-de-sac, roads that led nowhere, were rare in Melbourne in the 70s. This was the first one I'd seen, and I was keen to explore.

I told Lisa I'd do the honours and pushed off once, twice, with my right foot. My tartan-print cotton pinafore dress flapped around me – a favourite piece, sewn by Mum. The newly laid concrete footpath was clean and unmarked; I counted the scored lines as they whizzed past. Looking down instead of ahead put me into a sort of trance. By the time the front wheel got the wobbles, it was way too late. The scooter continued downwards but perpendicular to the path now and on its side, squealing metal, with my skinny body lying across the overturned footplate.

When the scooter eventually stopped, there was silence but for the roar of the cicadas. Rolling clear of the scooter, all I could see was bleached sky and blinding sun. I couldn't breathe much or cry – the only thing coming out was an odd squeak – but I knew I was just winded, had been there before, it would pass.

I gulped at the air and was just about to tell this good news to Lisa, when her face loomed over me, blessedly blocking out the sun for a second. She did not look as calm as I felt. 'Get up!' she shrieked, pulling on my arm, hauling me to my feet, staring open-mouthed at my chest.

Following her gaze downwards to the front of my dress, I was confused to find it was mostly dark red, not green-and-black tartan.

'Come on, we have to get home.' Her tone was grim.

I started to howl then.

Soon we presented ourselves to a man washing his car in a driveway one street back: a little girl pulling a stumbling, wailing, heavily bleeding other little girl in a vice-like grip.

'Mister, can you drive us home?' Lisa asked, her eyebrows knitted together in a scowl. She was not taking no for an answer.

I was horrified. We were not supposed to talk to strangers, much less ask them to put us in their car. 'No, no, no,' I burbled, terrified of what Dad would say about the ride, not to mention the injury and the mess I'd made of myself.

But we climbed into the back seat, and I tried not to bleed on the grey velour. Lisa squeezed my hand until the bones bowed, but I couldn't feel it.

After we banged on our front door, the seconds telescoped into an age. When Dad's frame filled the doorway, I was choking back the tears to launch an explanation – but he said nothing at all. He simply scooped me up and pressed me close to his chest as his long stride quickly took us to the bathroom, gore dripping a path down the hallway. Then he plopped me into the tub, dropped to his knees and peered closely at my chin.

I was confused and delighted. There was an urgency to Dad's care, and it made me feel important – not the least because it was just so darn unusual. After every other mishap I could remember, Mum had tended to us. Dad abhorred tears, treating them as a sign of weakness, even in little kids. 'Quit the waterworks,' he would tell us. But not this day. Between huge, noisy sobs, I wondered why.

Because it was a public holiday, I wasn't packed into the car for a trip to our GP. Instead, Mum and Dad arranged for a doctor to make a house call. Gently, he told me I'd ripped a hole in my chin the size of a ten-cent piece and that he would stitch it up, right there on the couch. Dad held one of my hands while this took place – with no anaesthetic shot, as I remember it – gently cracking jokes about the process to keep me from howling. None of this made any sense to me. Where was the scolding? Why was he being so kind?

The feeling of being special stayed with me for ages. I was used to seeking my dad's attention and approval – actually, I'd become a bit of an expert. I had developed a tough-kid, tomboy persona through the years of shooting trips, and I was good at words, both qualities that he valued enormously and would gruffly congratulate me for. This was different: I'd been vulnerable, a sobbing mess, and he had responded with tenderness. I had witnessed encouragement, pride and a willingness to teach his daughters the things he felt they ought to know, but never tenderness before that day.

I held that feeling close, even after, years later, we discovered Dad had found the basketball on the nature strip that Christmas afternoon and hidden it, then sent us on an unwinnable quest to find it. To teach us a lesson.

3.

The fly-wire door, sectioned by its painted frame, had a tear in the top half that defeated its purpose, big enough to let fat blowflies slip through from the blast-furnace heat of the early afternoon. It was a blistering day, and we were probably getting on Mum's wick. Everyone was wilting like weeds in this heat. 'Go next door and play,' she told me. The door gave a tortured scream as I slipped through.

Inside, I was cooler than at our place. Their parlour was dim, with dust motes floating in skinny shafts of sunlight, unwashed windows, heavy curtains. There was dark-wood furniture, a sofa with its green damask covering worn to threads, and square-piped cushions cratered from years and years of backsides. Old tunes from the 1940s were coming from a radio in the kitchen, muted because the door was closed three quarters of the way. Bonnie was in there, and the aromas told me she was baking, probably scones for the afternoon tea we'd have soon.

She had the visitor there again. I knew him only by his nickname, Lofty. He was old and tall, talking to me quietly in this parlour from another era. Last time he was here he'd been less bold, touching me only through the fabric of my shorts. He had left it at that. But now there was a change in tactic. Businesslike, Lofty removed a varnished straight-back chair from its place at the oval dining table and placed it – almost defiantly – right in the middle of the room. I climbed on it when instructed to, ascending to my execution under my own steam, but I turned my body to face sideways, a small mutiny. He placed his big hands on my shoulders and turned me to face him, talking in a whispered monotone, 'Be quiet, don't move, don't tell anyone,' as he arranged my clothing and underwear to suit.

I did not take in much of what he was saying because my brain was fizzing with fright, bright explosions behind my eyes, blood roaring in my ears, a hollowing in my gut. I didn't want his bony fingers to touch me, but I was a good girl who did what she was told – and anyway, I seemed to be somehow locked in place. So, I stood frozen while it happened. I was ten years old.

Afterwards I sat at the table, chewing one of Bonnie's scones loaded with jam and whipped cream, my forehead tipped as close to the plate as I could manage. My taste buds were dead, and swallowing was difficult. At the earliest possible moment, I fumbled an excuse to Bonnie and ran for home.

Our house was no longer the ramshackle jumble we'd found on moving day, and the yards were cleared, trees trimmed – a sharp contrast to Bonnie's tilting, rusted shack. I slipped inside and went straight to the bedroom I shared with Lisa. There I sat on the twin bed under the window, running my palms across the candy-pink chenille bedspread. This time I was not going to hide, I decided.

I walked on shaky legs to the kitchen, where I caught Mum taking a break at the table, a gossip magazine spread in front of her. 'I have something I need to tell you,' I wanted to say, but the tears overtook me so my voice came out broken between big gulps of air. I kept stopping and starting, but her face, inches from mine, was creased with concern, which gave me the strength to stammer through my confession. Mum told me I had done the right thing by telling her and that I was brave. Then it was over, and I was weak and dizzy with relief.

I ran-walked, stiff-legged, back to the bedroom. There I found Sam, who was just three, bouncing on her bottom, up and down on my bed. Normally this would have made me cross: she had her own room (a sore point with Lisa too), and she wasn't allowed in ours, pulling books off the shelf and mussing up my plastic horse figurine collection. But this day I was grateful to see her. Putting everything else out of my mind, I pulled her into a game of chasey around and around the bed. Although I was much bigger and faster, I pretended I couldn't catch her, and she let out peals of giggles, high and musical like handbells. Her eyes were huge with delight, blonde curls bobbing. I felt a stab of envy without really knowing why.

In bed that night I stared into the blackness, imagining police sirens blaring down our quiet street, blue-suited officers in their caps with the chequerboard trim storming Bonnie's house to cart my tormentor away. I don't know how I knew – no one in my life had ever talked about an adult touching a child in this way – but I felt in my guts what he'd done was not only wrong but illegal as well.

I'd picked my timing badly, though. My maternal grandparents Alice and Reginald arrived from England the next day, the first time my mother had seen her mum and dad in almost a decade. I knew how much this meant to her because I would spy on her as she broke open the airletter that came from her father every week without fail. She would use a dinner knife to split the fragile blue paper along the fold, revealing Grandad's spidery writing; there was limited space on an airletter, so he wrote as small as possible to fit it all in. Each week Mum drank in the details of the village life she'd once thought she was going to have.

Weeks had been given over to preparations for this month-long visit, bedrooms rearranged, sightseeing outings organised. There was no way a ten-year old's revelations could be allowed to change its course. But I was sure that once my grandparents were on their way back to England, my revelation would be addressed. I kept this to myself, though; Mum was already upset by any mention of their departure date.

After we'd waved Nanny and Grandad off at Tullamarine, I began waiting again each night for the flashes of red and blue to seep through our roller blind – but they did not come in the night, nor at any other time. Every day at breakfast and again at the dinner table I would search my parents' faces for signs of a *serious conversation* on the way, but the talk was always of mundane things like school and what was on the news.

Eventually, I had to face the most plausible explanation: I had been wrong. Maybe Mum and Dad had been to talk to the police at the red-brick station in Camberwell, and they'd been sent away with an admonishment to stop wasting the time of the boys in blue. The thought of it made me burn with shame, and I did the only thing I had left. I put it firmly out of my mind and swore to myself I would not raise it again. Perhaps everyone would forget after a while. And that would surely be for the best.

One thing had changed: Bonnie's visitor had disappeared altogether. Much, much later, I wondered if Dad had been sent next door to deal with Lofty; I imagined my father pinning him against the wall by the neck, his eyes bulging, face turning puce as he gasped for air – or Dad beating him senseless with his big bare fists, telling him to get out and never come back.

And I also wondered if, even in his fury, a door had opened a crack in Dad's mind. His daughter was a victim now, and victims are vulnerable.

It's the mid-90s, and I am home from Auckland visiting the family in Melbourne. I'm chatting idly with Mum and Lisa as we walk towards the front door, on our way to some outing.

'You'll never guess who dropped by the other day,' Mum says, and there is no weight to the words. She's just passing on a snippet of gossip she thinks might amuse us.

'Oh yeah? Who?' We are only half listening as we collect our bags from the hallstand.

'Lofty. You remember Lofty, from next door?'

There is a moment of pure stillness, which Mum does not seem to notice. My body has stopped moving, stopped working, is no longer accepting instructions from my brain – apart from my head, which swivels slowly until I am facing Lisa.

She is staring back at me. Our eyes, almost identical in colour and shape, are wide as oceans. We say nothing, but a look passes between us, and it lasts no more than a second, two at the most, but it carries a flood of memory and acknowledgement. In that moment we see each other completely. We do not need to speak; the horror and shame we have carried for twenty years, unspoken even to each other, is right there.

Once we have silently said to each other, *Yes, I see your pain*, I tear my eyes away and look back at Mum, then at the front door, at the doormat where he must have stood when he 'dropped by'.

I grit my teeth. 'Well. It's a good thing neither of us was here. We would have knocked his bloody block off.' The effort of holding my rage in check almost winds me.

Mum is staring at both of us in astonishment, and I wonder whether she remembers ten-year-old me plucking up the courage to tell her what happened to me between sobs. How could she forget? How is that possible?

But I don't ask. I can't open that Pandora's box – the effort is too much, and I'm caught off-guard. I'm not ready for the fallout. I pick up my bag and head for the car. None of us speak of it again for a long time.

4.

In primary school I was ahead of expectations for my age and keen-as for any and all of the lessons. I particularly loved the writing assignments and would slip into daydreams about the first novel I would author – it would be about ponies, of course. But once the bell rang for morning break, things were not so rosy.

When you're a child, the psychology of bullying, the why of it, is of no use to you. What do you know or care of the home life of your tormentors, the base ingredients of the spite-filled recipe they've cooked up to serve lucky you? Does it help, as you're pinched and pulled and taunted, to think about their low self-esteem, their need to act out, to be the popular one in their group? Does it matter to you whether they're good kids doing a very bad thing or the ones trudging the long hallway to the principal's office most days? 'Empathy' is not a word you heard much in the Australian schools of the 1970s, and you, kid, had no time for any of that – you were busy enough simply surviving lunchtime.

It takes only a small thing to make a target: something to mark you out, however subtle. It didn't take long for those with a nose for it to clock my deformity. The name-calling started with just a few of the older kids, but quickly I was 'Big Ears' to everyone. My ears stuck out at right angles, poking pink and obvious through fine mouse-coloured hair. Most days Mum tied said hair in two high pigtails, which left the offensive auricles on show. I was old enough to understand that appearance is important in life, but weren't ears just for hearing with?

One lunchtime I was lost in daydreams of the horse in *National Velvet*, my favourite movie, when I found myself trapped in a ring of older kids. They were circling like wolves, and for a few moments all I could hear was ringing in my ears. Gradually, the zingers emerged from the cacophony. 'Hey, Mrs Potato Head!' one of them shouted, and the chant was picked up by the group: 'Potatoheadpotatoheadpotatohead ...'

I let my eyes slide left and right, just once and not for more than a half-second, and evaluated my chances of escape. I was small and fast – an advantage, maybe. I swivelled, hoping to spot Lisa; she was much bigger than me and therefore *might* agree to save me. No dice. Even the other small kids had melted away and left me to the pack.

The chant rose in intensity until a boy stepped from the circle and lunged for his target. As he grabbed one ear, he gave a yell of triumph, but he couldn't maintain his grip when I thrashed to get free. He cannoned backwards, putting a few precious feet between us. Blood roared in my head, and I launched myself across the asphalt, hitting him ram-style in the stomach. It seems no one had imagined a retaliation, so it broke the spell for a long second; then

I was underneath a pile of bodies, a little upstart getting my just deserts.

I should have told my teacher or the school nurse, but I'd never seen a classmate go to the sick bay voluntarily, so that seemed too much of an unknown. What if they didn't believe me and I got into trouble? I should have told Mum and Dad; I was not a timorous child, more a rollicker – a right little smart-arse at times. Outspokenness was valued in our household, encouraged even. But I didn't want to tell them either, as that would have meant admitting a defeat I couldn't countenance. I could not let them know that school hadn't turned out to be the best thing ever; I'd been pestering Mum about it since I was three. Also, the bullying was obviously my fault. I was unsightly enough to attract the bullies; if my ears were normal, I wouldn't be ugly. And if I wasn't ugly, then I'd be safe.

That evening at the dinner table, Mum spooned peas onto our brown stoneware plates, a tumble of green to complement grey lamb chops and mashed potatoes, this being Tuesday. She asked me about my day at school. It was the question I had come to dread.

'Nothing much.' I could feel the tips of my ears burning bright with the lie. I imagined they were glowing like twin fireflies through the light coverage of mousy hair.

I glanced at Lisa and immediately regretted it. She was glaring at me, a fierce look on her freckled face. I pinched her leg and made a face that would have carried to the back rows of any theatre, but there was no stopping her.

She straightened her spine, pushed back her fringe and lifted her chin. 'Ali is being bullied,' she said bluntly.

The words, too loud, dropped into a space of silence. I squirmed, expecting trouble.

'What?' my parents asked. 'Why?'

Lisa gave a theatrical sigh and lifted her bony shoulders before letting them fall. Her body language said, *You should know this already.* 'It's the ears.'

There was another silence, and I stared into my water glass, wishing I could disappear. Mum and Dad were looking at me expectantly, eyebrows raised.

After a minute of silence, Dad tried to break the tension. 'Look, yes, your ears stick out – but hey, at least you don't need brakes when you're running downhill!' He had plainly decided humour was the way forward. 'You do look a bit like a taxi with its doors open.' He warmed to his theme. 'I've got a nickname for ya: Wingnut!'

My cheeks bloomed with heat, and I folded my mouth into a tight line, swallowing any chance of tears. I was conflicted, not sure why he'd added to the torment, but he just seemed pleased with his wordplay. I gave him a wan smile and thought this might be his way of showing solidarity. He had big ears, too, so I wondered if he knew exactly how I felt. Then a realisation wriggled grub-like into my brain: I'd seen boys with ears like mine at school, and they didn't seem to attract the same level of vitriol. This seemed unfair but the way of the world, and there was stuff-all I could do about that.

'Dad, pay attention. She's getting beaten up.' Lisa was having none of it.

'Alright, alright, keep your hair on. Here's what you've gotta do, Lisa.' He signalled for her to stand in front of his chair, then adjusted her feet, one forward and one back, moving her by the shoulders until he was satisfied with her stance. 'You hold your arms like this.' His huge hands covered hers, curling them into fists and arranging them at chin-height, one in front of the other. 'Next time anyone goes for your sister, you stand like this and tell them you'll knock their block off.'

Lisa threw me a smug glance. Now I owed her, and I knew she'd put deep thought into her preferred repayment.

But at school, it worked – at least for a while.

* * *

The idea of Lisa as combatant fit rather well, I thought. As the younger sister, I knew she had the requisite skills, because our early relationship – like it is for most siblings close in age – was a mix of glued-together partnership and all-out war. Although we were often out of the house for hours at a time with no one knowing or caring about our whereabouts (welcome to child rearing in the 70s!), living in the geriatric desert of Surrey Hills meant there were few other kids our age within walking distance. All our school friends lived much closer to Canterbury Primary School than we did, and when Lisa and I were young Mum didn't drive – so, not a lot of sleepovers or after-school hangouts for either of us. This forced us, despite our disparate interests and personalities, to hang together even more than other sisters did.

When it was war, though, there was violence of the slap, punch, pinch and Chinese-burn kind. Being the elder and quite a lot bigger than me, Lisa naturally set the rules. If I whined, complained, tried to change her chosen activity or attempted to assert any authority at all over my big sister, she would use violence with exquisite skill, beating me up until I stopped my bullshit and fell into line.

On the flipside, she was also willing to indulge me if she liked the sound of my latest plan or needed an accomplice for her own. One time, she let me tag along as she crisscrossed our suburb selling Girl Guide biscuits, even though I had no interest in helping her fundraise. I knew the pop star Johnny Farnham lived two streets away, and I wanted to see if we could meet him.

'This is it,' I said.

We hesitated at the gate of the white-painted brick bungalow. It was the prettiest house in the street, its windows shaded by wide-striped awnings. Mum would confidently point it out every time we walked past on the way to the tram stop, saying, 'That's where the pop-star lives!' But Lisa and I had no way to be sure it was his. We had never actually seen this superstar other than when he'd performed on our favourite Saturday night telly show, *Countdown*. I was sceptical. Surely bona fide pop stars lived in Toorak mansions or smart beachside flats in Albert Park. Why would a famous person choose Surrey Hills?

Lisa reached for the gate latch – but, overcome with doubt, I dug in my toes. 'I don't want to meet Johnny Farnham anymore,' I whined.

'Too bad,' she declared. 'We're doing it.'

As I stood open-mouthed at her bravery, she marched straight to the door and rapped on it loudly. It was answered by Johnny himself, seemingly ten feet tall, the sunlight transforming his blond mullet into a golden halo. Neither of us could speak, but Farnham worked it out and bought two packets of biscuits anyhow. When he thanked us and gave us that genuine megawatt smile, I thought I'd burst into flames.

Lisa rode that triumph and my adulation for ages afterwards. Adulation and loathing never balance the scales when it comes to siblings, though. I loved my sister – revered her at times, even – but I spent much of my time trying to escape her savagery and at least as much time plotting my revenge. I couldn't beat her at her game, because she would be bigger and faster than me until at least our mid-teens. But it was dawning on me that I could create the rules of a new game, one where she wouldn't see me for dust.

* * *

Lisa and I had once liked sharing a room. We'd spent hours sitting on the rug between our twin beds, playing jacks or pick-up sticks. Being able to climb into the other's bed when night terrors struck was convenient, if sometimes met with a sharp elbow to the ribs. But Lisa was into her teens now, losing patience with her preadolescent cellmate.

Dad had responded to our frequent fights by moving us into the largest bedroom, at the front of the house. He had spent a weekend building two sleeping platforms from chipboard and installing them against the back wall, with desks for homework underneath. This divided the room well enough, but it did not keep me from nicking Lisa's clothes or trying on the Maybelline products she had begun to spend her pocket money on.

'Stop. Touching. My. *Stuff*!' She grabbed my arm above the elbow, squeezing hard until I gave a yelp.

I tried to wriggle free, ducking under her arm, away from her bared teeth – before realising this move was more likely to pull my shoulder from its socket than get me out of her grip. 'Muuuuuuum!' I cried. 'Lisa's hurting me!'

This would usually have brought Mum from the kitchen, huffing in frustration because she knew valuable dinner prep time would be taken up with claim and counterclaim from her equally outraged daughters, red-faced and furious. But this day there were no approaching footsteps in the hall. Perhaps she was sick of our nonsense, but whatever the reason, I was plainly fighting this battle on my own.

Like many siblings, Lisa and I looked alike but did not share much in the way of personality traits or accomplishments. My older sister was a deeply creative child from early on, clever with her hands and able to grasp any art or craft quickly and with dexterity. But she was not a wordsmith, and in our household that meant she did not warrant respect. Having a normal-person's vocabulary left her exposed to ridicule. I had started to exploit this loophole.

I was still in her clutches, and my arm felt on fire, but I took a breath and brought myself back from a scream to something I hoped was approaching nonchalance. 'I really don't know why you insist on being so *pedantic*.'

Lisa hesitated, a hint of uncertainty rippling across her face.

I drew another breath and forced an edge of sarcasm into my voice. 'I mean, this *compulsion* for consumerism is unbecoming of you, if you ask me. Smacks of *avarice*.'

I knew what I was saying made no sense, but that wasn't the point: Lisa did not. She was properly confused, flushing with embarrassment.

She dropped my arm, and I crowed in triumph. 'Perhaps you could be a bit less *belligerent* next time.' That closed the deal, and I flounced out into the hallway, forcing myself not to rub my bicep where she had no doubt left angry red marks. I felt a rush of satisfaction – it had worked! Finally, I had a weapon to wield.

Once, when we were much older, I asked Lisa whether she remembered what we'd been like as kids together. I was not surprised to hear she didn't recall being savage. Her clearest memory was of a family dinner when she was in her late teens, about to leave home. Dad and I had been talking about politics, and she had wanted to add her opinion. But she'd somehow muffed the terminology. She was pounced upon like prey, ridiculed and then dismissed as Dad and I went back to pontificating in the language we owned.

'My counsellor explained it,' she said to me. 'You and Dad literally took away my voice.'

5.

My father was an extraordinary wordsmith. The English language and clever use of it trumped all; he would sidestep any emotion arising in the moment, leaving it in his wake like an All Blacks five-eighth slipping a tackle, if he reckoned he could land a zinger on his conversational partner. Grandiloquence was his special sauce: the fancier and more literary the speech, the better. Even as tiny children my sisters and I were sprinkled with snippets of Shakespeare, Dickens and Eliot like fairy dust and treated to the bon mots of wags from Oscar Wilde to John Cleese.

This might seem an incongruous mix: a giant, beer-swilling, muck-spouting hardman who could quote *Hamlet* or Wordsworth's poetry at will. But they were all like that, Dad and his journo mates – even the saltiest of them were poets. The craggy-faced Wrighty, for example – who looked like he'd stepped undusted from the page of a Banjo Paterson poem – was one of the finest writers of his age, able to turn the most mundane of daily happenings into a yarn worthy of a Stanley Kubrick treatment. When these guys gathered, the public bars would ring with both history's most meritorious prose and its foulest of cusses.

Dad had a saying for everything, which made watching the evening news a challenge.

A report on state politics? Dad: 'Labor's got it arseways foremost, as usual. They wouldn't know if someone was up them with an armful of deckchairs. If the Premier had one brain cell it'd die of loneliness.'

A story about groundbreaking brain surgery? Dad: 'I'd rather have a bottle in front of me than a frontal lobotomy.'

Goings-on in the criminal courts? Dad: 'That guy's in more shit than a Werribee duck.' (The semi-rural suburb of Werribee was where Melbourne's main sewage treatment facility was located.)

Sport? Dad: 'Too much coverage of cross-country ballet [rugby union] these days.'

The weather? Dad: 'It's gunna be cold as a witch's tit.'

The simple motions of daily life were a rich vein to be mined, too. Hungry? 'I could eat the arse out of a low-flying duck.' Leaving to go somewhere? 'I'm off like a bride's nightie.' In trouble? 'You're up Shit Creek in a barbed-wire canoe.' Acting strangely? 'There's kangaroos loose in the top paddock.'

He loved nothing more than a chance to rark Mum up about her English heritage, never saying 'I'm thirsty' when 'I'm dry as a Pommie's bathmat' was available. And she would invariably reply with a resigned, 'Oh, *Leigh*.'

The most creative and remorseless epithets were reserved for women, marinated in that strain of misogyny peculiar to the

Australian male of a certain age. Many referred to a woman's looks, considered fair game and treated like a sport. Any mention of an old girlfriend would elicit waggling eyebrows and tales of 'spearing the bearded clam' or the summary 'she banged like a dunny door', which managed to carry admiration and approbation all at once. Beauty in a woman was both revered and treated with suspicion, but woe betide you if you were less than lovely looking – what use were you, then?

His absolute favourite? 'If my dog had a face like that, I'd shave its arse and teach it to walk backwards.' (This insult was particularly pointed: Dad's dogs were by far his favourite household members.)

The weight of words, the possibilities inherent in their use, made an impression on me even as a toddler. I learned they could be both freeing and damning; could soothe and eviscerate, inspire and disgust, be loving and lethal. My lifelong devotion to words and their use came directly from Dad and is the reason I chose the trade I've spent my life in. But in our house, words were a double-edged sword. The gulf they cleaved between me and Lisa would take us decades to bridge.

Androcracy was Dad's preferred state – he loved being the head of the family. *Listen to my stories, laugh at my jokes, do as I say but not as I do.* In Mum's case: *Contort yourself into the small space of acceptability I have set for you.* That space had been moulded by all the hoary old patriarchal standards: *Do not ask for anything, as that is nagging; always be sexually available; bring me things I like but not those I don't. Don't interfere with my interests; have none of your own.*

The Sisters recognised this cruelty even though we were too young to articulate it. At the dinner table we would cut eyes at one another at each outburst. We learned not to try to catch Mum's eyes; she had no urge to acknowledge his brutishness, especially to us. My mother could out-stoic Marcus Aurelius.

There was a constant push and pull of imperatives in our house. Dad had a crass insistence on putting sex – or the scandalous lack of it in his marriage (*pity me, pity me!*) – front and centre, while Mum made desperate attempts to scuttle past those moments in the hope they wouldn't make an impression on our young minds. Despite her efforts, the message seeped in that sex was a man's right, and he ought to be greatly pitied if he did not 'get it' as and when he wanted. Dad would regularly tell us kids outright that his wife was frigid.

Adding a sexual put-down to any conversation, no matter how vanilla, was like a drug to Dad. Every woman was a potential target: from colleagues, his friends' wives and actresses on the telly to my mother. Any tiny reference that could be twisted to suit, was. Even my squeal of 'stop poking me' to a sister invading my space in the back seat of the car elicited a bitter chuckle and 'the chance would be a fine thing' from Dad. Sometimes this sort of comment was wrapped in the semblance of a joke, although unlike any other joke it had no set-up, build or punchline: only he saw the amusement in it. The room or car would go silent for that nanosecond women and children recognise when a line has been crossed. Dad would chortle contentedly into his pewter mug, and we would burn with an unnamed shame. His children felt horror without knowing why; his wife was also shamed.

When I think about how Mum must have felt in those moments, I can't stop my eyes from brimming. I couldn't tell you why, but above and beyond every other thoughtless cruelty and shameful thing my father did in my childhood – and I include his criminal behaviour – the piece by piece dismantling of my mother's dignity was his deepest cut. By my mid-teens, I was increasingly disgusted by this behaviour.

When I talk to my father now, most of the braggadocio that defined him for so long has fallen away. He never fails to mention how much he loves his wife. This is so out of character, after so many years, that it is a shock to me every time he says it. His voice wobbles and cracks as he begs me to understand how their relationship has changed 'in the last few years'. I know he's referring to his own attitudes: he is nicer to her now. *It's all changed, don't you see?* But it's too late – she is at the end of her life, and there has been too much hurt, towards her, towards The Sisters.

I know his dearest wish was that we would always look upon him as the intellectual, the boss, but also love him; he cannot have that anymore. He'll die with that knowledge.

* * *

By the time I was old enough to understand what journalism was, my father had left the profession. Yet it was in the blood: his father had been a journalist and later the editor of the *Border Morning Mail* in Albury, or so I was often told.

In the 1950s, Dad was working for *The Herald*, the evening newspaper of record in Melbourne, when he rose to the lofty heights of shipping correspondent. This was not as dull as it might sound: back then almost everything, including any overseas person of note, arrived in Australia by ship, so Dad was really in the thick of it. Like the other journalists in the *Herald*'s employ, almost exclusively male, he had to stick to a strict dress code – suit, tie, a folded raincoat across his arm – and always carry a shorthand notebook in his hand. Each reporter's shorthand skills had to be so precise that if he had the stupidity or misfortune to be run over by a tram, another reporter sent to the scene could simply scoop up the pages, take them back to base and transcribe them. The show, or in this case the story, must go on.

By the 1960s, Dad was moving into the nascent world of public relations. The 1960s and 70s was a boom time for proponents of the 'dark arts', with large US companies such as McDonald's and Coca-Cola arriving in earnest to promote their products. Dad was a natural: gregarious and loud, physically imposing, creative, a great writer.

His time as a journo may have come to an end, but he was happy to find one of his daughters keen to follow him into the fold. It was all I ever wanted to do. As soon as I had learnt to write, I'd started doing so obsessively, filling cheap lined notebooks with the contents of an excitable imagination. By the age of twelve, the idea of doing this for life – and being paid for it – had taken hold and would not be budged.

Whenever an adult quizzed me on my career plans, I would fix them with what I thought was the gaze of a hardened hack and say, 'I'm going to be a journalist.'

'Ah, the family tradition,' they would chuckle, sloshing their beers at Dad in salute.

It never occurred to me to doubt my ambition was anything but sound. Growing up in a house without brothers meant there was no sense of girls' roles being different from boys'. The Sisters were raised with the instinctive knowledge we could do whatever we put our minds to, and I have to thank my parents for that. But outside the home it was a different story. There were plenty of signs of obstacles to come, even in our family's close circles, had I been old enough to understand them.

One summer evening, Dad, Giffney and Wrighty were sinking beers and slapping mozzies around the garden table, and I was close enough to eavesdrop. Lying on the bright yellow mat of our little trampoline, I was rendered almost invisible to them.

'What's the Witch Bitch up to?'

'Making a public spectacle of herself as usual. You'd think she'd've learnt to keep her fucking mouth shut by now.'

I knew who they were talking about, although they never used her real name anymore.

Claudia Wright had been a glamorous, outspoken family friend who would arrive at barbecues, earrings jangling, and go drink for drink and quip for quip with the men. But I realised I hadn't seen her for ... How long? A year, two? And in that time she'd fallen foul of the blokes, enough to become a regular topic of conversation between my dad and his mates. This she-devil had plainly transgressed in some unforgivable way, given how often they returned to the subject when they thought we kids weren't listening.

Claudia had been married to Geoffrey Wright, and Wrighty was the man the blokes all looked up to (whether they would admit it or not) as the epitome of Aussie manhood. He was a bushman, a raconteur nonpareil, and a writer of extraordinary talent, famous in the trade. They all seemed furious that Claudia had divorced him. They did not talk about any other woman in the same manner – this Witch Bitch appeared to have an invisible power. I had the distinct feeling she had something to say that I needed to hear.

Claudia Wright was sacked from the Melbourne *Herald*'s women's pages in 1974 for upsetting too many of the establishment's delicate sensibilities, but she went straight into radio on 3AW, where she became a star. Without telling my parents, I listened to her morning show on my battery transistor, catching as much as I could before I had to leave for school. She talked about things that I didn't hear from anyone else, such as contraception and domestic violence. She even said 'cunt' in a live poetry reading on radio – and got away with it when the broadcasting authority ruled it was used in context! She seemed much larger than my suburban life, larger than everything I knew about Australian society. What the establishment, principally the Catholic Church, called her 'coarse speech and emotional screeching', I saw as a revelation.

It was the Church that brought her Australian radio career down in the end, convincing 3AW advertisers of her devilry and calling for boycotts. Aware the station manager didn't have the spine to fight her corner, she resigned live on air, telling the manager to 'fuck off' as she walked out the door. It was 1977 and she was one of the biggest names in broadcasting; even Prime Minister Gough Whitlam got involved in the resulting furore. A professional woman causing this level of fuss – with public swearing! – was unprecedented in the Melbourne of my teenage years.

Wright wore her demise as a badge of honour and did not let it stop her for a second. She forged on in Washington, DC, becoming an internationally renowned correspondent. She cut a wide trail for women, not just women journalists, and as a reporter she broke stories that echo to this day.

I never saw Claudia Wright again, but her legacy has stayed with me, as has the statement from the Women's Liberation Movement, released just after she was pushed out of her radio role. Wright, they said, was 'the latest in a long list of articulate women who had been robbed of their livelihood because they spoke the truth about women in society … for women everywhere who had no voice, Claudia was that voice'.

At the time, her treatment and her response to it made me both enraged and hopeful at the same time. As I entered my teens, I needed a voice like hers more than ever. Eventually, I told myself, I'd like to *be* like her.

6.

The Moores were at our dining table, knocking back riesling with Mum and Dad, regaling them with tales of station life. I'd been sent to bed, but it was worth the risk to eavesdrop.

Phil Moore and my dad had become mates in the Melbourne PR world. Then, a few years ago, Phil's company had transferred him to manage a cattle station it owned in the Northern Territory; his role was to develop business opportunities, including live cattle exports. The Moore family hadn't been there long when Cyclone Tracy swept through on Christmas Day 1974, turning Mt Bundy Station into a crucial staging post for the recovery effort. The aftermath of that cyclone was the first natural disaster I saw on the telly.

I would normally have had no interest in the tipsy dialogue of adult dinner guests, but I knew two interesting things about these visitors. One: although they lived four thousand kilometres north, they had daughters around my age at boarding school in Melbourne. And two: their life on the station revolved around horses.

At around the age of five, I had managed to convince my whole family to take riding lessons. We had gone several times to a school on the outskirts of Melbourne, where I was assigned a shaggy brown Shetland pony called Chocolate. My family looked awkward, as most beginners do, but I held myself plumb-straight, heels down, drinking in the instructor's cues. Sitting on Chocolate's back transformed me: the bullied child was made both powerful and empathetic. I felt a surge of love for the creature who (mostly) agreed with equanimity to the clumsy commands of my inexperienced body, and I felt wonder as my skills quickly increased.

Perhaps my parents had agreed to these lessons in the hope that would sate me. Riding horses and ponies is expensive, and Mum and Dad had little money for it. But they were out of luck – the lessons had only increased my obsession.

That night the Moores visited, I parked myself on the other side of the dining-room door, open just a crack, and listened to one of the most important conversations I'd heard in my young life.

'We tell her to put a sock in it,' said Dad, 'but she won't stop pestering us for a fucking pony.'

Mum said, 'Leigh, please stop swearing.'

'Once it's in their blood,' said Phil, 'you'll never get shot of it.' He laughed. 'Why don't you send her up with our girls for the Christmas holidays? She can stay all summer, ride the station horses. It'll be an adventure for her.'

There was a disbelieving snort from Mum, but Dad waved a hand for Phil to continue.

'We have a truck coming down this way at some point in the new year. I'll take Ali out in the ute to choose a brumby from one of the wild herds – we'll break it in for her and then put it on the truck.'

This was almost too enormous – and too exciting – for me to believe. I strained closer to the door as the adults discussed logistics, my brain tumbling like a sprocket searching for its matching link. There would be a plane flight, my first, and entry into a new and foreign world. I knew next to nothing about the Top End of the country, only that it was very different from the Melbourne suburbs and even the grey volcanic bush of the shooting parties. I imagined the ground would glow clay-red, and every bloke would look like Banjo Paterson's dauntless hero in 'The Man from Snowy River', with narrowed eyes under an Akubra hat, cracking his stockwhip as his hardy mountain pony raced to wheel the mob. We would ride all day, I thought, then wash off the sweat and dust with a swim on our horses in lazy brown rivers.

'It'll be wet season,' said Phil, 'gets pretty hot. She'll have to acclimatise to the heat and stay clear of the snakes. And the crocs – the salties are everywhere, and they're big.'

Perhaps no swimming in the rivers, then, I thought.

Phil was clearly enjoying the escalating alarm on my mother's face, and Dad dismissed her with a wave of his hand.

'She'll be fine. It'll be the making of her. Anyhow, she's a tough little nut, and she'll do anything to get near the ponies.'

***

Phil tossed our bags in the tray of the dust-caked Toyota and headed out from the airport carpark. He drove a little east and then straight as a die for Mt Bundy Station, an hour and a half down the Stuart Highway, known to locals as 'The Track'.

Next to me were the Moore sisters, Kathryn and Trisha, back from boarding school for the holidays. This would be the only time in the next eight weeks we kids would ride inside the ute's cab; once we were on the station, our place was in the tray of the ute. I still found it hard to breathe. Even the most punishing of Melbourne summers – when we often had to sleep stretched like cadavers under wet towels for relief – had nothing on this.

Phil kept up a tour guide patter as we rattled past the pub at the town of Humpty Doo (or 'the Doo', as he called it). 'They built that pub a few years back, and bugger me did it survive Tracy without a scratch. Best pub in the region, they reckon.' He laughed, and I suspected he might have had a beer or two in there from time to time himself. 'Biggest set of buffalo horns in the world behind that bar.'

I gazed at the famous bar: concrete floor, a roof and no walls. Just like the airport where the flight had pit-stopped at Alice Springs. Was every building open to the elements up this way? Would the homestead have walls? Anticipation and nerves churned in my gut.

The ute's aircon was struggling with four of us on board. Outside, the eucalypt savannah was punctuated by road signs to Wak Wak, Tumbling Waters, Rum Jungle and Tortilla Flats. Phil delivered another dire warning about salties as we swung parallel to the banks of the Adelaide River, a finger jabbed in the direction of Snake Creek.

Then we were pulling into a grassed compound, home to a low L-shaped homestead. I stepped into the scorching heat of the early afternoon and the petrichor scent of damp red earth overlaid with fragrance from a tropical jungle. The house was shaded by clusters of butterfly palms and mahogany trees, frangipani and hibiscus, and flanked by a billabong on one side. Vines crawled along the chain-link fence, and I stopped mid-pace, straining to see if the tendrils were in fact snakes – I knew they were waiting for the unwary at every step.

A shiver of excitement flitted down my spine as we climbed the few steps to the house, where Phil's wife Frances and the youngest sister, Gillian, were waiting. Kathryn and Trisha hadn't seen their mother since the spring holidays and fell on her with hugs and kisses. 'Hey, welcome!' Frances said. 'You all look like you need a cordial.' She peeled her daughters off and turned a kind smile to me before sitting me down at the kitchen table.

Remembering Mum's lecture about manners and being on my *very* best behaviour – a tall order for eight weeks, but it was only the first day – I waited until Frances turned back to the sink before flicking my gaze around the kitchen. Yes, there were walls, but the house was upside down; wood-framed windows close to the plasterboard ceilings were buttressed below, from knee-level to the floor, by glass louvres. I soon found they were in every room; they could be closed to keep out the heat of the day, then opened at night when the cooling breezes blew across the billabong.

'So, some rules,' said Frances. 'You'll have to stay inside for at least forty-eight hours to get used to the heat. After that you can explore, but you must be back here before dark.'

My gaze moved across the grass to the fence and the feral wilderness beyond. No way would I be staying out there after the sun went down.

'Make sure you put on mosquito spray before you go out,' Frances continued. 'The buggers are big as seagulls up here.' Her words floated above a cacophony of cicadas, louder than any I'd heard before. Behind her, gripping the windowpanes with marble toe-pads, were tree frogs the size of hamsters, acid-green and unblinking. 'Finish your scones, and the girls can show you the house.'

**

The homestead's horse paddock was beyond the back of the house. No surprise, it was there I wanted to head as soon as we were released from our two-day confinement.

'All in good time.' Phil grinned as he opened the screen door to his small crew of adventurers, swinging his arm in a wide arc to signify the massive possibilities beyond. The tour was for my benefit, of course; the Moore girls spilled past me, their leather boots hitting familiar turf.

'That's the cook's hut,' said Phil, 'and over there's the stockmen's quarters.' He pointed to rectangular board-clad buildings, smaller versions of the homestead. 'You're not to go anywhere near those.'

'Keep clear of the river, and watch where you put your feet at all times. And your hands – they like to climb the fences.'

Ah. Snakes again.

We eventually circled to the home paddock and the station horses. As Phil reached for the gate latch, an enormous chestnut gelding raised its head from foraging and nickered, ambling towards us. Its gleaming body swung in loose, easy strides, its ears pricked, until it reached the fence and pushed its muzzle at Phil's hand. I was immediately, desperately in love. Dusty, I learned in the next few seconds, was Phil's mount.

'Here's the one for you. Name's Fred.' He gestured past Dusty to a small, lightly built buckskin pony standing off aways. Phil looked down, briefly blocking the sun with the brim of his felt hat. 'He's got some go in him, but you can ride, I'm told. You'll handle him okay.'

'Thanks, Mr Moore. I'll be fine. He's perfect.'

Fred and I eyed each other with mutual suspicion.

'Well, you're a bit tall for him,' Phil added. 'But wrap your legs around and hang on – you'll get along.'

* * *

We of the X generation love to humble-brag about our 70s upbringings. Ask any of us and we'll regale you with tales of roaming the streets in packs, climbing on concrete playgrounds with barbarous equipment (to be fair, in 1977 an estimated sixty thousand children were injured by playground equipment in New South Wales alone), and all the ways we *almost died* when our mums and dads were nowhere to be seen – that's our jam.

None of it came within cooee of those eight weeks in the Far North. When I think back to the risks we took, the hair stands straight up on the back of my neck. Aside from the occasional careening ride into the bush on the back of the ute – one memorable day, we were chased out of thick scrub by a gargantuan water buffalo, with Phil booting the Toyota as fast as it could travel – most of that risk was our choice, the decisions we made ours alone, as we roamed the rolling countryside in a tight mounted cadre.

Fred the station pony was a bit more of a handful than I'd reckoned. Perhaps he was unaccustomed to riders trained in the 'pretty' English manner – or maybe he was smart enough to understand that without me on his back, he'd be spending the day in the paddock, flicking flies and grazing with his mates. In any case, he tried his level best to rid himself of this pest by rubbing against trees, ducking under low branches, and bucking, rearing or bolting. The kind of riding I'd been taught was not going to cut it. And the heavy stock saddles took a bit of getting used to: I was sitting further back with legs forward instead of heel, hip and shoulder in a perpendicular line. But this was a lot more comfortable for horse and rider alike on day-long rides, and I soon got used to the saddle. Fred, however, never stopped trying to get rid of me.

It was total, perfect freedom. For a city-bred girl only barely into my teens, this was the intoxication of a wildness I'd never experienced. Out of bed each day well before the sun reached its most savage height, the four of us would assemble sandwiches and water in the kitchen, pull on our boots at the screen door and head to the covered yards. Each night, after that blazing ball had dropped past the scrub-horizon, leaving the sky an empty vermilion canvas, we'd slump aching and spent into bed. Eyes on the window, I'd watch the constellations rise in the velvet spread. Sleep would catch me anxious to get up and do it all again as soon as dawn broke.

In the war, Mt Bundy Station had hosted a long list of Allied military camps: army motor pools, a US Navy radio detachment, an RAAF airstrip and the 8th Australian Cavalry Regiment, among others. Proximity to Darwin and the threat from Japanese forces had made the station an obvious staging point, and all these years later there were echoes of military life etched into the landscape. Although the outdoor movie theatre and sports oval were gone, the cricket pitch remained. Concrete bunkers dotted the landscape, some of them a few kilometres from the home compound; for us they were convenient outposts, their slab-roofs offering shade on our lunchbreaks.

We were allowed more and more freedom as the days passed – as long as we followed the rules – and eventually, that meant permission to camp out overnight. Kathryn was in her late teens, and Phil and Frances were confident she could keep the rest of us in line. She laughed at my excitement as we pulled together provisions for our first camp.

'What are these?' I asked her, turning over a shiny metal box like an oversized sardine tin.

'They're rations, left over from the war years.' She grinned as my mouth dropped open – I'd never eaten dinner that was more than thirty years old!

Sealed tight, they had to be cracked with a can opener and their contents rehydrated with boiling water. When we made camp that first night, rolling out our swags after checking for snakes, then building a little fire with sticks and brush, I watched Kathryn prep the food, my eyes wide with amazement as the grey flakes bloomed into meat and gravy. I'd never tasted anything so delicious.

* * *

The four of us pulled our horses to a halt at the top of a rise. Over the lip, the dirt track fell steeply away, levelling out to the plain more than a hundred metres below – perfect for some real fun, we decided.

As the oldest and therefore the boss, Kathryn sorted us into order. She took the first turn, urging her horse from a standing start to a gallop, faster and faster down the track until they reached the base of the hill and wheeled around to wait for the next rider. I was elated – this was real 'Man from Snowy River' stuff! Trisha and Gillian took their turns, trying to beat Kathryn's ride, and then Fred and I were alone at the top of the hill.

I gathered the reins and squeezed hard with my calves, urging him over the brow at a gallop, my eyes on the three riders tiny and toylike at the base. Fred and I had reached halfway when Kathryn waved her arms above her head. She turned to speak to Trisha, who also raised her arms. *How nice*, I thought as Fred's little hooves drummed a cloud of dust behind him, *they're urging us on. Perhaps I'll be the winner.* I pulled up beside them, glowing pink with effort and delight, and gave Fred a vigorous pat. 'That was great!' I looked up at three faces white with shock. 'What's the matter?'

Kathryn pointed back up the track, where a dark tail was disappearing into the scrub, leaving a wiggly trail across the red dirt. 'It's a king brown snake. We were trying to warn you. You rode right over the top of it.'

* * *

I dreaded the end of that summer. Having to fly back to the boredom of suburban life made every fibre revolt. I wanted to spend a year, maybe two, in the rhythm of station life, riding every day and sleeping with the intense arc of northern stars visible through the window.

Something had cracked open inside me, something I'd not really known was there until now. Back in December, the promise of unlimited access to horses had entranced me. Now, it was more than that: I'd become addicted to the freedom, the sense that with each passing day, I was growing in power, no longer an ordinary suburban child, no longer a powerless target of bullies. In this wilderness I was the tamer, not the tamed. The idea of giving up that freedom to be corralled among schoolgirls sounded like blue-gingham hell to me now. Not even twenty-six infected mozzie bites, which swelled up my right arm – and which Frances treated with calamine lotion – dented my fervour. As the days ticked down to the start of the school term I became insufferable, trying to wheedle permission to stay.

There was one last, crucial job to do: choose my wild pony, promised at that dinner party months before. I made sure to remind Phil of this as often as I dared, and eventually he loaded us into the Toyota and headed out into the scrub. It was an hour or so of bush-bashing before we came across the herd in a clearing – about twenty or so horses, mostly youngsters, which thundered off unhelpfully as soon as we appeared. I was aware the most crucial decision of my life was to be made in the billow of dust kicked up by a hundred hooves.

'Well, what d'you think?' Phil called from the cab. 'See anything you like?'

I was taking way too long, seized by indecision. Why wouldn't the bloody things stand still for one second? Eventually I spotted two identical chestnuts, the least scraggly and wild-looking among the bunch, and pointed at them. 'That one, or the other just like it.'

He peered at the horses, then back at me. 'Righto.' He took one more look at the herd before pulling a U-turn and heading back through the trees. Hanging on in the back, I tried to keep the red ponies' shining flanks in view, but after a few seconds they'd gone.

* * *

I can't be sure when that truck arrived in Melbourne, but it was months after I'd slipped back into my suburban life, pining for the outback and trying my best not to be sullen about how *boring* it all was.

I couldn't get a word of news out of Dad, no matter how often or how thick I laid it on. 'You'll just have to wait,' he would say. 'It'll happen – but not today.'

Eventually it *was* today, not that Dad told me that ahead of the ten-minute drive to the pony club grounds. As I wandered to the fence with a pocketful of carrot pieces for the ponies, Dad kicked the dirt, his eyes on the gate. There was a low rumble on the dead-end street, and I turned to see an enormous cattle truck turning into the gravel forecourt. I rushed to Dad's side, grabbing his hand and squeezing hard. This was it.

The driver swung down from his cab and lowered the ramp as I craned my neck, moments from welcoming that shining chestnut pony. My pony. I could have burst into flames.

The driver disappeared into the body of the truck, which appeared mostly empty, and re-emerged holding a rope in one gnarled hand. At the other end was Fred.

7.

The bullying had not stopped, but I'd at least learnt some decent camouflage tactics. Took me long enough. Every morning, under my very precise instructions, Mum would tie my hair in the most effective way: a middle part and low pigtails, with each elastic band fastened half an inch behind each ear, pulled tightly into place so they lay flat against the sides of my head – brutal, but bulletproof for the entire school day! When I was with the horses, to put my black velvet riding hat on, I would tilt it forty-five degrees to one side of my head, tuck one ear in, then lever it over my crown to tuck in the second ear. The other kids at the pony club would giggle if they caught me, but that was okay – better than having the ears sticking out beyond the rim of my hat like flamingo wings.

I became more and more obsessive about hiding them, walking everywhere with my head down in case the slightest breeze blew my hair back. Or in case anyone twigged that I had a face at all, with inadequate features that brought me grief. So, from small beginnings, an obsession with my appearance took root and grew like carrot weed in a neglected paddock.

I did not talk about this much, as Mum did not approve of us girls focusing on our looks. 'Vanity,' she said in her clipped English tones, 'is unbecoming of a young lady.' So I turned it inwards, making sure that once the daily tussle over the placement of my pigtails was done, I did not mention my ears again. I kept my tears confined to the bedroom, then made Lisa swear not to tell anyone about my night-time sobbing.

***

My wealthy great-aunt had convinced my parents to send me and Lisa to a private college after primary school. Her daughter was in the upper years at Strathcona Baptist Girls Grammar School, and although the fees meant my family would remain mired in financial strife for years, Mum and Dad signed us up.

While Mum missed the incense and drama she'd grown up with in the High Anglican church at home in Somerset, Dad was a committed atheist – a rabid one, actually. When the Jehovah's Witnesses occasionally ventured down our front path, he would tear his clothes off, wrap a towel around his waist and fling open the door, threatening to drop that scrap of flannel if they didn't get off his land, pronto. In his eyes, anyone who worshipped was a 'God Botherer'. It was curious to me, then, that they sent us to a Baptist school.

When Lisa started there in 1975, the school had only just dropped straw hats and white gloves as compulsory elements of the uniform. The teaching was quality, no doubt, but the atmosphere was stifling. Sex education was off the table.

As a nod to the subject we needed to know but which they couldn't bear to teach us, we had Embryology. This course was taught by the principal himself, the beet-cheeked, snowy-haired Mr Lyall, and I assume that *so* delicate was the topic, he could not bear to leave it to any other teacher. Embryology classes had gained legendary status because everyone knew they were really about sex and procreation *for humans*, but no one was allowed to say so. Instead we copied diagrams of chicken eggs into our exercise books.

I'm sure the school felt this had all been set up for our protection; it was strange, then, that the school did not seem interested in protecting us from sexual threats in the real world. When I was fourteen, Strathcona's Year 9 cohort all studied at a different campus in another suburb, reached via a walkway from the Hawthorn train station. A semi-regular feature of that path to school was 'the flasher', a mystery man who would wave his genitals around to groups of us walking from the train. He'd been there long enough for the legend to be passed down from year group to year group. While I was at the school, there did not seem to be any effective efforts, by staff or police, to remove this pervert – and knowing no better, we girls would bolt, screaming with laughter, if we came across him.

The clash between religion and the modern young woman I intended to be came to a head one day in Year 10, when I was fifteen. Our religious studies teacher was off sick, so a relief teacher gathered us all into the chapel, rolled in the boxy TV and VHS unit on its rattling trolley, and announced we would be watching a video to give us the 'facts' about our fertility choices. We cut mystified glances at each other – this kind of thing was rarely mentioned. But as the opening scenes crackled onto the screen, I twigged. There had been rumours floating around of a mysterious film that used gruesome footage to scare young girls into falling into line with the anti-abortion movement.

Abortion had been illegal across Australia – with a maximum sentence of life in prison – until just ten years earlier, but the increasing power and visibility of women's liberation groups in the mid-70s had lifted it from taboo subject to major political issue. Victoria, New South Wales and South Australia had changed their laws, and thousands of women in other states travelled to Melbourne and Sydney to get safe medical care. My generation of girls had watched the Labor prime minister Gough Whitlam publicly support legalisation on the evening news. When his government was notoriously and undemocratically sacked in 1975, the backlash began.

By the time my classmates and I sat cross-legged in that chapel, anti-abortion bills were being considered by both the Federal parliament and the Queensland parliament. If passed, these bills would have imposed long sentences with hard labour for social workers, doctors and nurses, and even the friends of women who dared help them access abortions. We may have been sheltered teenage girls at a private school, but we'd heard the right-to-lifers play 'foetal heartbeats' on commercial radio. We were aware of what was at stake.

As the opening scenes of the video played, all the hairs on my body stood straight up. My scalp prickled. I shifted slightly on the floor so I could study my classmates surreptitiously – their faces showed everything from boredom to simple curiosity to an unease similar to the expression my own face surely wore. I wondered if some of their hearts were pounding like mine, as though we all faced imminent danger. I could sit like a good girl and watch the scenes I knew were coming on that tape, or … what, fight back? A Strathcona girl did not cause a public fuss and certainly never spoke out against a teacher. It occurred to me I was about to step into the unknown.

I actually thought, *Consequences be damned*, as I pulled a face at a couple of classmates and stood up. 'Everybody *out*!' I hadn't planned it to come out as a scream, but there it was. Without taking my eyes off the teacher's face, I flung out an arm to point towards the door.

To my deep surprise, every single girl in the class stood and filed obediently into the sunshine.

Shortly afterwards I was caught by the assistant principal and given detention, but I reckoned, on balance, that was worth the trouble. The feeling that I had stood up for something important lit a small fire in my gut.

And it came with an unexpected credibility boost – even the cool girl group stopped by at lunchtime to congratulate me. 'That was kinda cool. Good on ya.' Their leader flicked her Farrah Fawcett fringe and gave me an assessing stare, her expression a mix of surprise and wary respect. I couldn't deny how good that felt.

* * *

I needed any scrap of respect I could gather. My ears had made me a target at Strathcona from day one, and the bullying had become much more intense over the years. By the time I hit fourteen, it was almost unbearable – and I had a bunch of practice bearing it by then. Scuttling between classes became an exercise in strength of mind; my peers seemed to find me an abomination and would follow in groups, hissing their insults. If I'd had a way to fight back, I like to think I would have used it, but there was no denying my ugliness and no easy fix for it, either. No amount of clever wordsmithery was going to change a physical flaw, and no matter how I tried to camouflage my ears, they had become – to my peers and to me – my defining feature.

My thoughts kept circling back to something I'd overheard at one of my parents' parties. A couple had been there with their pretty blonde daughter, who was several years younger than me. They were talking to Mum when I drifted into earshot with a plate of pigs in blankets that she had asked me to hand out. I watched as the woman brushed her daughter's satiny gold hair back from one side of her head. The girl's ear sat flat against her skull, like a perfect pink shell; her pale lobe was pierced with a silver stud.

'Yes,' the woman said to Mum, 'we had her ears pinned back when she was four. The doctors do advise you to get it done when the kids are reasonably young, because it's not a small operation.'

The girl pulled a face, wriggling free of her mother. I felt both sympathy and an intense envy as I watched her disappear down the back stairs, towards the shouts of kids on the trampoline. So, it was possible to fix me – possible, but not likely. A major operation would mean a major investment, as plastic surgery wasn't covered under the public health system.

* * *

The year 1979 was also the one when the young ladies of my class at Strathcona were formally introduced to boys for the first time. With only sisters, no cousins around, and horse-riding as my main pastime, after primary school I'd had almost zero exposure to young humans of the opposite sex. Boys were a puzzle I was keen to crack in any way I could. In Year 9, that meant I had to attend dancing classes with the Year 9 cohort from Carey Baptist Grammar, our brother school. This was a tradition at Strathcona, something the fifteen year olds liked to dangle over the heads of the younger students: 'Ooh-hoo, just you wait, you'll get your turn with the Carey boys when the time comes!' Although the Thursday evening classes weren't compulsory, we all pooh-poohed the idea for weeks beforehand and then signed up anyway.

But what would I wear? As a kid I'd hated dresses and skirts of any kind, ditto frills, flowers and pink; I would go to great lengths to avoid wearing anything other than shorts in summer and corduroy trousers in winter. In more recent years I'd spent my life in two different uniforms: the blue gingham and navy tartan of the school day, and the jeans, boots and jumper for the ponies after school.

'Lord knows I try, but I just can't convince her to wear anything but jodhpurs!' Mum would cry, a note of jollity hiding her embarrassment whenever I – scruffy, muddy and most times cross about being pulled from a book – was introduced to new adults.

Mum, bless her, recognised dancing class as a Code Red condition and agreed to free up some housekeeping money to ensure I blended in. Long leather boots with stacked heels, dirndl skirts and frilled-neck blouses with ribbon neckties were the vogue. We couldn't afford the real thing but found some vinyl knee-length boots the colour of heavy clay soil, with a chunky crepe sole. They weren't the ones the popular girls had, but they would have to do.

At the first class, the dance teacher announced, 'I want all the girls lined up on *this* side of the hall.' He swept an arm to his left, backing away simultaneously, like an eighteenth-century nobleman inviting his paramour to the quadrille. Spinning on the spot, he eyed the boys, who'd already worked out by process of elimination where they were to stand but waited for the instruction anyhow.

We girls teetered on our brand-new heels, backs against the dark wood wainscoting, as freezing draughts pulled like the eddies of a stream at the hems of our skirts. As terrified as I was by the boys lined up opposite us, I began to look forward to the promised partner dancing; at least we might conserve some body heat in this mausoleum of a school hall.

'Each boy will choose a partner and invite her to dance,' boomed our instructor in tones as formal as a royal page announcing a white-gowned debutante to the Queen.

This seemed unfair – why weren't we girls allowed to do the asking? The idea of speaking up popped briefly into my head and then was dismissed; calling attention to myself didn't seem to fit the occasion. We girls, in our skirts and new heels, some with a hint of frosted lipstick, were there to be modest, decorous examples of young womanhood, not protestors of the patriarchy. I stared at the toes of my clay-coloured boots, too nervous to look across the fifteen-metre gulf at the boys. I felt fascinated and terrified just by their maleness. Shaking from nerves and the cold, I glanced along the line of my classmates to see if they were reacting as I was. Curiously, some of them seemed absolutely at home, flicking mascaraed eyelashes at the boys they liked the look of. I closed my eyes and wished I had that kind of confidence. But I knew, in my breaking heart, which classmates would be snapped up first.

No boys looked at me, and I wasn't surprised. A growth spurt had caught me up to my classmates in height, but I was still the same old angular, flat-chested, big-eared Ali.

Most of my friends ended up with a boyfriend from those classes, and at teenage parties I watched as those couples moved from kissing to hands under shirts. The stocky, dark-haired boy I liked was also at those parties, but I had to be happy with imaginings of how the smooth heat of his skin on mine might feel; in fact, humiliatingly, he stayed as far away from me as he could. I'd twigged that attention from boys unlocked another level of life achievement. There was power in it, I knew – everything I saw around me told me so. I also knew that my deformity was the most probable reason for his rejection. By day my ears attracted my peers in the worst possible way, and after school they repelled the people I actually wanted to notice me. By the end of that year I'd had more than enough.

* * *

After Samantha was born, Mum had begun saving to fly home to England, every two years or so. Each time she took Sam with her – a practical decision as Sam was little more than a baby and the idea of leaving Dad in charge of her was ludicrous – but there was no money for Lisa and me to go with them. We dreaded those weeks – sometimes more than a month – that Mum was away, when life went from ordered to slapdash and unpredictable. We were used to making our school lunches every morning, but we tired very quickly of having cheese toasties for dinner every night. In our childish way, both Lisa and I resented Sam for her good fortune, refusing to be charmed by her cute English accent which stuck for at least a few days after they returned.

One time, Mum and Sam arrived back just before the summer school holidays, and Lisa, Dad and I had dressed up as if we were walking into a church service on Sunday, instead of an airport arrivals terminal. After a long flight with a toddler, I knew Mum would be craving our smiles and hugs, looking forward to a happy family reunion, but this time I couldn't give it to her; as soon as she came through the sliding doors to the arrivals lounge, I burst into noisy tears and threw myself at her, begging for the surgery. She took my hand, making soothing noises and promised they would talk about it.

Otoplasty was a major procedure back then and hardly essential surgery – I never did find out how Mum and Dad managed to pay the thousands of dollars it must have cost. In truth, when they called me into the kitchen a few weeks later and told me they had booked the private hospital stay, I was too terrified they might change their minds and didn't dare to ask.

During the consultation appointment, the surgeon's cool fingers probed my ears – calmly, as if it were nothing at all! – while I vibrated with excitement.

'So,' he said, 'Alison.'

I could only manage a squeak.

'What I will do is make an incision behind each ear, cutting through the cartilage and removing the excess which is holding them out.'

'Okay!' I said shakily.

'Then we will fold the ear back and secure it with stitches, which we'll have to remove after about ten days. That will leave you with scars behind each ear –'

'It's okay, it's okay!' Why was he faffing about scars? I could not have cared less.

'Is it a very risky operation?' Mum asked. I could hear the worry in her voice as she pressed her knees together on the straight-backed visitor's chair.

I gave her a pleading look.

That half-hour in a bland consultation room changed my life altogether.

When released from the surgery, I wore a turban of white bandages and had to sleep sitting up for a week. With great glee, I told everyone at pony club I'd had brain surgery.

On my return to school after the summer break, it was as if my life had been cleaved into distinct halves: deformity and post-deformity. No one seemed to notice my appearance had changed, but the bullying had stopped. A miracle.

* * *

I'd always been a solid and mostly invisible student. Having set my course years before – I would be a journalist if it killed me! – I focused on the humanities.

In the middle of my penultimate school year, my English teacher called me aside after class. I was one of her favourite students, or so I liked to think, and she had never delivered me anything lower than an A-plus.

'So, Alison, what is it you want to do when you leave here?' Still marking assignments with firm strokes of a red pen, she waved a hand towards the rows of empty wooden desks.

I felt a swell of excitement. I was about to reveal to someone who mattered – someone other than Dad and his drunk journo mates – how I was going to spend my life; how I would use my (only) talent, one that she was closely familiar with, to build a career.

I took a deep breath, suddenly nervous. 'I'm going to be a journalist.' I emphasised the rightness of the statement with a firm nod.

This pulled her attention from the essay papers; she looked up at me, a wrinkle deepening between her eyebrows. 'Really? Oh, I don't think so. Will you? Why don't you reconsider, look at nursing or teaching instead, like the other girls in your class?'

This was not at all what I'd expected, and the mental image I'd had of her proud smile, the words of quiet advice and encouragement – fuck, even a simple 'good for you' would have sufficed – disappeared in a puff of cartoon smoke. For a second I thought I must have misheard her, which left me standing mute with a look of horror on my flushed face. Then a wave of disgust and betrayal swept from the top of my head to my feet.

As upset as I was, I also felt embarrassed for her. Why had I not twigged to how clueless, how ignorant, how *backward* her thinking was, this teacher I had so admired? This was 1981, not 1951!

She was looking at me expectantly. I could argue, I thought – explain my heritage, try to put into words why the path I'd chosen was the only one for me. Teaching and nursing were fine, caring professions, but not for me. Was it worth even attempting to explain?

I stretched my mouth into an utterly fake grin. 'Oh yes, I'll definitely consider that. Thank you!'

If she heard the heavy loading of sarcasm, she did not react.

I wanted to get to the bathrooms before I burst into tears, but I squared my shoulders and forced myself to walk, not run, from the room. *You absolute bitch. I'll show you.*

* * *

At Strathcona, I was grateful to have at least one or two friends at any one time. From the age of around fourteen, my closest friend was Katie. We developed an intense bond, spending most of our time together in and out of school. Katie was an exquisite ballerina – although she hated me calling it that. 'The word "ballerina" is only for the top professional soloists,' she would scold me. She had huge dreams to match her talent, and I loved that she wanted something *other* than the standard goals we were steered towards at school. She was determined to achieve what we both desired more than anything: to *get out of this place*.

At fifteen she cracked it, auditioning for the Australian Ballet School and gaining a place among the country's top handful of student dancers. I was sorry to lose her from school but stayed in close touch; we wrote letters to one another and spent as much time together as possible. I often told her I loved her, completely unselfconsciously, and there was no sexual element to it – that simply did not occur to either of us.

In my final year at school, as exams approached, my mother approached me one afternoon as soon as I walked in the door from the tram. 'Alison, come into the kitchen. I need to talk to you about something important.'

I dropped the heavy blue schoolbag in the hallway and peeled off my blazer, then followed her in. She drummed her pink-lacquered nails on the Formica countertop and wouldn't meet my eyes. This was new – Mum had no problem being strict with her girls and did not hold back if she had 'a bone to pick' with us. But today there was something strange in her manner, as if she was unsure of her ground. I slumped onto a dining chair and waited.

Her mouth, with its customary swipe of Rimmel Heather Shimmer lipstick, was tucked into a tight hyphen before she spoke. 'Your exams are less than two months away. They have to be the most important thing in your life right now.'

'Uh, yeah? I guess so, of course –'

'I'm concerned your friendship with Katie is a distraction. She's at the ballet school, and you've got to focus. I've decided. You're not to see her at all, not until you've finished school.'

This was also a puzzling departure for Mum, who was happy to leave us to make decisions for ourselves. It was one of the traits I most admired in her.

I could see Lisa hovering in the background, plainly roped in as support for Mum's argument. I shot her a look, which she ignored.

'What?' I said. 'Why?'

'You're spending way too much time together,' Mum said through pursed lips, before turning abruptly back to the stove.

Lisa left the room at a similar warp speed.

I was burning with outrage. As I stood, dazed and on the verge of tears, a new thought squirmed at the back of my brain. There had been something odd about Mum's delivery – a little too prim, even for this delicate English rose. I smelled a rat.

In the bedroom, Lisa would not look directly at me, feigning disinterest as she flicked through a magazine. She wasn't going to get away with that charade. 'Oh, alright,' she said, *'fine* – Mum thinks you're lesbians.'

I goggled at her, stunned. This hadn't even occurred to me, and the fact that Mum was taking the notion seriously was astounding.

And so what, I thought angrily, if it had been true? My father's politics were often, as he liked to put it, 'Somewhere to the right of Genghis Khan,' but there'd been no hint of homophobia in my upbringing, or not that I recalled. To my mind, lesbian relationships were a thing some women were into, and that was cool – that wasn't me, but all power to them. I had felt, exactly, neutral about the subject.

Until that moment. Until, however misguidedly, 'lesbian' was a label directed at me. I didn't know how I felt now.

'Look,' said Lisa, 'just do as you're told. It's only a few weeks, and then you'll be out.' She flicked the pages of her magazine as if it were nothing at all.

8.

A pony cost money, and money had to be earned. Soon after Fred had come clopping off that truck from the Northern Territory, my parents had made it clear the ten dollars needed to feed him each week would come from me. My first job, at fourteen, had involved pulling weeds in the baking sun at a plant nursery. By sixteen, I'd graduated to the new standard in teen employment, which every young person lusted for back then: a job at McDonald's.

The first Macca's in Melbourne had opened seven years earlier. My dad had the PR account for the company's foray into Australia and organised the opening. There was a ceremonial filling of a time capsule with newspapers, coins to the value of a Big Mac and, oddly, a copy of the 1973 federal budget. Dad added a canister of 'air' filled with exhaust fumes from our car. He also took my mum to the empty store for a candlelit dinner before it opened, just the two of them.

By 1980 McDonald's stores were popping up in every suburb, and any self-respecting teenager knew how to speed-quote the Big Mac slogan in less than five seconds. Lisa had been working for a couple of years at a local outlet. I pestered her relentlessly to get me on the hiring list and squealed with joy when I was accepted to the training programme, underpinned by the Macca's shibboleth: 'If you have time to lean, you have time to clean.' Management took this seriously, and the shifts were long and often frantic, serving lines of hungry punters that sometimes snaked right out the door (drive-throughs were years away).

Our workspace was a perfect hunting ground for anyone with wandering hands. Cramped, with narrow walkways between the grill, counters, drink and dessert stations, the paths we trod a thousand times in a shift were like dark alleys where our bodies belonged to anyone present. We had to squeeze past our workmates every couple of minutes, and on each shift there were unwanted touches and sexual comments that turned our stomachs and had us silently fighting back tears when our parents came to pick us up at home time. I learned never to bend from the waist to empty the bin or to gather ingredients from a low cupboard – if I did, the slick navy polyester of my work-issued trousers would stretch across my bum. Instead, I'd twist sideways and drop from the knees, ankles together, keeping my workmates in clear view. Because we had no name for this treatment, we did not know how to tackle it, or even that it could or should be tackled.

While there was a camaraderie among the 'crew' that made the work enjoyable, there were also entrenched gender roles that did not. Girls were for counter service, for refilling the veggie containers and the fries station, and for cleaning. Only boys could work the grill – hot and hard work, but at the top of the kitchen-status tree for sure. I had come across gender-segregated playgrounds where boys played cricket and girls were not allowed, and now I was finding a similar state of affairs in my workplace.

As Lisa and I were lolling around on our beds one evening, I asked her what she thought of this injustice.

'I guess ... it's not really fair, but it is what it is,' she said sagely.

'Well, I don't accept that,' I huffed, and began plotting to overturn the stupid rule.

If I'd been mature enough to notice the irony inherent in their edict – that society wanted women in the kitchen but apparently not *this* kitchen – I would have used that as part of my strategy. As it was, I just pestered the various managers on every shift for at least a year until they'd run out of excuses. I became the first female at our branch to work the grill.

One of the shift managers, a hulking eighteen year old called David, had been paying me extra attention. We began dating, if you could call it that. After the disaster of dancing class and my first experience of boys the year before, I was astounded to be shown any attention, let alone by my tall, blond, broad-shouldered, handsome boss.

David was what we girls, hunkered behind the freezers and giggling uncontrollably, would call a *spunk*. The two-year age advantage he had on me felt like a chasm; this was an *adult*, I thought in awe, who was sneaking admiring glances through the burger hatch at *me*. Whenever I called out a question for a customer, and David ducked his chiselled face, topped by the paper hat of the grill leader, below the stainless-steel shelf and held my eyes for just a moment longer than necessary to answer, I thought, *Holy heck!* The operation on my ears had worked, it seemed, like a bloody magic spell.

Most of our time at work was spent flirting 'surreptitiously' – we thought no one could tell, but duh, everyone knew. Most of our time together outside work was spent in his parents' garage, getting up to sexual mischief on his father's tool bench. By that I mean an array of kissing (with lots of tongue) and touching, over and under clothes. I had a terror of someone – oh god, please not his father – walking in on us, so I would keep one eye on David's blond head bobbing about and one on the doorknob in case it turned, but that never came to pass.

I thought things were going well. I wrote flowery letters to Katie at ballet school about how clever I'd been to choose someone older and therefore more mature than the boys our age. I was in love, or so I firmly believed.

The relationship ended when I put my foot down. What I did was repeat 'no' again and again and again in my best good girl voice whenever David decided it was time for us to have penetrative sex. He did not ask out loud – such a thing would have been unusual then – instead trying to take advantage of moments when we had our undies down. But at sixteen, I did not have 'intercourse' on my to-do list; I intended to stay a virgin for the time being.

When David finally twigged that I was serious about this, he dumped me without ceremony. I was distraught, and angry, and on top of all that I had to front up to work the next day and treat him like my boss (which he still was) as if nothing had happened.

This quickly became excruciating. I'd invested a bunch of florid imaginings in this guy, and he was now refusing to say a single word to me on shift. Within a month, he'd had me transferred away from my friends to another outlet. I went with my tail between my legs, believing my banishment was somehow my fault – I had broken some unwritten rule and had to go. Resisting would have been fruitless, and anyway, good girls did not make a fuss. But I loathed working at the new store and eventually engineered my own demise.

McDonald's relied heavily on upselling – 'Would you like fries with that?' – as a sales tactic, which I thought was both redundant and rude. To my sixteen-year-old logic, surely customers already knew what they wanted when they placed their order. On the rare occasions my parents were feeling flush enough to splash out on fish and chips, we planned the order to the cent and argued over how many fried potato cakes we *really* needed. Why would we, polyester-garbed servants of a fast-food behemoth, second-guess another family's order? It just did not make sense.

One shift on the front counter I was caught by the manager, who bent and hissed halitosis breath an inch from my face, *'Suggestive sell!'*

I turned back to the line, and when the next customer, a guy in his twenties, placed his order, I said sweetly, 'Would you like a new car with that?'

I was fired on the spot. After spending two hours sitting in a tree in the park, wondering what my parents would say, I thought, *Fuck it*. And went and worked in an ice-cream parlour.

***

In the fraught and utterly banal rhythm of coming together and falling out that sisters share, Lisa and I managed to stay close throughout our teens. Once I was old enough (with enough makeup on) to pass as eighteen, she and her mates would allow me to tag along to King Street nightclubs like Inflation, with its echoes of New York's Studio 54, and the Underground.

The two of us would get ready together at home, crowding the bathroom mirror, laughing and excited as we wielded teasing combs like witches' wands on our permed hair. Sam, with her straight-cut fringe and baby face, jostled behind us and pleaded to be included, while Mum hovered with anxious advice at the doorway.

'Mum, don't worry,' Lisa would say, 'I'll look after her – she'll be fine with us!'

And I always was.

Within a year, Lisa had met David, and that era of closeness ended abruptly. He was her first boyfriend, and although I couldn't fathom the attraction, they were inseparable.

Bedrooms were shuffled at our place, and Lisa and David installed an enormous waterbed in hers. On the rare occasion he wasn't there, I would wheedle my way in and lie gingerly on the bladder, feeling the water sloshing within its blond pine frame. I didn't dare ask Lisa what that amount of movement meant for David's nocturnal visits, which I knew were almost nightly, but I wondered how on earth they could keep their balance. Mum refused to expose Sam to such debauchery, so David came and went via a ladder propped against the side of the house underneath Lisa's window.

When I was in my late teens, Sam and I were bridesmaids at Lisa and David's wedding, held at a rustic estate in the Yarra Valley. In the photos, my dad and his mates are frozen in celebration: glasses raised, eyes unfocused, heads topped with the bridesmaids' flower coronets as a joke. David does not crack a smile in the photos, not even once. I am also unsmiling; when Lisa threw the bouquet from the steps of the olde-worlde homestead, I felt only emptiness – and fear for her.

Their only child, Benny, was born less than a year later; before he turned one, David had vanished. But by then, Lisa and I had separate existences, drifted far apart like sticks thrown from a bridge. My relationship with my sister hadn't withstood this interloper.

* * *

In early 1983, we were experiencing the worst fire season in decades, thanks to years of drought. One February night I'd been clubbing in town. Stepping into the street at midnight to catch the last tram home, I was startled to find the city cloaked in an eerie red haze, particles of ash swirling in the darkness, catching in my hair and clothes. Fires had been burning in spots across South Australia and Victoria since early in the day, but by evening a violent wind change had turned those spots into raging fronts, some of which were approaching Melbourne's outskirts on several sides.

When I turned the key in our front door an hour later, I found Dad awake, dressed and pacing the living room, simmering with suppressed energy. 'Get changed. Get in the car. We're going to save your horse.'

I'd had no idea the fires had spread south-west of the city during the evening, and were heading towards the rural suburb where my horse was kept, and I stood locked in confusion for a moment, foolish in my tube skirt and heavy makeup. But I knew better than to babble – he wanted compliance, and quickly. I washed my face and was standing in the darkness by the car within minutes.

Through empty streets we raced towards the fire zone in the outer east, me sneaking glances at Dad's face, a grim mask of determination lit by the red glow off the approaching Dandenong Ranges. At the foothills, blue-and-red lights scythed through the smoke: a roadblock. I watched Dad tower over the group of cops on the roadside, eddies of lambent embers spiralling around their bodies and faces, all of them smutched by black ash. Whatever he said in those few intense moments was enough to convince them, because incredibly they waved us through.

The mission was a bust: the horse was safe and had never been in danger. Curiously, Dad seemed exhilarated rather than stroppy as we retraced our route home. I suspected Mum would not be sharing *that* feeling, and I dreaded what she would make of our recklessness when she woke. But although the rational part of me knew what a dangerous stunt it had been, I couldn't help but see Dad's impulse as just a little bit heroic.

Later, we would learn twelve firefighters had perished when their trucks were overcome by the blaze, on a narrow track just a few kilometres from that roadblock.

I spent all the next day, groggy from my hangover and too few hours' sleep, perched on the couch in my pyjamas, watching news of the fires. All four channels suspended normal programming and were broadcasting rolling coverage of the tragedy, which they'd dubbed 'Ash Wednesday'. It was the first extended live news event I can remember.

In one replay of footage from the day before, a reporter was stationed at the end of a blackened gravel road, gum trees incinerated to sticks behind her. She was young and, I suspected, new to the job, clad unwisely for the assignment in a light summer dress that repeatedly caught the swirling wind. She clutched at the skirt with her free hand as it billowed about the tops of her legs, the drama of the moment heightened by the odds-on chance she'd be showing her undies to millions of viewers. She never once loosened her grip on the microphone or faltered in her commentary, gravely listing the loss of lives and properties with just the smallest vibration – of what might have been fear – in her voice.

As I watched her, I thought, *That's what I want to do.*

***

I was part of the final tranche of inductees who entered the journalism craft in the old-school way: via a cadetship. This was a four-year, on-the-job apprenticeship where you graduated each

January from absolute shit-kicker to advanced shit-kicker, and then emerged from the chrysalis to become a D-Grade journalist, then C and B and so on.

Cadetships were already scarce as feathers on a fish, but in the middle of the 1983 recession, the deepest since World War II, my timing was dreadful. The typewritten begging-letters I posted, heavy with emphasis on an almost perfect English exam score, got a polite and regretful 'no' from both major metro papers. The *Herald*, double-spaced, told me I'd only narrowly missed out and to try again next year. But they would say that, I thought.

On Dad's advice, I widened my scope and wrote to every provincial newspaper in the state, then bit my nails down as I waited for replies. Only one came back in the affirmative: an offer for a first-year cadet place at the Warracknabeal *Herald*. I had never heard of the joint, so Dad dragged the atlas from the shelf, blew off a cloud of dust, and pointed a stubbed forefinger at a tiny speck on the map, 330 kilometres to the north-west. 'There you go, Warracknabeal. It's in the Wimmera. Wheat country.'

'What's it like?'

'Dry. Flat. You'll be the tallest thing for miles!'

He was finding all this suspiciously funny. All I could think of was the yawning distance between the tiny town and my busy social life in the bars and clubs of the Melbourne CBD. I did not have my driver's licence and had no hope in Hades of owning a car anytime soon.

Dad could see me wavering and gave me some of his trademark blunt logic. 'Whaddaya going to do instead?'

'I could work at Safeway and try again next year ...?' I already knew this was not going to wash.

He closed the atlas with a decisive snap. 'Tell them yes. Stay a year, then you can try again for the metros. But stick it out for a year.'

The town of a couple of thousand residents was a dusty, sun-bleached hamlet on the banks of the Yarriambiack Creek and on the traditional lands of the Wotjobaluk people. It boasted the Royal Mail Hotel (one of four pubs in town, the Royal Mail was a white-painted, double-storeyed, rectangular edifice dating back to 1899), a racecourse, and the Wheatlands Agricultural Machinery Museum. This last claim to fame was central to the town's particularity: it lived and breathed wheat and sheep.

The town also proudly boasted a twice-weekly newspaper. The Warracknabeal *Herald* was a family-owned publication run by generations of the Wards. My offer of employment came from its editor Audrey Hoffmann, a local woman in her early fifties. I did not clock how unusual it was to have a woman putting out the paper. With the addition of myself, the entire reporting staff of the eight-page gazette would be female. What trailblazers we were.

I wrote back, accepting the position. My pay would be $90 a week.

* * *

By the end of my first week, and especially after a sleepless Friday night of listening to the town drunks brawl on the pavement underneath my window at the Royal Mail Hotel, I'd had quite enough of pub life.

The *Herald* had come up with the idea of introducing me to the town via a single-column story, basically a plea for someone to give the girl a break and rent her a flat. In the black-and-white picture, I looked ridiculously young and nervous, with my very ill-advised fluffy cropped haircut, trying to appear the seasoned journo. The one-bedroom relocatable cabin I eventually found for thirty dollars a week was bleak because I had little to furnish it with. No matter – there was my first job as a reporter to get stuck into.

And I was the only on-the-road reporter, so I was all in, all the time, with any reportable goings-on from Dimboola and Jeparit to the west and as far north as Rainbow and Beulah. Sport, crime (not much of that around), weather, Country Women's Association meetings – they were all in my patch. Once a month, a whole day was given over to local council meetings in Horsham, a veritable metropolis of twenty thousand residents half an hour's drive south.

This made my lack of a driver's licence a problem, but I'd had a couple of lessons from Dad and a couple with a taciturn instructor from the RACV, so I booked a test at the town's police station, conveniently located right next door to the *Herald* office.

On the day, I wandered in to find a beefy officer, at least as tall as my dad, stubbing out his last Winfield Red in an overflowing ashtray. He crushed the packet in a huge paw and smiled. 'Well hello, little lady. Is the car out front?'

I nodded, gesturing to the *Herald*'s company sedan parked at the curb.

'Bonza. You can drive me down to the milk bar for some durries.'

Once shoehorned into the passenger seat, my tester did not appear to need much from me. After the stop for ciggies, he directed me around the block a handful of times and then to the blacktop ramp to the railway station.

'We'll have to do the handbrake start here,' he said. 'It's the only slope steep enough.'

I passed.

***

Not even out of my teens, unpublished aside from a few essays in the Strathcona almanac, suddenly I was writing stories to fill at least half of a twice-weekly newspaper. That the publication stretched to a maximum of eight pages, including agricultural machinery ads, mattered not at all: the hands-on training was absolute gold.

There was no option but to work fast. 'This paper won't write itself!' the patriarch of the Ward family would boom. Arriving back at the office from the day's assignments, I'd scoop up a handful of seven-inch copy paper, flip open my spiral notebook, and start clacking away at the drab-green Remington International. First, the catchline, top right-hand corner, and the intro par, then zip, *click-click-click* with a new page and three more pars, typing frantically until the margin bell rang and the lever was pulled for the next line. I finished every article with ENDS, in caps.

Mrs Hoffmann was kindly and helpful, always happy to explain the ins and outs of town life, and to warn me whenever I was off to interview any of its more crotchety inhabitants. I'd slip the numbered copy pages into Mrs Hoffmann's desk tray. Every word was carefully subbed with a blue wax pencil by this expert, searching for literals (errors), and heaving herself out of her chair from time to time to check facts in the cuttings room. Being a local of many years helped her greatly – with no internet, fact-checking relied on her encyclopaedic knowledge of the town, its people, and its history. For me, being allowed to make mistakes and then have them corrected by a sharp mind with a blue pencil was a huge luxury.

But while my reporting skills were on fast-track, my mental health was tanking. I came to dread any break in the workday. At lunchtime I would head to the bakery and gobble a slab of chocolate slice, literally eating my feelings. Once work was over, the day emptied of human connection, and I would trail home to the prefab, make myself dinner (generally some variation on instant noodles) and lie on the mattress on the floor, desultorily flicking through the few available TV channels. Without a phone at first, I spent too many evenings in the public phone box on the main street, placing collect calls to Mum; I'd sob, and she would cluck sympathetically, and once I'd calmed down she'd pass the phone to Dad to talk some sense into me. There was little either of them could say to console me, other than counting down the weeks and days until they could visit or until I could cadge a lift to Melbourne for a weekend. Most often, Mum would tell me – in her bracing English tones – that I would make friends soon enough and then, magically, my life in the bush would be transformed.

But the townspeople – particularly those my own age – seemed closed off to me for reasons I didn't immediately understand. My tentative efforts to make new friends were rebuffed, and I seesawed between trying much too hard and withdrawing into myself. In the winter I put my name down for the women's netball team in a desperate attempt for connection, but I spent the entire season running around the court without once being passed the ball. I can see the comedy value of it now.

There was good reason for all this, at least in the locals' eyes: I was an outsider. In the midst of the most savage recession in decades, driven by interminable drought, jobs had disappeared like mist on a Wimmera morning. And there was I, swanning in from the bright lights of the city, swiping one of those precious jobs – on a one-year contract, too. Newcomers to a town that size can't escape scrutiny, and the bush telegraph would have been hard at work. They knew I wouldn't be hanging around for long.

I did manage to make some friends. After a few months, I moved from the prefab into a dilapidated wooden villa on the outskirts of town – recently condemned and therefore cheap as chips at a tenner a week – with the other outsider, a young woman on transfer from a bank branch in Shepparton. I was also befriended by an older farming couple, who gave me dinner once a week and allowed me to bring my horse up from Melbourne to their property. They were incredibly kind, almost like surrogate parents, but to this day I can't recall their names.

* * *

I don't remember other crucial facts and people from my time in Warracknabeal either, which is a bewildering and uncomfortable feeling. It's as though I long ago scrubbed my mind clean of all detail. The only thing left is the eidolon of loneliness, welling up whenever I try to bring those memories to life. I'm ashamed of that gap in my recall.

Years later, I was sitting by the open fire in my parents' front room, sipping sherry with Mum. She'd been having a clean-out, she said, and had found some buried treasure. 'Look, it's the letters you wrote to me from Warracknabeal.' She grinned and offered me a sheaf of envelopes.

'What the heck?' I slid my thumb under the flap of the top envelope, yellowed with age.

The first three paragraphs were in my handwriting but in a voice I no longer recognised as my own. From the page came roaring an anguish so powerful, my head snapped back in horror. Burning hot with revulsion, I stuffed the pages back in their casing and tossed the lot into the flames.

'Ali! Why don't you want to keep them? Are they that bad?' Mum seemed taken aback.

'Yep, they are that bad. Let's please not talk about it, ever again.'

It took me forty years to even allow the memories to rise and be recognised.

In the beginning they were like flashes from the muzzle of a gun: brief and terrifying. They would come from nowhere and stop me in my tracks, and I would stand or sit confused for just a second, before realising what was forming and stomp on them as quickly as I could, pushing them down to the unexplored base of consciousness, literally shaking my head and body to remove them.

Sometimes they would bubble up while I was driving, which in a strange way makes sense. Experienced drivers rely on muscle memory for the basics, leaving mental space for things like the chatter of the radio. I remember one early instance, on Auckland's Northwestern Motorway. As I was driving in the left lane towards the Hobson Street off-ramp, sweeping under the overpass, there was a glitch – like my brain was a computer being hacked.

For a brief second, I was back in the lounge room at Surrey Hills two decades before, lying with my back pressed awkwardly into the seat of the green vinyl couch and with Dad's huge hands heavy on my bare thighs.

I'm having a panic attack, I thought, and instructed my brain to concentrate on breathing, *in, one two three four, out, one two three four. Focus on the left-hand exit lane, check your following distance, breathe.*

Over time, I became an expert at this.

9.

Dear Alison,

We're pleased to hear you've had a productive year at the Warracknabeal *Herald*, and thank you for applying again to *The Herald and Sun News Pictorial*; however, I'm sorry to inform you that our policy is to avoid poaching cadets from other newspapers.

You are welcome to get back in touch when you've completed your cadetship.

Yours sincerely,

Bruce Baskett

Chief of Staff

The Herald and Sun News Pictorial

The letter sent me into a panic. I'd done what I'd promised to do: stuck it out for a year in the bush. I'd never considered escape back to the city might not be easy.

Dear Mr Baskett,

Thank you for your letter. I understand your policy, but am planning to leave Warracknabeal and relocate back to Melbourne in December regardless.

I hope this might make you reconsider taking me on as a second-year cadet.

Yours sincerely

Alison Mau

Baskett's response, which I imagined was written with a heavy sigh (oh, *alright then*) offered me a place as a copygirl: the lowest rung on the ladder. It would be a step backwards, a big one, with another five years before I'd graduate to D Grade.

'I could almost train to be a doctor in that time!' I moaned to Dad on the phone.

That was probably the fortieth time, given our calls were approximately weekly, he'd had to listen to my impatient yearning to get back to Melbourne, to the metros, where I thought my real career would begin. He listened to my rants with varying levels of patience depending largely on the time of day and his alcohol intake. But he was always practical, and his belief in my ability to stick it out never wavered.

If he'd had a few beers, I would make myself as comfortable as I could in the phone box, sometimes seated on the floor with the silver cord stretched as far as it would reach, while he recounted stories of his early days at the Melbourne *Herald* and his later role as a photojournalist on Fleet Street in London. Grit was always a feature of these tales – sticking it out was what he expected of me, and we both knew I did not carry that expectation lightly.

On this occasion, he laughed. 'What are your options?'

I wrote back accepting the job before Baskett could change his mind.

* * *

The role of the copygirl or copyboy had been right there in the name, until that very year. The most junior of staff, their main tasks were picking up the wads of off-white paper as final pages zipped from typewriter rollers, sorting the original 'books' from the five or so carbon copies, running them to the subs desk (for scarification, if there was even the smallest of errors), and then bringing them to the Lamson pneumatic tubes to be whisked away for typesetting. But that January, the *Herald and Weekly Times* had taken a tentative step into the future. The typewriters had vanished, replaced on each reporter's desk by a beige box, roughly the shape and size of a portable television. These word processors had a single purpose ruled by a complex set of commands and keystrokes.

While my job description had lost a crucial element – the copy! – the rest of it remained. I fetched endless cups of coffee, emptied the stinking mounded ashtrays, and ran down to the newsstand for packets of Winfield, Stuyvesant and Craven A cigarettes.

Copykids were not permitted to write. The very thought of allowing words from such a stripling to grace the paper would have been greeted with astounded snorts. The only exception was the gig guide: a section with short write-ups of pop concerts and pub band performances. One of my debut articles for the *Herald* was a breathless dissection of Elton John's Too Low for Zero Tour concert at the Melbourne Sports and Entertainment Centre.

***

A bollocking in the bullpen was nothing out of the ordinary: we were all accustomed to having strips torn off us by the new chief for some error or other. But it rarely happened to a senior reporter. And I could see that this time it was happening to the only senior female journalist in that male-dominated newsroom.

'What's going on?' I whispered to Nick, the cadet whose copykid shoes I'd stepped into on my first day. He'd taken me under his wing, becoming my drinking mate and invaluable guide to staying out of trouble with the bosses.

We pressed ourselves against the back wall of the newsroom.

'I think they're going to send her home?!' His thick black eyebrows were almost at his hairline.

The closed ranks of the *Herald*'s patriarchy were slowly opening up to women, but few had yet risen to her level. She was the chief state political reporter, a figure of awe and wonder for little fish like me. But the chief was windmilling his arms, gesticulating at her clothing. I stood on tiptoe, taking in her simple black suit and sensible heels. She was holding her ground, giving as good as she got. The argument escalated.

Another cadet slid in beside us, and we both bent our heads for the whispered update. 'He's furious she's come to work wearing *pants*.'

'What the …?' I ran sweating palms down my pencil skirt. There had been nothing in my induction to indicate women were restricted to dresses and skirts at work.

We watched wordlessly as the chief delivered his coup de grace, and the furious reporter stalked out with her bag slung over her shoulder. In an hour she was back, skirted this time – and humiliated, no doubt.

I had a strong urge to talk to her about it, find out what she thought, but I didn't dare. Copykids did not bother their seniors about anything if it could be helped, certainly not about touchy subjects like this one. How would I even approach it? 'Uh, hi, saw you being utterly demeaned today, what's it going to take to get gender equity in this goddam place, huh?'

At the pub that night a group of us juniors discussed how bizarre the scene had been – this was the mid-1980s, not the 50s! She had been neatly dressed; in fact, she had been dressed the same as the other senior reporters. The sheer regressivity of the chief's edict astounded us all.

I soon learned the chief had a bee in his bonnet about female staffers and their attire in general – and one morning it was my turn. I'd been out the night before and hadn't got home to change, turning up for a 5 am start with a quick stop in the ladies loo to rub away the panda smudges under my eyes.

'Mau. In here.'

I looked up to see the chief's famously luxuriant eyebrows drawn together in a scowl. At five foot three, he had a voice much larger than his stature.

I scuttled over on my four-inch stilettos, and as I came to a stop in front of him, we both clocked how comical the height discrepancy must look. A full foot shorter than me in those heels, he had to crane his neck to address me. 'Don't you *ever* wear those *FUCKING* shoes in here again.' He looked up at my gaping face and waved a dismissive hand. 'That's all.'

* * *

I was late again, belting up Flinders Street at a flat run. Already dreading the scolding I'd get from the chief, I barely noticed the group of dark-suited men turning into the foyer of the *Herald-Sun* building. I raced past them into the open lift and stabbed at the button, turning to the doors as they slid closed – right in the scowling face of Rupert Murdoch.

Oh wonderful, I thought, *that's my short career over and done with!*

We'd all been following Murdoch's three-way battle with Fairfax and the billionaire Robert Holmes à Court for control of the biggest newspaper empire in the country; that day he had come to claim his victor's spoils. His newly acquired staff of journalists were hardly rolling out the welcome mat: two of the company's senior editorial leaders had already resigned in disgust, and the leaders of our union were dead against the purchase.

Journalists tended to spurn any suggestion of editorial interference, and the newsroom simmered with antipathy that day.

All of us were collected in tight ranks, our arms folded. I skulked at the very back of the pack, hoping Murdoch wouldn't spot the minion who'd left him high and dry in the foyer an hour before. Lucky for me, he'd either forgotten all about it or had bigger things on his mind – I never heard a thing about it.

* * *

After four years at the *Herald*, one as a copygirl and three as a cadet, I was doing okay. My work had even recently made the front page for the first time, a huge thrill for any young newspaper reporter. But the gap in my progression nagged at me: I had done my first-year cadet duties back in Warracknabeal and then an extra year as a copygirl. By rights, I thought, I should be graduating with the others of the same age and experience.

The exam to test our shorthand skills – the *Herald* insisted its journalists used Pitman shorthand, which was considered superior to the other system, Teeline, but was harder to learn – stood as the final hurdle in the progression to graded journalist, and the bar was high: 120 words a minute or you failed. The exam was held in a building across town, in a stuffy room where the scent of fear hung heavy in the air. It was held once a year, and there were no re-dos. We knew this was make or break. I turned the paper face down on the desk and glanced around the room at my fellow cadets, seeing a few dejected faces and some satisfied smirks. I was fairly sure I'd passed.

When the results came out, I walked straight to Mahogany Row, named for the wood-panelled offices of the executive class. I strode into the plush antechamber of the big boss. 'I'd like an appointment with Mr Hinton, please.'

His secretary eyed me with suspicion. 'And you are?' Cadets did not generally come anywhere near the editor's office and certainly never to request a personal audience.

'I'm a third-year cadet, and I should be a fourth year – that's what I want to talk to him about.' I was shaking with nerves, and this last bit came out in a tangled rush.

She raised a pencilled eyebrow, keeping her eyes on me as if I'd nick the silver at any second, and thumbed through a large diary. 'Alright then. He can see you on Thursday. For ten minutes.' She snapped the book shut.

When Thursday came, I put my argument to the editor. He listened politely as I reeled off my reasoning and finished with my excellent shorthand score, trying to pull off an air of confidence I certainly didn't feel. Who was I to make demands, let alone one that would catapult me over an entire year of work? So when he said yes I was astounded, stuttering my thanks and scuttling back to my desk. I decided not to tell my fellow cadets right away; they would learn of this anomaly soon enough, and some of them would hate my guts for it. C'est la vie.

One person I did want to tell immediately was Dad. I called him as soon as I got off the tram to the flat in Fitzroy I shared with three other cadets in my cohort. While his response was more laconic than effusive – wasn't it always? – I could hear the pride in his voice. I felt I'd been chasing that all my life.

10.

For a bunch of women of my generation, the sexual revolution had delivered a condundrum. Two decades on from the release of the Pill, we'd been promised the freedom to explore our own pleasure. But whatever we'd imagined sexual freedom would look like, in practice the patriarchy had not quite finished with us.

The rules for sex remained in place: you were still a 'slut' if you pursued it and 'frigid' if you rejected it. If you were not 'nice', then you were a 'bitch'. This tightrope was impossible to negotiate. The worst thing you could be was a 'cock-tease', responsible for whatever a man, whether you knew him well or not, might choose to take as his cue, his right – your fault, either way. The other side of the sexual revolution's shiny coin was the new expectation that if you'd popped that cherry you would be *always* available, *always* keen and *always* skilled at pleasing your lover in ways that would make your mum blush beetroot.

But hey, we women were having fun … careful fun, in the era of HIV/AIDS. At one point while working at the *Herald*, I was going out to dinner or gigs with four different guys, and they were all lovely. When three of them got whiny about exclusivity, I called them from my office phone, one after another, and as gently as I could dumped them all on a single morning – too much trouble! But the signals were sometimes more confusing.

Matthew was the first person I really fell for. I met him in the bar at the Phoenix Hotel. A young writer for the rival daily *The Age*, he was, by a long shot, the most beautiful man I'd ever seen, dark and intense – and *completely wrong* for me. I fell for him immediately.

Matthew styled himself as an intellectual. A Marxist in the poser sense, he wore all-black polo-neck sweaters and carried copies of Sartre. We had a year-long affair that was mostly sex, but I fancied myself in love. I was devastated when he announced he was moving to Sydney. There was no suggestion – not even a hint – that he'd like me to move there with him, and although I agonised over it, I couldn't bring myself to ask directly.

On our last night together, he left me with the 'compliment' that he'd have 'a hard time finding someone who fucks like you do'. Gee. Thanks.

After three months of pining and a number of pleading phone calls from me, Matthew (grudgingly, I think) agreed I could come to Sydney for a week's visit. For thirteen hours on an overnight bus, Cold Chisel playing through the tinny headphones of my Walkman, I imagined an ecstatic reunion. Everything had changed, of course, and we spent two uncomfortable days in his inner-city terrace flat together, before he kicked me out. He'd caught me flipping through a copy of *Cosmopolitan* and could not, he claimed, be in any kind of relationship with someone who read such low-brow muck. Matthew wasn't a bad guy, though – he was young and trying to work out what he wanted from life, just like the rest of us.

A week later, at a campsite on the New South Wales coast, my mate Nick from the *Herald* introduced me to his best friend. Straight off the plane from my humiliation in Sydney, a new entanglement was the last thing on my mind, and Shaun – laid-back, smart, funny, perceptive – was the polar opposite personality of the intense and brooding one I'd imagined myself in love with just a few days earlier. *No more men*, I'd told myself, *not this side of thirty!* And Shaun did nothing other than be himself (not that I could see, anyway) to seduce me. But he seemed genuinely interested in me as a person. When the week at the beach was up and we returned to Melbourne, I told him I wasn't interested in anything short of commitment. He called two days later to ask me out on a proper date.

Shaun taught me what an equal partnership could look like. We spent winter weekends at a chilly Torquay beach house, where he would wind his limbs around me to fend off the draughts that whistled up between the floorboards. I was literally wrapped in love.

We were together for more than two years, and while we both made mistakes, I botched it up in the end. I imagined I was on some career fast-track, while he just wanted to surf. (And why not? We were barely out of our teens!) With an overblown sense of *my destiny*, I decided these two things did not align, and I ended it.

* * *

The problem with knowing at the age of twelve what I wanted my career to be, I found, was that within a few years I had pretty much achieved everything my pre-teen brain had imagined. By twenty-three, I'd been working as a reporter for five years and was beginning to get itchy feet. Many of my friends were leaving on their big overseas experiences, following streams of Aussies and Kiwis to London, or on backpacking odysseys in Asia. I decided a three-month break from the mundane would give me time to think about what I wanted to do next – and if my bosses at the *Herald* didn't want to give the time off, I'd quit.

A couple of months after I'd booked my ticket to London I was at a rowdy journo dinner party when I heard a former colleague, Michael – who'd left the profession for a government press sec role – discussing that he was looking to hire. I was very drunk and halfway through an expletive-riddled rant about how appallingly low-paid we were at the *Herald* despite our cohort's five years' service, so all I really heard of Michael's pitch was, 'It pays thirty-eight thousand a year.'

This sounded like untold riches compared to my meagre salary.

'I'll do it!' I slurred from the other end of the table, shooting my hand into the air.

Michael grinned at me. 'Perhaps we should discuss it tomorrow, when you're feeling, uh … a bit more normal.'

We did, and Michael agreed to hire me for the position of media liaison for the Health Department, starting on my return from Europe.

* * *

The flight to London was the first time I'd left Australia since I was a toddler, which made the 24-hour stopover in Hong Kong my first experience of a foreign city. When I told a friend in Melbourne about this, they put me in touch with their friend Hugo, an English finance specialist, who volunteered to act as my tour guide.

Back then, organising the meet-up meant an exchange of letters and a leap of faith that he would show up. On arrival, I was relieved to see him waiting at the airport as planned. Soon he was speaking to me with intense, arm-swooping enthusiasm about his adopted home, particularly the rivers of money to be made in those twilight years of British rule. A fine tour guide, he escorted me around backstreets and markets, then up Victoria Peak for the famous view across the colony.

We had a fancy dinner at a banquet restaurant, followed by a polite verbal struggle as I insisted on paying for my part of the meal. Then we headed into the hectic neon-lit streets and the overwhelming flow of people, cars, pedicabs and bicycles to a succession of packed and raucous nightclubs.

It was the early hours of the morning when we found the mid-level hotel I'd booked for one night, a pencil-like tower stretching up into the haze. In the brass and marble foyer, I began to say my thank-yous and goodbyes, but Hugo insisted: chivalry impelled him to walk me all the way to my room. He was the smiling epitome of British charm.

'Hey, that was so great,' I told him when we reached the door. 'I don't even know how to thank you for showing me around.' I slid the key into the lock and cracked the door open before turning to face him. 'Well, this is me. Gotta get some sleep before my next flight.'

The passage of seconds slowed to a crawl. Hugo lunged across the metre or so between us. I stumbled a half-step on my heels, instinctively tilting backwards from the waist, stiff-backed, confused. He caught me by the upper arms, way too forcefully for chivalry, then the Mr Nice Guy schtick was gone as he pushed his face into mine, gripping me tightly.

The force of his weight sent shock and adrenaline coursing through me. *What's happening?*

The door slammed back against the interior wall, revealing a perfectly made bed in a tiny square space. My suitcase, with my travelling dreams packed innocently inside, was at the end of the bed. All of Hong Kong was spread beneath the single window.

In that instant, an improbable number of thoughts cycled through my head. Had I invited this? I'd been ... well, me. Curious, excited, intensely happy to be experiencing something new. Chatty, sure, but not overly flirty.

I snapped back into the moment, grateful for the first time for being tall – several inches loftier than he was. 'No,' I said. 'This is *NOT* happening.'

Here was a situation that might have gone a number of ways. Fight, flight, freeze or fawn: these are the options the body and brain have to choose from in moments of threat or attack. None are guaranteed, none are a conscious choice, each one happens fast, all are designed to keep us from being hurt or killed. The body chooses. Hormones released from the hypothalamus activate the adrenal medulla, which release epinephrine and norepinephrine, flooding the bloodstream. The bladder loosens, the heart accelerates, muscles contract, pupils dilate, hair follicles become erect.

That night, my body believed I could overcome the threat. I pushed with everything I had, tipping Hugo off balance long enough for me to slip inside and slam the door. He yelled the usual insults, not caring how many tourists were slumbering in nearby rooms. Finally, as I leaned panting with shock on the inside of the door, I heard him curse, under his breath but so filled with venom he might as well have been holding a megaphone.

A pause, then footsteps dulled by the deep hallway carpet. Then silence.

* * *

I did not sleep. Another day, another long flight, and in the dark hours on board my mind chewed relentlessly over the night before, analysing, self-blaming, circling back. By the time the plane landed in London I'd completed the necessary mental gymnastics and decided to try to put it behind me and be more wary next time. What other option was there?

After a couple of weeks with my grandparents in Somerset – my first visit since that trip with Mum and Lisa when I was just a toddler – I took the train back to London for the start of my Contiki tour. I'd booked the three-week sprint around the highlights of Europe as a way to prepare myself for a more lengthy period of backpacking – border crossings, changing currencies, that sort of thing. I did not imagine for a second it would change my life entirely.

In the 80s, Contiki was legendary for its late-night, party-hard code. After nights of binge-drinking, we were fogged by hangovers as we slithered onto the bus each morning. My memory of Paris to Amsterdam via Italy, Austria, Switzerland, Monaco, Liechtenstein and Germany is not exactly a sharp, blow-by-blow timeline.

By day three, I was in a casual sleeping arrangement with the 'courier', Craig, a sweet Canadian with floppy blond hair, not that much older than myself. I thought I might be in love, in the misguidedly intense manner you have when you're young, but I was (duh) just another in a long line of lovelorn travellers looking for connection in unfamiliar territory. A relationship beyond the boundaries of the Holborn Street departure and the ferry ride from Hook of Holland back to London was never on the cards.

Sleeping with the crew was, in hindsight, a tactical mistake: it set me apart from the group, and not in a good way. My fellow travellers either seemed resentful or mocked me relentlessly for the 'special treatment' (wink, wink) I was apparently shown. Some just refused to talk to me. With all of my hair flicking and moon-eyed gazing, I deserved their scorn in spades, no doubt. But I did become close with a couple of girls from Boston who spent hours on the bus regaling me with idioms from the US. A sample: 'In Australia we say "drunk" or "pissed" – what do you call it?' 'Oh, in Boston "pissa" means "awesome". Now, "drunk" – that's "twisted", "toasted", "I'm sheets", "half in the bag" …'

The situation with Craig led to a mystery that remains unsolved to this day. Midway through the tour, I was approached by a crew member. The message they carried was a delicate one.

'We, uh … You need to come and see the nurse,' they told me.

'Oh. Really? How come?' I'd left my sunglasses in the room, and the morning sun was giving me hell for last night's drinking.

'Well, you might be, uh …' Their voice dropped to a stage whisper. 'You might have caught VD.'

That floored me. I had no symptoms of a venereal disease, but I knew that was no guarantee of anything. And although I had no clue how this person would know whether I had or had not come into contact with what we'd now call an STD, the unearned shame that flooded me stopped me from asking any questions. Why was I filled with shame? The crew member wasn't inferring the speculated condition had come from me, and even if it had, there ought not to have been any ignominy connected with that. Thanks, patriarchy, you win again.

Beetroot-red to the roots of my hair, I followed the polo-shirted messenger, eyes firmly on my sneakered feet. As we walked, my escort said brightly, 'We can treat it, it's simple – you'll just need to come with me.'

There seemed to be more crew gathered with the nurse than strictly necessary. The nurse (*was she?*) produced ampoule and syringe, and indicated a down trou. Once again, soaked in humiliation, I didn't ask questions but pulled down my shorts and underwear and was stuck in the bum with a large needle.

I never spoke of this again – not even, as I recall, to Craig, although I should have given him the third degree. I wasn't stupid, I knew my stuff. I'd been careful.

Years later, after I'd moved to New Zealand to work in television, a former Contiki staffer told me 'the jab' was a semi-regular prank on the Europe circuit. It was played on naive passengers who had the temerity to sleep with the crew. If this is true, the prank was a cruel but ingenious one: who would want the particulars of *that* intervention spread beyond those already in on the joke?

I was gobsmacked, thrown back into the mortification of that moment, decades ago. I managed to choke out, 'What the ...? That's awful,' with a strangled laugh. The former staffer seemed mildly apologetic, and we shrugged it off with rueful smiles.

The knowledge that if it had been a prank, it had also been a physical assault with a weapon didn't strike me until later still. But I don't know which version is the truth. For the sake of who knows how many other unwitting passengers, I do hope it was all legit and done out of concern for my health. If not, well, I hope the ears and consciences of everyone involved are burning right now.

* * *

There was one experience on the Contiki Europe circuit we heard about long before the bus pulled into that stopover: the party at The Fridge. This was some kind of disused bunker – small, concrete, airless – transformed into a tiny nightclub and packed nightly with writhing, sweaty bodies.

It was late September, the weather still warm in the southernmost stops, and in the windowless Fridge, it was stratospherically hot. We were all tripped up on herby shots of Jägermeister, which at 35 percent alcohol was the favoured route to inebriation. The drinks went down and the volume up, and the party quickly hit that ideal level of frenzy where everyone has lost track of time and inhibition, no one laughs at your dancing, and all that matters is the music.

As the church organ strains of George Michael's 'Faith' came on to delighted squeals from the crowd, I glanced around and saw him. He was leaning against the wall a little apart from the crowd and not – pointedly, I thought – dancing.

He was tall, much taller than anyone else in the room. Slim build, broad shoulders. Thick, longish black hair. Dark eyes. He was not drunk, or if he was, he held it better than the rest of us. A touch of the aloof, but by no means on his own, chatting to a tight knot of people who all seemed to be vying for his attention. I watched them for a while out of the corner of my eye, asking a staffer who he was: Simon, a Kiwi, one of the senior Contiki couriers, a rising star in the company. I weaved my way unsteadily, bumper-car style, through the throng to be introduced.

The two of us talked for a bit, and although hampered by the Jägermeister, I put on the flirt as best I could. Later I couldn't remember what we said. I did know I'd made no better impression than the probably hundreds of other passengers who tried to play siren for Simon every summer season.

* * *

It was early October when we reached Amsterdam, our final stop. The long, flaring tail of summer, still hanging on in Southern Europe, was absent here, swapped for bruised-purple skies and carpets of red and gold leaves along the canals.

In the spotty mirror of our hostel bathroom, I barely recognised the face that gazed back at me: pale, puffy, slit-eyed. 'You look about eighty years old,' I scolded myself aloud, making a pledge to lay off the drink … for a few weeks at least.

The ferry crossing from the Hook of Holland to Harwich was brutal. Bilious from the rolling waves, I huddled alone on a plastic seat, face to the wind. Suddenly, Mr Rising Star was in the seat beside me, chatting amicably, plainly in much better health than I was.

Simon suggested a movie in the onboard theatre, and I nodded and followed him. But I saw only parts of it between lurches to the side of the boat to vomit into the steely waves of the Channel. He suggested dinner in London the following night. I wondered why he was bothering with me at all – a shivering, puking wreck – and I turned him down, pleading prior plans. 'Oh, well, perhaps we'll write?' I wrote his name and postal address in my Filofax, and we left it at that.

Weeks later, backpacking in Europe with my cousin, I was calling Mum and Dad from a phone booth near the Ponte Vecchio in Florence when the door was flung open and my bag, which I'd stupidly placed on the chest-high metal bench, was lifted cleanly away. By the time I'd turned from the phone there was just the thump of footsteps as the thief disappeared into the dusk.

My first thought was not for the traveller's cheques I'd have to replace: it was for the Filofax with the names and addresses of everyone I knew in it, gone forever.

And then, for some reason I could not fathom, I thought particularly of the latest addition. Someone I barely knew, whose surname I couldn't even recall. I thought for a bit about going into Contiki's London HQ and asking for his details, but the idea was too humiliating. *I'll never see him again*, I thought. It felt like a loss.

* * *

The postcard arrived at my parents' house a few days before Christmas, sent from Canada, where he was visiting friends.

I'm snowed in and bored, Simon wrote, *so I'm holed up in a public library writing to a few people. How are you?*

We fell into an easy but fitful correspondence, weeks passing between letters as he worked the seasons in Europe and I threw myself into my new job as media liaison for the Health Department in Melbourne.

It was 1988, and Victoria's Labor government was pressing ahead with radical responses to the growing HIV/AIDS crisis. It would become the first state government in Australia to introduce needle exchange programmes and safe injecting rooms, to much outrage from conservatives. The AIDS unit, staffed by pioneers of the fight for funded drugs for HIV patients, took up a whole floor of the Health Department's city headquarters. I spent much of my time there, consulting with experts on safe-sex public messaging campaigns – while trying not to blush at the huge posters all over the walls, showing scenes a private school girl from the eastern suburbs had certainly never encountered before.

But outside of work, I was spurred on by a growing need to escape from the low-rise backwater town of 80s Melbourne. I decided to use my grandparental right of residence to move to London as soon as I could.

Halfway through 1989, the letters from Europe stopped altogether. At first I assumed Simon was busy, then that he probably had a girlfriend – what did I know, perhaps he'd got married …? Six months passed without a word, but I found I couldn't put him out of my mind. I pulled his last letter from its shoebox and re-read it; he'd said he would be heading home to Auckland at Christmas. A plan formed.

In Melbourne's CBD, there was a shopfront library of telephone books, one for most major cities in the world. After taking the tram down from the office in my lunchbreak, I pulled the Auckland book from the shelves and combed through it for all the Dallows, copying them into my notebook. There were about fifteen, from memory. I was accustomed to searching for information in the analogue world – for a journalist in the 80s, just about every story began with the White Pages.

This fact-finding mission coincided with an opportunity that seemed too good to pass up: a friend had told me of a spot coming free in his Hampstead flat. I would finally be moving to London.

One evening just before Christmas, I told my best friend and flatmate Shauna about the phone books and the list, over a meal of her excellent pasta at our little walk-up flat.

'What should I do?' I asked.

She let rip her glorious laugh. 'Make the calls, of course.'

'Really? Are you sure? Seems, I dunno … kinda desperate?'

'So what? You're never gonna know if you don't call.'

It took several Jim Beam and Cokes for me to work up the courage to start dialling. After five duds, my next call was answered by a woman. 'Yeah, this is Simon's place, but he's not here right now.' She sounded annoyed or bored or both.

Almost certainly his wife, I thought in a panic. 'Ah. Could you tell him I called? I'm … um … a friend, I met him in London. But I'm in Melbourne. He can call me back … ah, if he wants to …' I gave her the number, waving an arm furiously at Shauna, who was rolling around on the carpet in fits.

'Okay.' The line went dead.

Not long after, on Christmas Eve, Shauna and I were propped at the bar in Greasy Joe's, our local, thoroughly drowning our sorrows and bitching about men being useless and *rude*. It had been four days, and there'd been no call back from Simon.

'Why do we care so much?!' I wailed in her ear, as the bar erupted to the first strains of Neil Diamond's 'Sweet Caroline'.

'Beats me, roomie.' She waved at the barman for another round.

Around midnight we rolled up the concrete stairs to the flat, clutching each other for balance. It took several goes to get the key in the door, but once we'd stumbled inside, the first thing I saw was the blinking red light on the small beige box in the corner of the living room. A message. On our answer machine.

Suddenly sober, I pressed the button.

A very deep voice filled the room. 'Hi, it's Simon. Got your message. Call me back.'

11.

I was running late, so late. Half an hour until the moment Simon and I would meet again, and I'd already cocked it up. I'd dreamt about this moment for months, but today time had slipped through my fumbling fingers. The universe was conspiring with my chronic indecision – the evidence: a pile of discarded clothes on the twin bed in my room, the casual but careful hair and makeup I'd redone twice, and the Hampstead Tube station where at least two trains should have materialised by now to take me into town. It would all come to nothing if I didn't make it in time.

Simon and I had made the date by phone, months ago, on one of those long late-night calls between Melbourne and Auckland. When I landed in London, he'd told me, he would be leading a tour in Europe in the early season. 'I'll be back in London on 28 April,' he'd said. 'Let's meet the following day, at noon in Trafalgar Square.'

It was warm for the end of April, not the usual soft spring day. I was sweating (ugh, so not attractive!) by the time I'd pistoned my legs up the steps from Charing Cross station and barrelled into the square, hair flying. Stupidly, I hadn't accounted for the tourists – in my mind's eye, Simon would be the first person I'd clap eyes on. But every inch of the square was packed with sightseers. How carelessly they wandered, as I weaved at a run through the crowd, suddenly no longer confident I'd know his face.

It was twenty past twelve. He might quite reasonably have left, having made the assumption he'd been stood up.

Then there he was, a little distance off. He was leaning against a wall in jeans, a polo shirt and sunglasses.

The immediate realisation I would have known him anywhere. The sheer relief of it. While my head was strict – *be cool, be cool* – my legs refused the order, breaking into a run, propelling me straight at him. Bye-bye insouciance.

He absorbed this projectile blonde with just a raised eyebrow. 'Oh. Here you are. I was about to leave.'

I tried to keep my voice below a shriek. 'I'm not always this late [a lie] but the eleven-thirty train was cancelled. I probably should have got to the Tube earlier. Anyway, sorry, sorry …' My apology bumbled on longer than necessary.

He cut me off with a smile and those flat Kiwi vowels. 'Okay, all good. What would you like to do? Shall I show you my favourite London spots?'

The rest of that day exists in my mind as a set of Polaroid snapshots, some bled of colour and unfocused, some saturated and clear as if no time has passed. My first ever taste of Long Island iced tea, in a Covent Garden bar; a late afternoon movie session during which I was so overcome by his proximity, his shoulder just a couple of inches from mine, that I couldn't remember a single plot point in *The Hunt for Red October*; a visit to Ronnie Scott's, the famous jazz club in Frith Street, Soho.

Eleven hours, a swapping of origin stories, several arguments. Years later we would laugh about the number of times I stalked off, offended. But this early inkling of how different we were was ignored as our mutual attraction took root.

Simon was only in London for a week, but by the end of that time I was – as my father might say – gone for all money.

Back when I'd moved to London a few weeks earlier, I'd fallen into a situationship with a fellow Aussie journalist. He and I went on dates and had perfectly lovely sex, but each time we met up he gave me the 'don't get too attached, this is just a casual thing' speech. And each time I warmly assured him I wanted it to stay that way too, but he didn't seem to believe me.

After my first earth-shaking week with Simon, I took the journo aside at a picnic on Hampstead Heath and said, 'Sorry, no more dates.'

He seemed astounded and genuinely hurt. 'Are you telling me …' he paused, overcome '… that you like this other guy *more than me*?!'

'Um. Yes, that's what I'm telling you.' I couldn't think of anything else to say.

I had always been a one-guy kind of girl – a committed monogamist – and I tended to fall hard and early. The way I felt about Simon after that first week was way too intense for the circumstances. If he'd said, *Hey, let's get a flat together*, I would have jumped at the chance. Instead, we were kept apart by practical considerations; his job travelling Europe for three, six or even eight weeks at a time meant we saw each other for a weekend a month at best. In private I railed against this, but there was nothing to do but accept it and get on with making friends with the people around me.

Long-distance relationships of the kind we had are like riding in a car with a learner driver. You might wish you had the wheel, but your destiny is in another's hands. You think you know the rules of this road and how to implement them, but it's not up to you, the one pining at home, to negotiate those twists and turns. And in my union with Simon, it was way too early for us to be setting rules anyhow.

So, I would write, long outpourings on brittle blue-lined airmail paper, trying to leaven the longing with amusing tales of London life.

* * *

I had to find a job. I didn't want to pull pints in a sticky-floored pub; naively, as I blew through the few thousand dollars I'd brought with me, I clung to the belief I'd get work as a journalist.

I'd arrived in London at a time of political upheaval, dragging my suitcase off the train from Heathrow and into the midst of the poll tax riots on 31 March 1990. My first glimpse of my new home was a post-apolcalyptic landscape of burning overturned cars, shattered shop windows and mounted police spurring their horses at unarmed protestors. Anti-Thatcher sentiment was at its height – and there was, I assumed, *lots* of news to be written.

Three months on, I'd almost run out of money.

Despondent and half-cut at the pub one Friday night, I was chatting to a Kiwi journalist I'd met. He pointed to his boss at the bar – a tall, bearded man with the slightly shambolic look of the English aristocrat.

'I'm going back to New Zealand for six weeks, and I know he needs to cover my shifts – may as well ask, eh?' the Kiwi suggested.

That man at the bar, Peter Ewence, was the co-owner of Intervoice International, a TV production company. He did not want to hire me at first, and I couldn't blame him – I'd never written for telly before – but in desperation, I told him I'd work for free for two weeks, and he could make his mind up at the end, keep me on or boot me out. He stroked his beard thoughtfully and decided he liked the deal.

I was still at Intervoice eight weeks later when fate handed me another opportunity. 'Bring a nice jacket to work on Monday,' Peter told me over pints at the pub. 'We've landed a new contract, and I want you to do a screen test.'

There were two problems with this idea: I did not own a jacket, and I did not see myself as on-screen talent.

'Just humour me.' He sighed. 'I'll see you, with a jacket, on Monday.'

Peter's production company was an early cog in the wheel of a brand-new form of broadcasting the news: the 24-hour satellite news channel. BBC World Television had been formed to go head to head with CNN, and Intervoice International was gaining respect as a contract provider of programming for the BBC's insatiable round-the-clock beast. The new contract, however, was with Taiwan's flagship TV channel, run in partnership by the country's defence force and its education department. The head of CTS Taiwan wanted a European correspondent to beam into the nightly news: a small role, just a couple of minutes, right after the first commercial break.

There was no formal training for becoming a newsreader, so I had to make it up and hope I had 'it', the thing that gets people to watch. Every day for weeks, I had been sitting in the control room and watching our presenter Mary Nightingale host *World Business Report*, so in the screen test for CTS Taiwan I simply pretended I was her. I must have been a good enough facsimile because I got the job. But I didn't sound like her, and that was a problem.

'Er, I'm terribly sorry and all ...' Peter said to me, again with the beard-stroking. 'I don't mean to be rude, but we can't have you speaking like you do on-screen. You'll need to have elocution lessons. We'll get someone over from the BBC.'

He needn't have worried; I wasn't offended – having accepted the role, I was determined to do anything I needed to do, to knock it out of the park. And I found letting go of my Australian accent fairly easy once the coach had explained the basics of craniofacial function. In the Received Pronunciation of British English, the vowels are made by dropping the jaw; in Australia, the lips and jaw draw back, creating nasal vowels. Simple! In a very short time I was on the air five nights a week. After one question from the stunning and very regal female news presenter in Taipei, I would deliver my two-minute answer from our tiny London studio.

I'd had about an eight-week head start when Iraqi troops crossed the border into Kuwait on 2 August 1990 and took the country within twelve hours. The Gulf War became the focus of every news channel, and I went from a two-minute autocue read to eight or nine minutes live and unscripted Q & A at the top of the CTS bulletin every night. That's how I *really* learned to be a news presenter.

Peter insisted I also learn to produce and present *World Business Report* on a roster with Mary, and even to direct the programme from the control room. That last role was terrifying – I don't recommend that job unless you have nerves of steel.

I wrote to Dad about my job, excited to share my success and bask in his praise. I was crushed when he made it abundantly clear that journalism meant *words in print*, not 'some gussied-up talking head on the goggle-box'. It was as if I'd let the side down.

* * *

In 1992, Peter asked me to travel to an international conference in Taiwan to give a speech on the rise of satellite news broadcasting. 'Ah, my specialist subject!' I wisecracked to him as we argued over his choice to send me – surely, I thought, he should be the one to make the address to all of those learned colleagues? I was just a beginner in the broadcast news world.

When I arrived in Taipei, I realised that it wouldn't have

mattered if I'd stood on that conference stage and sung 'Mary Had a Little Lamb': it seemed everyone in the country knew my name. Whenever I poked my head out from the marbled hush of the Grand Hyatt, they would point and shout, 'Alison! *ALISON!*' and follow me down the street in groups, laughing and chattering. It was my first ever experience of being in the public eye, and although Taipei was just a few years out of martial law, I never felt unsafe for a minute in this invigorating city full of kind, beautiful people.

On the final night of the conference, the head of CTS invited the keynote speakers to a banquet in his private dining room. He finished the meal with a flourish by presenting each of us with a huge replica Ming vase, at least a foot and a half high. Some of us got the giggles as we considered how on earth we'd fit the thing in our carry-on luggage for the trip home.

But the vase wasn't the only gift I failed to appreciate that night. The genial American sitting to my right at the table was professor emeritus at the Columbia University Graduate School of Journalism. Columbia was the best journalism school in the world – even I knew that.

Over coffee, he made me an offer. 'Ali, you should come and do postgrad study with us.'

'Uh, I don't actually have a degree, so I wouldn't qualify.' I had finished most of a BA in Journalism at RMIT while a cadet at the *Herald* but had never graduated.

'But you have easily enough industry experience to make up for that.' He gave me his card. 'Think about it. And call me.'

It was a sliding-door moment. I could see his offer was genuine, but there was something impossible about my mind's-eye picture of myself moving to New York and walking in the footsteps of the greats. It didn't fit. I would be pretending, I believed, just like I'd pretended to be Mary Nightingale when I auditioned for the on-screen job and as I had when I'd given my speech at the conference the day before. And I would be among actual journalism graduates from around the world who had no need to pretend.

So I let the decision drift and went back to London, carrying the huge box with the vase in it – fake, like me! Six months later, sick of the dark and cold and pining for a decent beach, I moved home to Australia. Passing on that offer is one of my few professional regrets.

12.

'Whaddya get up to in your time off? I'll bet you're fucking your way round town, just like your dad did, aren't you?' John Sorell leaned back in his chair, tickled by his own joke, his large beer belly shaking under his business shirt.

From London I had presented and produced programmes for major international broadcasters, but Sorell wasn't interested in my professional experience.

This job interview was unlike any I'd ever attended, and I'd done plenty. I was also no easy mark: you could not have grown up in the house I had, a third generation Aussie journo, without a skin like a Northern Territory water buffalo and an understanding of how brutal the news business could be, especially for women. My early years had prepared me for any and all kinds of sexist bullshit – or so I'd thought. Here, within minutes of sitting down, I'd had my work experience dismissed, and now the man I hoped would hire me was drilling me about ... my *sex life*?

I knew of Sorell, of course. He was a titan of the Melbourne news business, his name spoken – sometimes in whispers – with both fear and reverence. For years he'd written the 'On the Spot' daily column in the *Herald*; he'd gained legend status after a scoop interview with Red Adair, grabbed mid-flight after Sorell convinced the cabin crew to swap his seat with the one next to the famous American firefighter. For that, Sorell won a national Walkley Award for Excellence in Journalism.

In the early 1970s Sorell had been the editor of the *Sunday Observer*, pushing the salacious tabloid to ever-higher circulation numbers with a formula of 'tits, trots, TV and track'. That charming description of the paper came straight from the horse's mouth, in a 1975 student magazine interview with *Observer* publisher Maxwell Newton, who also freely admitted the publication was a 'vulgar paper of entertainment' that did not 'try very hard to inform'. Sorell had been a clever hire for that purpose, pushing the boundaries of scandal reportage and lifting readership year on year. At the pinnacle – or, might I say, nadir – he was apparently responsible for the headline 'My Billy's No Poofter – Sonia Tells' atop a story on rumours about former prime minister William McMahon's private life.

Channel 9's owner Kerry Packer snatched Sorell away in the late 70s to run GTV-9's Melbourne newsroom – the fact that Sorell knew nothing at all about television news (and told the magnate as much) mattered not at all. Packer wanted a hard-arse journo for the job, and Sorell fit the bill in spades. In the fifteen years or so he'd been at the helm, he'd taken Nine from the doldrums to the top spot in the ratings. By the time I sat across from him, he was known to all and sundry by the twin monikers 'The Bear' and

'The Admiral'. That man could strip the flesh from your bones with a single narrowed-eye glance.

I knew his reputation, but his ugly question knocked the breath out of me regardless. For a moment I blinked mutely, wondering what Dad had to do with this. How did Sorell even know my dad? The shock of it fogged my brain, and it took me a moment to realise that they had been contemporaries in the blokes-own world of Melbourne journalism in the 1950s and 60s. They would have known each other well – had probably been drinking buddies at the Phoenix Hotel, a few staggering steps from the *Herald Sun* building.

Heat was spreading from my neck, engulfing the businesslike makeup I'd carefully applied for the interview. *Fuck this guy.*

'I'll give you a go,' he told me. 'Six months. As a reporter on *Melbourne Extra.*'

The local current affairs show was new to the Nine line-up, created as a lead-in to the nightly news bulletin at six. I was given no contract, just a brief typewritten letter of offer, signed by Sorell. That letter survived my habit of losing things, thank god. In a few short months, I'd need it more than any other piece of paper I'd ever been given.

* * *

Newsrooms of the past were tough places, loaded with rivalries and soaked in ambition, just as Hunter S Thompson wrote all those decades ago. In a triumph of cognitive dissonance, they were often also, fondly, described as 'families'. If GTV-9 was a clan, I had the strong feeling I'd been cast as the unwanted stepmother when I walked through the famed Bendigo Street doors on my first day. A stranger with a weird hybrid accent, in a flash suit from Harvey Nichols, I stuck out like the proverbial banged thumb.

My first task was a small one: a short filler story for that night's bulletin. Afterwards, I took the audio cart to the chief of staff for checks.

'*MAU*. In here.' Back from his three-hour lunchtime pub session, Sorell pinned me with a laser stare from the door of his office. The cart was clutched in his massive paw. He was pulsing with offence.

I picked up my notebook and scurried over.

'What is this shit? I need you talking like an Aussie, not like some Brit toff. If you don't have an Aussie accent by the start of your shift tomorrow, you're gone.'

'Yes, of course,' I stammered. Once again, dammit all, I was blushing crimson.

'Well? Don't just stand there like a stunned mullet. Fuck off and fix it.'

I spent the rest of the afternoon slumped at my desk, turning over my piteously few options. I had not a flyspeck of doubt he'd carry out the threat. Maybe he already regretted his decision to hire me and this was the easiest way to get rid of me. Forget any visions of telly stardom, I needed this job to pay the rent and bills on my hovel in the inner-eastern suburb of Kew. After three years in London, leaning into those elocution lessons, how on earth was I going to put it right in less than twenty-four hours?

After the 6 pm bulletin had been and gone, after the last newsroom pissheads had shuffled off for the night and the place was largely empty, I scooted down the corridor and found a solitary audio technician still at work in a booth. 'Please could you help me?' I asked him. 'I have to change my accent by tomorrow.'

The soundie sighed and slid a blank cart into the recorder. 'Have you got a script? Get in the voice booth.'

Over the next few hours, we recorded the same few sentences over and over, listening back ad nauseam as I ironed my vowels flat one by one, coaxing the nasal drone back into my voice. The soundie, bless him forever, got right into the spirit of the task, giving feedback after each take. It was after midnight when we packed it in.

The next morning I was able to give The Bear what he'd asked for: a perfect Strine drawl indistinguishable from any other in the team.

That was the first bullet to dodge. There would be plenty more.

**

'*MAU*. In here.'

'Yes, John?'

'I'm sending you out to interview Lisa Curry. She's doing some charity launch thing – they've made her ambassador. You'll have to chuck her a few questions about that, of course, but what I really want you to get is her comment on the boob job.'

My mouth fell slightly open. 'The … The what?'

He sighed heavily at having to deal with yet another moron. 'The boob job. The rumour is that our golden girl has had her breasts enlarged.' He trilled the 'r' in 'breasts' like a Vaudeville comedian. When there was no appreciative chuckle from me, he rolled his eyes and continued. 'Her PR attack dogs will instruct you not to ask anything of the sort. But I'm telling you, this is what the viewers wanna know. *DON'T* come back here without a comment about the boobs.'

The champion swimmer Lisa Curry MBE, OA, was indeed Australia's 'golden girl'. She'd won seven Commonwealth medals. Competed for Australia at three Olympic Games. Held Australian records in every stroke bar backstroke. She was beloved – for her own achievements, and also for marrying the champion Ironman and Olympic Bronze Medal kayaker Grant Kenny. They were the epitome of the Australian dream couple of the era: bronzed, blond, strong and fast – winners who looked great in their togs. (Albeit not as good as Lisa Curry would have liked, as it turns out. I would not be telling you this story had she not talked about her choice to get breast enhancement surgery in her own memoir in 2022. It was her story, her terms.)

'Why would I do that?' I asked Sorell. 'Surely that's her private business.' *Ah fuck it, you fool, you've let the words come out of your mouth*, I thought. *Why* did I keep sabotaging myself? Did I have a dole wish?

There was a pause while Sorell gazed gimlet-eyed at me. I imagine it was much like coming face to face with a cheetah on the savannah. But surprisingly, he didn't pounce. 'Of course it would be, but she's a role model, looked up to by millions of young kids. I wanna know whether she thinks getting a *boob job* is a good look for a role model. And as I said, don't come back without it.'

I thought about Sorell's justification for the entire car journey to the interview venue, a sports oval way out on the city's fringe. There were multiple issues here, not least the just cause and hard work of the charity Curry was representing. I knew if I asked the blasted question as ordered, next to nothing about the charity would feature on-screen that night. Oh, no. Instead, there would be old footage of Curry swimming, as well as multiple clips and still shots of her in a swimsuit, all plastered over conjecture about her body – which I would have to voiceover.

According to the UK's Ethical Journalism Network, intrusion by the media must be justified if the public interest is to be used as a shield. The reasoning must be explained clearly to the public. One test for the public interest is to ask what impact the story will have on people. Who will suffer? Who will benefit? Does wider society benefit from publication? That day, the answers to those three questions were plainly: Curry would, no one apart from salivating geezers like my dad, and no. A resounding *NO*.

Yet I remained in a frenzy of indecision even after we'd parked the news car and walked, carrying the tripod and mic case, to the large tent erected for media interviews in the centre of the footy oval.

As foreshadowed, a coiffed-and-lacquered PR woman clasped her taloned digits around my arm and said firmly, 'No personal questions, you understand?'

This would normally have made me push the envelope – journalists are not generally given to bending to instructions from the PR world. But this situation was not normal. I would almost certainly be unemployed if I didn't arrive back at Channel 9 with the goods. And if I asked the question, I'd be betraying every ethical fibre in my body.

I didn't ask it. And yes, back at base there was a bollocking waiting for me, the biggest of my career, before or since. I didn't bother trying to explain – there was no point in arguing when The Admiral was tanked, as he always was after his 'lunch' at The Grand Hotel. He would have swept away my namby-pamby views on the public interest with a guttural roar.

For years afterwards, I thought of that day as a low point in my newsgathering career; recalling it made me burn with humiliation, as if I'd failed not only Sorell and Channel 9, but myself as well. It was only with the passing of decades – and a better understanding of feminism – that I realised I'd done the right thing, not the easy thing.

But I was on the money about one fear: my days at the top TV news channel in Australia were numbered.

* * *

Sorell made people into stars, including women like Jo Hall and Tracy Grimshaw who became some of the biggest names in the business. He also once hired a sixteen-year-old schoolgirl to present the weather in a bikini. His news ethos of tits-and-arse and sport, in that order, kept Nine at the top of the ratings for a quarter of a century. But what I saw of the culture he fostered in the newsroom, for women at least, was misery.

If the Nine newsroom wasn't a hostile working environment for women, I don't know what would be. It was like each day we were walking the slimmest of tightropes – making sure Sorell noticed our work and liked it (we all learned how to interpret his grunts, and you rarely got more than a grunt) but not drawing his attention in any other way. Often, and always when he arrived back from the pub at four, there was no place to hide. He would holler across the newsroom, commenting on our bodies, demanding to know who we were fucking and what we liked to do 'in the sack'. The sheer specificity of those questions would knock the breath out of you. We learned to self-police, keeping a straight face if we could, or ducking off to the bathroom as surreptitiously as possible if the tears came. The stress of it got to most of us, and the injustice of it was a frequent topic of hushed conversation.

One night, close to midnight, my phone rang. A newsroom colleague, in tears, gulped to get the words out. 'How do you stand it? What can we do?' she pleaded. I didn't know what to tell her.

By the early 90s we'd all heard of 'sexual harassment'. The term had been coined in 1975 by Lin Farley at Cornell University and popularised by an article in the *New York Times* the same year: 'Women Begin to Speak Out About Sexual Harassment at Work' (it was published on page thirty-eight, in the 'family/style' section). Over the next few years, dedicated feminist lawyers built case law and defined pathways to justice through the *1964 Civil Rights Act*, and they fought for compensation for their clients through the Equal Employment Opportunity Commission. Their brave clients were mainly black women, the groundbreakers of sexual harassment case law.

In 1980, the brilliant lawyer and scholar Catharine MacKinnon developed a legal theory cementing 'hostile work environment' as well as 'quid pro quo' forms of harassment. The EEOC and US courts began to use both definitions. That same year, Dolly Parton, Jane Fonda and Lily Tomlin tackled the issue of working for a sleazy, sexist boss in the hit movie *9 to 5*.

And just a couple of years prior to my tenure in the Nine newsroom, we'd been glued to the TV coverage of the 1991 Supreme Court confirmation hearings for Judge Clarence Thomas, where his former employee Professor Anita Hill testified, against her original wishes, to the sexual harassment she alleged to have experienced while working for him.

A fellow reporter on *Melbourne Extra* was Tracey Spicer, one of Australia's best broadcasters. In her memoir *The Good Girl Stripped Bare*, Spicer tells of witnessing Sorell roar across the newsroom at another female colleague, 'I want two inches off your hair and two inches off your arse!' Spicer went on to become a star at Channel 10, in a newsroom environment starkly different from the one at Nine.

The legendary foreign correspondent Hugh Riminton was also at Nine in the late 1980s and 90s. In his gripping memoir *Minefields*, he recalls one example of the nightly newsroom gatherings where everyone was expected to get stuck into the contents of the fridge in The Bear's office. Sorell, having reportedly downed six bottles of red wine at lunch, waved an unsteady hand at his female reporters and loudly queried of his editor, 'George! Which one would you fuck first?' In recalling this incident, Riminton muses about 'why so many young men and women put up with it'. Sorell's thunderclaps, he posits, bonded the people working under him 'in the trenches', and great friendships were made. More complex, Riminton claims, were the relationships Sorell had with the women he made into stars – these were the people he was most proud of, Riminton says.

But we all wanted to make Sorell proud; he had unlimited power to shape or to tank the careers of everyone in that newsroom. Whether we were one of his favoured few or not, we deserved to do our work without fear and near-daily humiliation. I'd been brought up in a family that, even with all its faults, taught The Sisters we could do whatever we put our minds to. And I was no ingenue – I knew full well what it took to make it in the news business. For one thing, a *huge* capacity for drink was a non-negotiable, and I'd been developing that since my late teens. But I had my boundaries: I would not sleep with bosses, and I should not have had to do good work in an unsafe environment.

What were my other options? Well, there's the rub – I had none. I had to get on with it and take the knocks.

***

While I played the Faustian game, higher powers even than The Bear were working to bring us down. *Melbourne Extra* was a dud, and it was axed little more than a year after launch. Most of the staff were absorbed into the wider newsroom, but I was for the chop – last in, first out.

It took every crumb of courage to bring up the issue of money with Sorell. 'Will I be paid for the three months left on my agreement?'

'Fuck off,' he said. 'You'll get this week's pay.'

I couldn't just leave without protest: I had bills to pay. I discussed it with the family around the dinner table and with Simon, who'd also come home from London and was splitting his time between Auckland and Melbourne.

Dad was unimpressed by my plan to demand what I knew I was owed. 'Christ, you want to take on The Bear? You'll never work in the business again!'

I made an appointment to see Ian Johnson, the station's general manager, renowned as a reasonable man and a steady hand to balance Sorell's bacchanalian excesses. He greeted me with a kind smile.

'As you might know,' I said, 'John has told me he's letting me go, effective immediately.'

'Yes, and I'm sorry to hear it. It's unfortunate when a show is dropped, not all staff can be redeployed. I want you to know it's nothing to do with your work. Of course, that probably doesn't make you feel any better.' His eyes crinkled under eyebrows thick and lush as a faux-fur throw pillow.

'The problem is, John's refusing to pay me out. He says I don't have a contract so he doesn't have to pay me anything.'

Johnson glanced at the manila folder in my hand.

No point drawing things out, I thought. I handed the letter – with Sorell's signature in a flourish of blue ink at the bottom – across the polished wooden desk. 'I'm owed what's left of this, and I want a cheque by Friday. I think Nine would consider it fair, especially considering the conditions we're working under in that newsroom.'

'Can you explain what you mean by … conditions?'

I told him, in as explicit terms as I dared, about Sorell's harassment. 'I just want to leave with what I'm owed – I don't want to have to pursue a complaint in the courts,' I said primly. Even to my own ears it sounded ludicrous. Who was I to take on the giant of the news business, the most powerful man in the industry?

Johnson's reaction was not what I expected. 'One of your colleagues has already made a complaint. You'll have your money by Friday.'

***

John Sorell remained at the head of GTV-9 News for another decade, handing the reins to Michael Venus and retiring in 2003.

In 2009, I was in the office at TVNZ when the phone rang. It was Dad – the 'bearer of bad news', he said. 'I just thought you'd want to know. John Sorell died. It was a heart attack.'

There was a long pause.

And then I said, curtly, 'Good job.'

I don't know what Dad had been expecting, but it wasn't that. 'Steady on, Ali. That's a bit harsh, isn't it?'

'Dad, he was a creep. He made all our lives miserable. Don't you remember?'

I never could find any mention of any harassment case against Sorell reaching the courts. I do not know whether he was cautioned – who would even have tried? – or spoken to about his behaviour. Perhaps he was protected by payouts and non-disclosure agreements.

Through my work as an investigative journalist, I would come to recognise a pattern. A woman is harassed in the workplace; the woman makes a complaint, expecting it to be taken seriously; the woman is the one hurried out the door – or she leaves by choice, unable to bear staying in an unsafe workplace. Her harasser remains, and his career goes on untouched.

In 2002, John Sorell was interviewed in the *Sunday Age* and called his reputation as a difficult man to work for 'an urban myth'. 'I think I'm a fair boss', he said. 'I don't think I'm too tough,' he said. 'I have so many people I've worked with for so long, they'd leave if they weren't happy, wouldn't they?' he said. The kicker – like a kick in the guts – was in his closing comment: 'The fact we operate as a highly successful family is more important than operating as an autocratic, dictatorial person who rules by fear.'

I'm someone who knows how dysfunctional families work, and all I could think was, *How ironic. How delusional.*

As if families aren't often ruled by fear, with a happy and successful face presented to the world, masking dark truths. Sorell's fantasy of the Channel 9 'family' was a response I've become too used to hearing from harassers when they're faced with the truth of their behaviour: it's called gaslighting.

* * *

After being booted out of Channel 9, I was dead-set certain I'd never get another job in Australian media. I'd only been back in the country three months and had hardly made much of an impression, so I did not figure on anyone's hiring wishlist.

Over beers at a forlorn farewell gathering at the pub, a very kind colleague tried to buck me up. 'What you need is a bit of exposure to the people who matter. A few of us are going to Sydney for Mike Munro's fortieth. I'll get you an invite, you can talk to the bigwigs, make a splash, you'll get a job no worries.'

This seemed improbable. Munro was a household name, having for years been a correspondent on *60 Minutes*, the pinnacle of television current affairs – and I would essentially be crashing his birthday party. But I thought it was worth a shot, so I booked my flight, wincing at the cost, and went anyway.

As I boarded the plane to Sydney, I was stricken by nerves and already feeling like a fraud. Worse, I had developed a heavy head cold, and by the time we landed at Kingsford Smith I was feeling rough as guts. I stopped at the airport pharmacy and bought strong cold meds, promising myself I would not make the mistake of mixing them with alcohol.

I don't remember much about the party at Munro's beautiful Sydney home, because of course I broke that promise. I downed several glasses of champagne and had a chat with the legendary Mike Willesee – he asked me what I thought of the football, and I burbled on about Aussie Rules, not knowing he meant the Sydney League teams, ouch.

Then suddenly I was waking up on the boards of the expansive deck, flat on my back, with a crowd of flashily dressed telly stars peering down at me, murmuring their concern.

Fuck. I'd passed out cold.

If you've ever passed out in public, you'll know your strongest impulse on waking is to pretend everything is fine.

'I'm fine!' I said, jumping to my feet. 'Really, I'm fine!'

The next time I woke up, I was slumped on a garden swing-seat with the protective arm of a complete stranger around my shoulders. 'You passed out again,' she said gently, before explaining who she was: a senior producer at Channel 9's Sydney HQ. I assume my face was a mask of abject horror, because she laughed. 'Don't worry. Look, you're already old news!' She pointed to the rolling lawn, where a few metres away an unconscious partygoer was being hauled off by his hands and feet.

That was it, though. I'd made an impression, but as the girl who'd fainted, twice, at the media party of the year. I'd never live it down.

It's 2018, and I'm at home in Auckland, checking my phone. I have three missed calls from Lisa, then one text message: *CALL ME*.

My older sister doesn't normally use all caps. It's an emergency.

I call back, and she picks up on the second ring. She is screaming, incoherent. The grief and rage pour down the line from Melbourne to Auckland, where I am standing with the makings of dinner spread across the kitchen bench.

Immediately, before she can even catch her breath, I know the purpose of this call. I knew this conversation was coming, we both did, for more than forty years.

But then Lisa gives me new information: our father's use of children's bodies for his own sexual gratification is not just confined to her and to me.

This news literally knocks me off my feet. I sit down heavily on a dining chair and think, *It's good I'm here by myself tonight*, as she screams and screams.

Benny. Her son, her beautiful son. The boy she raised almost completely on her own, since her husband walked out no more than a year after his birth. Raised him 'on the bones of her arse', I used to tell people admiringly, speaking of the courage and goddamn strength she had, putting one foot in front of the other, day after day, working jobs she sometimes hated to give him the best she could.

'His own grandson.' We breathe the words together. 'How could he?'

'I'm so sorry, I'm so sorry,' I repeat over and over.

Eventually she calms enough for us to talk more, turning over the possible and impossible, talking after all these years about confrontation, about justice. And after we shared an unearned and unspoken shame for so many years, now it is out and I share her rage. It wells from us and pools between us, big enough to fill the Tasman.

After we say goodbye, I move to the couch and sit in silence, staring at nothing for I don't know how long. For the first time, I let the memories come in their entirety. I do not stop them at the brink. I do not gatekeep. I let myself remember being ten, eleven, twelve.

It's night-time, and everyone else is asleep, but I have been brought to the lounge – or perhaps I came out to get a glass of water? – and laid on the couch. This happens without words: Dad just takes my wrist, not forcefully, and arranges me as he wishes, and my body slides down from sitting to lying as he pulls off my pyjamas. The television is still on in the background, *The Don Lane Show* or some other late-night thing; I keep my eyes tightly shut and see the bright flashes of fright explode behind my eyelids again.

As I lie frozen, for some reason unable to move, the main thing I feel is abject terror. There are others in this house: my mum, my sisters. Any one of them could walk through the lounge-room door, at any moment, and witness my shame. I keep my eyes firmly on the door as he touches me, clever in his method, starting small and progressing until, in later encounters, he makes me touch him too. He does not rape me, but he destroys me nevertheless.

Until Lisa called that night, I had never told a single soul.

13.

Pure chance brought me to Aotearoa. After that disastrous night in Sydney, I'd applied for jobs in Australia and got none of them, which cemented my conviction that I'd be better off moving overseas again. The house in Kew was cold and damp through the Melbourne winter months, and I had little energy – and even less money – for socialising. I suppose I was depressed, but in the early 90s therapy was something wealthy neurotic Americans took part in, not skint twenty-somethings in Australia.

Simon had been in Auckland for a few weeks. The night before he was due to fly back to Melbourne, he called me with a suggestion. 'There's an ad in the *Herald* jobs section today, for a presenter of a business programme. That sounds like you.'

Bless his practice of reading the paper front to back, even the classifieds!

I spent the next day typing out a new CV and sending it off, with a copy of my showreel on VHS tape, in a courier pack. Within days, courtesy of the production company Communicado, Simon and I were on a flight to Auckland for a screen test and interview. They hired me on the spot.

After years of recession post-1987, the Kiwi economy was stirring again. I was co-presenter on *Made in New Zealand*, a show that helped to inject confidence into the business sector by highlighting successful companies. I then moved to another Communicado show, *Eyewitness* – forgettable, best described as 'current affairs lite', and no relation to the beloved 1980s news programme of the same name.

Communicado also hired Simon for a presenting role, an opportunity that came about when a young TV3 reporter and former stock trader called John Campbell failed to turn up for his audition slot (thanks to their talents, both would go on to be two of the most respected broadcasters in the country). Simon helmed the news segment on TV2's edgy *Newsnight*.

One day I was walking to the TVNZ studio to film the links when *Newsnight*'s executive producer stopped me in the corridor. They were changing the line-up, he said, and he wanted me. 'You're the only contender I'll consider, so when you go talk to the boss, remember you're in a strong position.'

When I met the boss, who'd come from London with a formidable reputation for wrangling star talent at the BBC, I suspected he was unused to women asking for more money than he was intending to offer. I shook with nerves all the way through a tense verbal struggle. I insisted; he refused to even consider my 'ridiculous' demand.

In the end, I stood and smiled as sweetly as I could. 'Okay. Well, I already have a good job, so let's leave it at that.'

He turned a vivid shade of red and told me to 'talk about the weather for a minute' while he composed himself. I got the number I was looking for. It was the only time in my television career I was in the driver's seat on money, before or since.

Newsnight was the first time Simon and I had worked together as part of a presenting team, something the rest of the media seemed fascinated by. It made absolute sense to us: we respected each other's talent and ability in the studio, and at work we treated each other as colleagues first.

By then Simon had bought a house: a two-bedroom board-and-batten cottage with sweeping views of North Piha beach. We had been living together in rental homes since moving to Auckland from Melbourne, and this move, to me, marked a more serious commitment. But try as we might, we couldn't entirely align our expectations of what a committed relationship should look like.

In 1994, we split up. I moved into a Parnell apartment with a flatmate who would become a lifelong friend. I intended the move to be final.

* * *

Back in the 90s, news anchors in larger markets overseas weren't really treated as celebrities in the way they were here. Our telly journalists subbed in alongside All Blacks and Olympians for a share of the limelight. So you might scoff when I say this, but hand on heart it's true: I never saw working in television as a route to fame or money, although it brought me some of both. In this, I was my father's daughter. Television news was simply news in another format, a visual way of telling the story, and the story was *always* the most important thing. Plus, the real privileges of the job were not the nights out or the entry to exclusive corporate boxes, but the experiences you'd never get in any other profession.

In 1994, when the New Zealanders AJ Hackett and Henry van Asch were taking bungy jumping to the world, I flew to Queenstown with my executive producer and a crew to film a piece about their Kiwi company. I'd become a little obsessed with their story, just about wearing out the videotape of their thrilling jump from the Eiffel Tower in 1987.

My team and I were in Queenstown to try, for the cameras, a new offering: heli-bungy.

I felt completely calm as I sat on the open side of the chopper, feet on the strut, ready to go – but only because AJ Hackett himself had strapped my feet to the bungy rope, in the carpark at Coronet Peak.

'Keep your eyes on me!' he shouted, over the *whump* of the chopper blades.

I couldn't stop myself peering down at the tiny-looking trees that stuck out of the snow like blackened matchsticks.

Hackett held up a gloved hand, his fingers spread apart. 'In five … four … three … two …'

Unable to wait any longer, tipping forward, flying free and weightless for long, long seconds before the bungy's stretch took my weight and I bounced, two, three times. Then there was a ten-minute chopper flight back to the carpark, with me still upside-down below the full stretch of the cord, making lazy circles in the freezing winter air.

After the pilot lowered me gently onto my back in the snow – what skill that bloke had! – and van Asch untied my feet, the producer's face loomed into sight above me. 'Uh … we missed the shot when you first came out of the chopper. Would you be willing to do it again?'

'No.' I laughed manically. 'No, I am not. Once was enough.'

On another occasion, the editor of a prestige glossy magazine called the TVNZ publicity department with an almost unbelievable offer. 'They want you to learn to fly,' the publicity manager told me, 'and then write a story for the mag about the experience.'

I was stunned into stupidity for a moment. 'What? Fly a plane …?'

She grinned. 'Yep. They say they'll pay for your lessons, right up until your first solo flight. Then if you want to take it further, you're on your own.'

I'd never had a particular urge to learn how to fly, but faced with the prospect of lessons on a platter, I was keen – for two personal reasons that I mentioned to almost no one. Number one: I would be required to develop basic mathematical skills I'd ignored for many years, a significant personal achievement. And number two: here was another opportunity to impress my father. Flying had been Dad's passion as a young man; throughout my childhood, the house had been dotted with pictures of him at the controls or smiling proudly from the pilot seat of a light plane.

It took me fourteen hours of training by a kind and extremely patient flight instructor at Ardmore Airport before I was ready to go solo, and I only ever did it once. I walked away from the Cessna that afternoon feeling extremely fortunate to have done that, on my own, and lived – but I had no wish to do it again. And yes, my dad was very proud.

But my family could also bring me down with a thump. In 1994 I was chosen to cohost the first Christmas in the Park, a spectacular show in Auckland's Domain, and I walked onstage to the cheers of a 250,000-strong crowd – exhilaration and terror were wrapped tightly together into one moment. As I gazed out at the mass of people, I thought, *This is what Mick Jagger must feel like.* A great example of how *that* kind of thing can go straight to your head. Luckily when I posted a VHS copy of the performance to Mum, she phoned and said, 'Your bra strap was showing.' Thanks for keeping me grounded, Mum.

***

Four months after I moved out of the Piha cottage, I retraced my steps and fled back to the known. At that point, Simon and I might have benefited from some professional help and set the groundwork for meaningful communication, the kind that carries a relationship through hard times. Instead, in 1996, we got married. In July the next year, our professional partnership was also cemented: we became co-presenters on TVNZ's *One Network News* weekend edition. Not everyone was thrilled with that outcome, but the critics who dubbed us the 'Ken and Barbie of newsreading' were easy enough to ignore. We worked well together and were quietly happy with the way our on-screen careers were progressing.

Growing up, I'd felt ambivalent at best about the idea of having children. I certainly liked them – I'd supplemented my pocket money all the way through my teens with babysitting, like many teenagers do – but apart from that, I'd never given it much thought. And I had absolutely no experience with babies. But it was as though getting married – a definitive leap in commitment in that relationship – gave me permission to examine how I really felt. I struggled a little with the *conventionality* of this life progression (marriage, babies – not very feminist of me!), but on the flip side it wouldn't derail my career – the weekend newsreading role meant I was essentially a part-time worker – and I knew Simon was really keen for kids. Within six months, after a lot of thought, I realised I felt the same. Our first child, a girl, was conceived almost exactly a year after the wedding.

Weekend shifts at TVNZ were usually more relaxed than the weekdays; there were fewer staff in the newsroom, and there was less news breaking locally. But on a Sunday in August 1997, we'd all be tested by one of the biggest stories my lifetime: the death of Princess Diana.

I'd been called in early via a terse and breathless call from our producer. 'Diana's been in a car crash. She's injured. Dodi is dead. Get in here now,' was all he said.

In '97 the news had been dominated by stories of Diana's romance with the heir of the Harrods fortune, so I knew exactly what he was talking about. But when I got to the office, and for hours afterwards, we had no idea that earlier reports of the Princess's condition – hospitalised with broken arm – would end like this, with official word of a world-changing event coming from French officials.

There was a long, long second of silence, as if the words had vacuumed all the sound from the newsroom – and then choreographed tumult.

I looked for the senior news director, Norm Sievewright – our commanding officer at such moments. Behind round tortoiseshell frames, his eyes were already on me. He mouthed a single word. 'Run.'

The fifty-metre bolt from my newsroom desk to studio three took about fifteen seconds. Thanks to the kilos I'd gained since finding out about the baby, it was more of a lumber than a sprint. By the time I'd sat down and the lights on their black metal gantries burst into life, Norm and the control room team were ready. With the *One Network News* horns already ringing through my earpiece, I grabbed the wire lying on the desk and clipped the mic to my jacket. The autocue blinked empty under its black hood in the camera facing me. There was no script, just Norm's voice in my ear: 'Speak!'

So, I broke the news of Princess Diana's death to any New Zealanders watching at 5 pm on a wintry Sunday, ad-lib. The name of the hospital, the time of the crash, the deaths of two others in the car, speculation about the paparazzi's pursuit – that was all we had. The update took less than a minute and ended with my promise to bring further details as soon as they came to hand. We had under an hour until the main news bulletin, and that hour would be bedlam.

Above: Mum and Dad in the 1950s. Left: Maureen Prosser, improbably dressed for the beach. Right: Leigh Mau, the very model of a young newspaperman.

Left: Mum with her father, Reginald Prosser, on her wedding day, in front of the Church of St John the Baptist, Frome, England, January 1962. She would have had no idea what awaited her, thousands of miles away.

Me, age six, having taken great care to cover my ears for the photo.

My sister Lisa (left) and me, watched over by Mum, outside our pre-renovated house in Surrey Hills, 1971.

Above: Mum at the kitchen window at Surrey Hills in the early 1970s. The rebuild, done entirely by Dad (with some help from us kids), took years. Below: The house after its spruce-up. Dad turned the one-level cottage into a four-bedroom split-level.

Astride the Shetland pony Chocolate, at my first ever riding lesson, c.1970 – a chance to leave the bullies behind for a day.

Me with my sister Sam in 1975, the year of Lofty and 'next door'. My neighbour Bonnie's house is in the background.

The Sisters together on the backyard swing in 1976. Left to right: Sam, me, Lisa.

Class picture from Canterbury Primary, 1974 – the one surviving image where my ears are somewhat on show. I'm third from the left in the second row.

ABOVE: At Mt Bundy Station, Christmas 1977. Having convinced Gillian to let me ride her beautiful bay station pony, Cinders. One of the compound's accommodation buildings can be seen in the background.

RIGHT: Left to right: Me, Kathryn and Gillian in the cool of the evening at the Adelaide River Show Society, Northern Territory, summer 1977.

LEFT: Me, Mum and Sam with Dad waiting in the Suzuki outside the Surrey Hills house, 1977.

BELOW: Having made the transition from cattle station to pony club life, Fred still often tried to get rid of me – but we had many adventures together.

With my closest friend Katie, age 16, dressed for a midnight performance of the Rocky Horror Picture Show. Dirndl skirts and flouncy blouses were big in 1981.

LEFT: At Lisa's wedding in 1984, age 19 and plainly not thrilled about the day's events.

BELOW: With Lisa and baby Benny in the mid-1980s.

RIGHT: Training for a one-day event on my second horse, Sonny. Riding's always been my idea of perfect freedom.

BELOW: A shot taken for the magazine coverage of our UNICEF-sponsored trip to Papua New Guinea in 2007. Georgina is in the black T-shirt. *Courtesy of Helen Bankers.*

Left to right: Sam, Lisa and me in the early 1990s, on Portsea Back Beach, a few kilometres from where we'd holidayed as teenagers.

RIGHT: In the Fijian Yasawa Islands, the day before my wedding to Simon, April 1996.

BELOW: Me and Mum on one of her visits to New Zealand, late 1990s. This shot shows the height difference between Mum and her giant daughters!

With Karleen at Whangapoua Beach, the Coromandel Peninsula, 2010.

Right: The Sisters in 2015.

Below: Left to right: Me, Lisa, Mum, Dad and Sam with Charlie the dog, at Surrey Hills in 2015.

Among the leaders of the 2017 Women's March in Auckland, on the day of Donald Trump's inauguration.

Riding Bex along with friends at Muriwai Beach, having realised a lifelong dream to live on my own land with my horses. I think my face says it all about how life has turned out.

The lights went off with a metallic *thunk*, and I sat for a few long moments in the dark, staring vacantly at the camera. The rush down the corridor had left me gasping.

As I walked back through the control room, I was surprised to find the entire crew still at their stations, gaping at me wordlessly. I was immediately on my guard, self-doubt flooding the spaces that a moment earlier had been filled with adrenaline. 'What? Did something go wrong? Was it okay?'

'It was incredible. You were ... so emotional. You could see how choked up you were.'

Squirming, I set them straight. 'No, not emotional – just out of breath.'

In the flurry of activity before I returned to the studio an hour later, I made an unwitting miscalculation that led to a minor scandal: I hadn't thought to change clothes.

Tom Bradley was my co-presenter that night, and as I introduced coverage of Diana's death to what was by then a much bigger audience, the TVNZ telephonists began to take calls from enraged viewers: 'Why is Alison wearing white?' 'Surely your newsreaders should be dressed appropriately for such terrible news.' 'Shame on her!' Details of the calls filled a full page in 'the log', the big book that sat on a shelf in the corner of the newsroom and was surreptitiously leafed through by presenters from time to time. We'd cast guilty glances over our shoulders, hoping not to be sprung by colleagues but unable to tear ourselves away from this record of what the public thought of us. For a few days, my ledger wasn't pretty.

I was struck by the depth of feeling Diana's death unleashed. I'd never been an acolyte of the princess. Her wedding had been a special event in my family home, thanks to my royalist mum, but I'd watched the spectacle with a teenager's wary disdain. The puff of a dress that engulfed her was a fitting metaphor for the ceremony and what happened next. I pitied her as the tsunami of coverage washed over us. Anyone born after the mid-1980s would struggle to believe the sheer volume of stories about Diana and how often she stared out – like a hunted animal – from magazine covers. In the 90s, the writers of think pieces made origami of themselves trying to parse why, if she hated the public scrutiny so much, she would make 'chums' of some journalists, release information behind the scenes, and smile at paparazzi as often as she scowled and hid. It seems obvious: she craved a tiny bit of control. More than a decade later, I would have a taste of how that must have felt.

The day after her death, I passed the head of news in the studio corridor. We spoke for a bit about the funeral details that were beginning to come through from London. The event was likely to stop most of the world in its tracks the following Sunday, and *One Network News* would of course be covering everything.

'You should host it,' he told me.

'Really? On my own?' The notion of any woman in New Zealand – other than the renowned newsreader Judy Bailey, of course – being trusted with an event of that size and import was unusual enough to make me wary.

'Yeah. Why not? You're the Diana Girl now.'

14.

'Ali, you're not supposed to put on any weight at all until sixteen weeks,' said the doctor at my first antenatal appointment, when I told him I'd put on twelve kilos. I laughed and, apart from eschewing seafood and soft cheese, went on my merry way. I was one of the very fortunate ones, the ones who 'bloomed' without any debilitating morning sickness or gestational issues. My only issue was 'blooming' a little too much: this was the first time since my teens when I felt free to eat without giving a thought to keeping my body within the accepted boundaries. And eat I did.

Our daughter arrived smack-bang on the day she was due, which, we would later joke, suited her personality perfectly! Our kindly neighbours had offered us their city apartment if and when we needed it, which meant we hadn't had to worry about a mad fifty-minute dash from Piha – instead, I wallowed like a hippo in their large spa bath until Simon finished work a few hundred metres away at TVNZ, and we drove in relative calm to National Women's Hospital. While Simon found a park, I waddled up to the nurses' station and found the place in an advanced state of chaos.

'Everyone's gone into labour at once!' the charge nurse told me with a wink. 'You're the last one we can take tonight – if you'd been any later we'd have had to send you on somewhere else. As it is, we'll have to put you in the multiple births suite.'

That turned out to be a cavernous room the size of a university lecture auditorium, with a single bed and all the beeping machinery in one corner; I supposed they needed the space for extra medical staff when there were twins or triplets due. Once I was settled, my midwife Noreen asked for an anaesthetist to come and prep me for an epidural, and we were on our way.

I was looking forward to the experience. I knew it would be hard, I'd had plenty of people tell me that, but in a funny way I was keen for that challenge. And I knew I wanted to do it alone or as close to alone as was practical. Simon was there, of course, to 'help' – not his fault, as there really is very little a man can do in that situation unless he's a nurse or the obstetrician – but I was not on board with having sisters, in-laws, besties or doulas in the room cheering me on as I pushed a human being out of my body. My loss, perhaps, but no thank you.

After an hour of pushing, I was grateful to see the smile on Noreen's elfish face. Then she waved a large mirror at my bottom half. 'Here she comes. Would you like to have a look?' There was a delighted smile in the woman's Irish lilt.

'Ewww,' I huffed in the spaces between contractions. 'No, thank you.'

'Okay, no worries.' She put the mirror down. 'Oooo, she's a redhead!'

'What? Give me that mirror!'

And so, Simon and I saw our little girl appear with a puff of pale red-gold fuzz on the crown of her head.

The birth had been smooth and, thanks to the epidural, not overly painful. It wasn't until Paris had been placed on my chest and had her first feed that things went awry. Noreen had been manipulating my stomach, but it had been ages, and the placenta was nowhere to be seen.

My obstetrician was a small, slight woman with tiny hands, for which I was about to be very grateful. She came in to give me the bad news. 'We'll have to take the placenta out manually.'

Hmm, *manually*. I wondered, in a fog of post-birth hormones, what that might mean.

'It means we'll have to take you to surgery now. Do you understand?'

I was so tripped up on birthing drugs that I would have said yes to anything. And after the staff had settled me on the operating table and topped up my epidural, I did say yes to a large group of medical students crowding into the room to watch. Completely off my face, I just waved them in with a silly grin, thinking, *Wow, it looks like the whole hospital's in here*. They jostled around the foot of the bed as the obstetrician prepared her work. *Oh*, I thought hazily, *they're really getting in there for a good look, eh?*

I began to feel a little uneasy as she talked through what she was going to do: no special instruments needed, just her fist pushed up my vaginal canal, through my cervix, to bring the pesky placenta out. *So that's what she meant by 'manually'*.

It was only later, when the drugs wore off, that I thought about what had just happened. I reflected on the number of people who had watched this intimate procedure from inches away as I'd been spread, in the most vulnerable position possible, on the table. I was surely not a stranger to them all – my face was regularly on the television, so at least some of them knew whose vagina they were staring at. I had been awake, sure, but in no state to give consent, not really.

After I woke in the recovery room, nestled under a high-tech duvet-type thing filled with warm air, I considered raising the issue with the recovery nurse. But it had been hours since I'd seen my new baby, and my body was vibrating with the need to hold her. That was my priority, I decided – any worries about informed consent would have to wait.

* * *

Those hormones were followed swiftly by a bunch of others, seesawing through my post-birth body until I barely knew which way was up. I'd heard about the day three baby blues but had felt so good for the first two days that I foolishly thought I'd escape them somehow. Paris was feeding and sleeping well, and it seemed silly to take up a bed at the postnatal centre for more than two nights, which had me going home on … day three.

That same day, my mother flew over for a two-week support role. She arrived from the airport to find me crying uncontrollably over the baby, in the basement bedroom of my in-laws' house.

Meanwhile, on the floor above, the 'welcome, baby!' barbecue crowd continued to celebrate. My sobs were coming so hard that my nipple kept popping out of Paris's mouth, which made her cry too, her little ginger-fluffed scalp turning bright red in outrage.

'What on earth is going on?' Mum demanded.

I'd been down there for ages and apparently had just been missed, and the wailing had led her right to the spare bedroom's door.

'I just want to g-g-go hooooome.' I knew I sounded like an overtired toddler throwing a mega-tanty, but I neither cared nor had any way of stopping.

Mum patted my head, marched upstairs and stood on tippy-toe to whisper in Simon's ear. To my great relief, within minutes we were packed into the car and headed to Piha.

I did not know anything at all about children when Paris was born. I'd never changed a nappy in my life. And stubbornly, I'd refused to consider going to antenatal classes because I didn't like the idea of all the fake huffing and puffing in front of a roomful of strangers; instead I'd relied almost entirely on Heidi Murkoff's *What to Expect When You're Expecting*. A few years after I first read it, the book came under fire for catastrophising every small thing that might go wrong in a pregnancy and even allegedly tipping some women into eating disorders. Avoiding antenatal classes was a stupid decision on my part – worse, because it came from vanity – as I effectively cheated myself out of the new mum's group that many women find so helpful. While we had Simon's parents to call on, and they were terrific, they didn't really fill the gap that my own mother or my sisters might have. Rasing a child without your *whole* village around you is a challenging and sometimes lonely road.

I was thankful to Mum for flying over to spend the first couple of weeks with us. She was gentle with her advice and never once overstepped, which I imagine is easy to do with clueless new parents. By the time she'd gone, we were in a workable rhythm.

This was helped by the fact that every time the baby cried, I felt a rush of excitement to see her. Even for the 3 am feed, I was happy to haul my body out of bed and jog the few metres down the hall to her. I probably had high levels of oxytocin post-birth – I just felt so privileged to have this gorgeous creature to look after.

Paris wore nothing but nappies for the first three months of her life, one of the hottest summers Auckland had experienced for years. Time passed in a beautiful daze. Simon would spend hours holding her in his lap while watching test cricket on telly. In the evenings, he would drive to work at TVNZ, and I'd take her out in the pram or the front pack to feed the ducks in the pond on the other side of Garden Road. Then I'd bathe her and massage her chubby pink body as the sun poured in across the waves from the west.

When Paris was five weeks old, I went back to weekend newsreading, feeling fortunate to have part-time work that fit so easily with my baby's needs. The makeup crew were happy for me to park her in the little office next to the makeup room, and I would come down the hallway from the newsroom when she was due to be fed. She never once woke up.

While I often felt exhausted, I felt no reason to complain. Our house was tiny and easy to keep, and the beach with its glorious late summer splendour was just a short, safe and traffic-free walk away. At seven weeks, Paris was already sleeping through the night.

A perfect baby. How bloody lucky we were.

* * *

When Paris was eight weeks old, I took her on my own to Melbourne for her introduction to the wider family. There was a big boozy barbecue in the backyard that Saturday afternoon, with at least fifty of the old guard gathered in celebration. On the Sunday night, Mum wanted all of us to herself. She created a tableau of a typical Sunday night dinner when we were kids, making a roast lamb leg, pumpkin, peas and spuds, and her legendary chocolate cheesecake for dessert.

Mum called her grandson to the table, but he pretended not to hear her. She tried again. 'Darling, come and sit down for dinner!'

Ten-year-old Benny feigned nonchalance and looked everywhere but at his grandmother. Sam and I smiled as we watched his still-round face.

Mum's face, in turn, showed he was skating close to the edge. This was a rare family dinner with all of us in one place, at home, around the table. But for some reason, Benny was standing directly outside the closed spare bedroom door where his baby cousin was sleeping – and he wasn't budging an inch.

It occurred to me, suddenly, that he had been there on and off for most of the day. 'Hey, Benny,' I said, 'what's up?'

'I'm looking after Paris.' He'd blushed bright red, uncomfortable at all the attention, but his voice had a hard edge to it.

'She's okay, honey. She's sleeping. Come and eat!'

'No, thank you. I'm not hungry.'

Dad was getting angry now, and he spoke to Benny in his most instructive tone. It was the tone that had made all of us, even Mum, obey instructions immediately for as long as I could remember. 'Ben. Come and sit down, *NOW.*'

But the boy would not move from the bedroom door. Even Dad let it go, eventually, although he left Benny in no doubt how much trouble he was in. When Lisa and Benny left that evening, Mum gave the boy a plate to take home, still puzzled at his behaviour. Benny thanked her politely but said nothing more.

* * *

On a stunning summer's day after Paris turned two, I sat with her on our deck and watched while she picked up tiny squares of food from her highchair tray, lifted them to her face, and considered whether she might, maybe, acquiesce to putting them in her mouth.

Amazing, I thought. *We've managed to keep her alive for* two whole years.

This seemed an enormous achievement, given how little Simon and I had known about raising babies.

What kind of mother did I want to be? The enormity of the task ahead was overwhelming. I sat in thought for long minutes while a soft on-shore breeze blew back the red curls from her peachy little face.

Minutes earlier, I'd hung up the phone from a call to Mum, our weekly check-in. We'd talked for more than an hour in the end, the cordless phone cradled under my chin as I folded washing and put it away in the powder-blue drawers in Paris's room, then chopped carrots into sticks for her at the kitchen bench.

Those calls were our only connection for months at a time. I missed Mum intensely but tried to manage it with logic, scolding myself for being so sniffly about it. *Think about how she had it for a minute, would you?* She hadn't seen her parents for *years* after leaving England that first time with Dad, and she'd been much younger and more naive than I was. I had a memory flash of a butter knife on fragile blue paper, and then Mum sliding her frost-pink fingernail into the slit, unfolding the airletter flat to read her father's news of home, her only connection with the family she loved.

I'd been home a couple of times, but I didn't see my family as much as I'd have liked. Dad found air travel uncomfortable, so they'd only visited us once together since Paris's birth. Although Mum came over more often, she hated leaving him at home on his own. 'Let him eat cheese-and-pickle sandwiches for a week, it won't kill him!' I would cajole as she fretted about how he'd cope alone.

I thought about how much I loved her and how deeply I wanted my child to feel that same connection. I thought about what I could take from the way she had rasied The Sisters, her precious girls. What she had done right, and where – whether from her own choices, or from the circumstances she'd found herself in – she might have gone wrong. How much would my influence shape my child's life? Overcome by the size of it, I thought that if I could choose just one thing to give my children, and stick to it, then that at least would be something.

I decided that this one thing would be honesty. It was the thing, looking back, that my own childhood had lacked, and by my early thirties I was beginning to piece the reasons together like a puzzle. My mother's insistence that all was well in her marriage, in our household – that was a lie. My father's insistence that he loved his wife above all others – another lie. I gradually uncovered the truth when old enough to pick up clues about the affairs he barely bothered to conceal.

At a family barbecue when I was sixteen, Dad pulled me over to introduce a woman I'd never seen before. She was young, and glamorous in a swirling, multicoloured sundress. Lustrous dark hair spilled over one shoulder. She and Dad were standing close to each other, almost touching.

'This is Helen,' he said. 'She's a teacher.'

Helen smiled encouragingly, and I said 'hi', but I wasn't looking at her – I was distracted by Dad. There was something odd about how he was pulling at his beard and spilling his words fast as he thrummed with an unfamiliar energy. The usual laid-back verbosity missing altogether. 'Helen's an English teacher, actually. I thought she could, you know, come round home a couple of times a week and tutor you. Give you some help.'

This was beyond bizarre. Dad knew I needed no help with

English – I was one of the top students in the state in the subject. I'd never got less than an A on any assignment.

In that instant, the realisation of what was going on between them struck me like a physical blow. 'No. Thank. You. I don't need your help.' That was addressed to Helen, but I stared at them both, lacing the words with as much disgust as I could muster. Then I turned and walked away.

I didn't tell Mum what I'd seen, but I wondered whether she knew, and if so, why she and Dad continued to live inside a lie. It seemed like the worst kind of self-torture, this acceptance of deceit and betrayal. I would break that chain by telling my child the truth, no matter what. *Parenting is a long game*, I thought. At least when Paris was grown, she would be able to say her mum always told the truth about the big things.

***

When Paris had been around a year old, I'd got pregnant but miscarried at about ten weeks. I had felt some sadness but hadn't fallen too much into grieving; I was content enough to trust my body to do again what it had before. I told almost no one, and Simon and I agreed to keep trying. But eighteen months passed. We began to worry then, going so far as to book a fertility appointment.

In the winter of 2000, I realised my period was two weeks late. I peed on the pregnancy test stick in the Koru Lounge toilets on the way to Queenstown for Winter Festival – a bit random, but I had to know. Mid-flight, I whispered the result across the aisle to Simon.

He reached out to me, a look of pure bliss on his face, and we held hands for the rest of the flight. Every time the flight attendants had to get past, they excused themselves with a laugh.

When I'd been pregnant with Paris three years before, we'd argued about finding out the sex of the baby *in utero*. I wanted to know – I figured there'd be enough surprises waiting for me in the delivery room – and Simon did not. We'd compromised and found out at thirty weeks. This time, I was happy to wait until the baby was born, and we told the radiographer not to say anything. Unfortunately for him, the screen told the whole story.

'Wait. What's *that*?' Simon pointed to a spot on the image.

The radiographer looked at him and then me, confusion on his young face. 'I ... uh. You said you didn't want to know, so ... I ...'

I waved a hand, laughing, indicating he didn't need to panic.

'Is that ...?' Simon asked insistently.

'Yep, that is a penis right there.' The radiographer sighed with relief. 'It's a boy.'

A boy. That was really something for me to chew over. I had no brothers and no male cousins, and I'd been overseas for most of my nephew's early childhood. Bloody hell, I had no real experience of males under eighteen! How would I deal with a boy? How would I know what to do? This nagged at the back of my mind for months as my body grew and changed for the second time. Here was I thinking I'd nailed this mothering caper, and now I'd been thrown a curveball.

I needn't have worried. Born on Black Friday in the middle of a hurricane, Joel was just as wonderful as his sister – if a little more demanding, and a little less reliable on the sleep front. Parenting was harder with a toddler as well as a newborn, but again we were in a more fortunate position than most. Back then, TVNZ operated an on-site creche, so Joel was just two floors away from me when I again went back to part-time work five weeks after giving birth.

Simon and I put as much of ourselves as we had available into raising our kids, who have grown into kind, hardworking, empathetic adults. I love them more than anything else on earth.

The landscape is just as I remember when I was that scruffy, gumbooted kid learning to gut a rabbit. There's a drought, a bad one, so everything I see from the window of the rental car is beige and gold, and parched.

At least three times a year I fly to Melbourne, hire a car from Tullamarine Airport and drive west to visit my daughter, who is studying Music Theatre at Federation University in the town of Ballarat. I try to time each stay to coincide with her end-of-term productions, and I adore witnessing the passion and skill she pours into her work. I go to every performance I can catch, staying at Airbnbs and choosing a new 'local' for my morning coffee each time. Ballarat is a handsome town, renowned for its grand Victorian architecture from the gold rush of the 1880s, when it was briefly among the richest cities in the world.

Ballarat is also cloaked by an invisible pall – perhaps not evident to everyone, but felt by survivors. It gets stronger the closer you get to Lyons Street and St Patrick's Cathedral. On the iron-spiked fence that rings the bluestone church, thousands of coloured ribbons flutter and flare in the breeze: a tribute to the scores of children who were raped and abused by the priests there. It's both beautiful and monstrous.

After the call from Lisa that changed everything, my visits to Ballarat allow me to take part in a secret council of war. My older sister and her son Benny come up from Melbourne and stay with me. At night we will go to the university theatre and cheer my daughter on; by day, we plan to talk about what we might want to happen next.

The first time we sit down together to talk, in the living room of a gloomy Victorian-style terrace house, it's difficult even to start. There we are, the three of us, on the edge of a vast sea of hurt, our toes curled into the earth lest one of us slip and start talking – and then what will happen?

The easiest way in, I decide, is just to jump and ignore the freezing shock. 'We have choices, and nothing is set in stone, so we can take as long as we like,' I say, as if we're discussing a house purchase or a holiday booking, but it breaks the ice.

We have placed ourselves separately around the room, like three points of a triangle. Benny is on a long black leather couch, and Lisa in an armchair, while I pace the plush red rug, back and forth, and their eyes follow me. It's a wintry day, and the room is cold and shadowy, fitting for our task.

'We should think about whether we want to call the police,' I say.

It's the first time this has been uttered within our group, and the statement settles heavily between us. The decision would be a legitimate one, we all know that. If all three of us were to testify in a criminal case, Dad would likely spend the rest of his life in jail.

I use what I've learnt from my work as an investigative journalist, stepping Lisa and Benny through what we would face as witnesses in the trial of our father and grandfather. Many, many survivors have told me what it's like to be a witness in the trial of their abuser. Many hadn't realised they would not be a party to the case – 'Just a witness!' they said in tones of disbelief. And many hadn't realised the prosecutor wasn't their lawyer but instead was working on behalf of the Crown.

On the other hand, accountability – delivered in the form of a guilty plea, an apology or a conviction, or through a restorative justice process – can set you free, sometimes. It can help you heal. Lisa and Benny need to know all this before they decide. I leave the decision in their hands, especially Benny's. I will do anything he wants to do, and he can take all the time he needs.

15.

In 2004, Simon got a call from the head of news, who told him to pack his bags: he was expected on the next flight to Fiji.

He'd been away a few days when there was a knock at our front door. I'd been working early shifts on TVNZ's *Breakfast* programme and was sleep deprived, hence I wasn't in the best frame of mind when I opened the door, Joel on my hip and Paris peeking around my legs, to find a nervous-looking young man. He said he was there to get my comment 'on the breakdown of your marriage'.

I was astounded. 'I'm sorry, what? Where did you get that idea from?'

The journalist shifted uncomfortably, gesturing to the driveway. 'Well, his car's not here, so where is he?'

'Who the hell are you anyway? What publication are you from?'

He gave the name of a trashy 'women's' magazine.

I let him sweat for a moment. 'Simon's in Fiji, working. There's a coup on …? In case you hadn't noticed.' It had been all over the news for days, and I gave him the full force of my sarcasm.

He narrowed his eyes. 'Well, Alison, people are talking about you. And if it's got as far as us, then you really should be worried.'

Then he turned and ran down the stairs, leaving me open-mouthed on the doorstep.

***

Sometimes I think of my marriage to Simon as a superyacht: sleek and gleaming, every stainless cleat polished, every rope tidily coiled. A casual observer, lacing their boat shoes on the dock, might look up and think, *Now there's a handsome vessel! Must be a good time aboard that beauty.* Even the water this ship sits upon is calm, nary a ripple bothering its shining surface.

But below the waterline, unseen, there is a breach, a hole too tiny to notice. At first it admits only a bead of water – but as the years pass, the breach gets bigger, and the outside begins to come in. Is invited in. Almost imperceptibly, the vessel lists – and eventually, inevitably, you are over the side and in the dark waters, swimming for your life.

Of course, a marriage is not made from teak and brass and sailcloth: it is a relationship with needs. It needs care and maintenance just like a sailboat does, but a romantic pairing, if it is to last, must also start with a basic compatibility. An understanding of similar life goals. Conversations that lead to understanding, about loyalty, and honesty, and what is the truth that will be carried into your old age together. That's a lot to put on a fledgling relationship – particularly one that has been stop-and-start, mostly formed by hearts grown fonder through distance as well as the tidal flow of absence and coming together.

I eventually came to understand that Simon and I had done none of that groundwork and did not have the mix right to begin with. Within a few years, although we were working daily alongside each other with a flawless professional relationship, we were so far apart on the fundamentals that it was never going to last.

But I did not want, at any time, to accept that. And there were good times, of course there were – wonderful times. Our children brought a lot of joy to both of us, and I'll always remember the look on Simon's face each time I told him I was pregnant.

* * *

Eight years after I'd got married in a white lace dress on a secluded island in the Fijian Yasawas, I went home to Melbourne for a visit. As usual, I travelled alone with the children. When they were very young, I stopped staying for more than a night or two at my parents' house on any visit, and when we did stay, I slept in the spare room right next to the kids' trundle beds and kept a close eye on them. Often we stayed with Lisa or with friends. I couldn't put a name to the caution I felt, but it prickled at the back of my brain, swimming just under the surface of conscious thought like the shadow of an eel in a bushland lake.

I knew Mum treasured these visits, and so did I. While the kids played with Lego or threw the chew toy for Oscar the Jack Russell, we would sit on the green vinyl couch together and talk. This time,

I had something big to tell her. I craved her input: who could advise me if not my mum? But I feared her reaction.

Tucked under her arm – not easy, considering our height difference – eventually I blurted it out. 'My marriage isn't working. I don't know how to make it work.'

She was concerned, I could see that, and a little bit shocked.

I had a flash of memory from twenty years back: Lisa had just announced she and her husband David were to split. He'd walked away and left her, actually, so there wasn't much to do either way – but Benny was just a baby still, and Mum was distraught. 'I never thought I'd see the day,' she told me, 'when there'd be a divorce in this family.' She'd waited until there was no one else around and then whispered it to me like a witch's curse. Her words, time-travelling all the way from 1987, parked themselves in my head.

She picked up my hand, held it in hers. I ran my fingertips over her pale knuckles, already grossly swollen with arthritis. 'You'll do what you need to do, of course,' she said. 'Just promise me one thing. Promise me, before you make any final decision, you will do everything in your power to save the marriage.'

Relief washed over me. I'd said it, but I hadn't meant I was going to do anything about it. Just putting the thought into words was dangerous enough. I was testing it out – surely it was safe to do that with Mum. Who else in your life could you do that with, if not your mum? And there had been no explosion from the person whose opinion mattered so much.

I was too tightly wound to catch the reference, the one layered underneath, to an event forty years earlier. The one that had lived like a parasite in the lie of Mum's own marriage, for all those decades. 'You've made your choice, and now you must go back and live it.' That was Nanny Alice Matilda Burbage Buddon Prosser, putting her foot down to 29-year-old Maureen after she had crossed the seas to Somerset with her two babies, sailing for six long weeks to escape. I didn't catch this reference because Mum's version was not the same – time had passed, the world was different. She was not *instructing* me to do anything. Anyone would have said her advice was reasonable to a fault. 'Do everything in your power.'

I looked right into her eyes and swore to her I would.

But our marriage, by then, had become a labyrinth with no clear exit. It seemed an impossible task to follow the threads back to trust and understanding, and there were so many threads in a god-awful tangle. Each path that looked promising would wind in on itself, leading us back to the same differences, the same argument. But for the next few years, while staying seemed impossible, leaving seemed even more so. I chose to dig in, pretending to myself and the world that nothing was awry.

* * *

The CEO of UNICEF called my mobile phone in mid-August 2007 to say they'd decided on Papua New Guinea. They'd invited me to be a national ambassador the previous year, and I'd known they wanted to send me on an overseas PR mission ever since – but PNG was a surprise.

Most charities are savvy about the use of 'celebrity' to raise their profile, and while some sections of the media regard this as a suspect practice – what on earth could a pampered, overpaid television personality really know about easing suffering? – the charities do it because publicity is hard to come by, and it works a treat. UNICEF's New Zealand office was sending several hundred thousand dollars a year to PNG AIDS relief projects, mainly focused on women and children, and they knew I'd done some work for the New Zealand AIDS Foundation over the years: a way to continue the contribution I'd valued so much at the Health Department in Melbourne years before. A perfect fit.

I'm not sure if their head office in Wellington had thought the practical stuff through as thoroughly as they might have, in retrospect. We were four women on our way to one of the most dangerous places on earth. The only one among us with any relevant experience was Georgina, the UNICEF media officer, a Londoner with ten years as an international aid worker in Somalia, Sudan, and Rwanda at the time of the massacre. Hell, she had even lived for a year in Gaza *on her own*.

After a month of hep A jabs and malaria tablets, we flew up via Cairns in mid-October and were delivered straight from the plane to UNICEF HQ in an office building right in the heart of the capital. Port Moresby is notorious for its violence, but from eight floors up it is beautiful, with steep red-brown hills huddling closely round a sapphire deepwater harbour. Our local liaison Noreen showed us to the boardroom for a safety briefing from the Head of UN Security for the region, a Belgian man named Jean Luc, and

I'll never forget the look on the poor man's face when he took stock of the four of us sitting on the other side of the table. His whole demeanour said, *Fuck, how the hell do I keep this lot safe?*

Jean Luc took around half an hour to scare us witless, explaining in his emotionless French accent how PNG was more dangerous than Afghanistan (!) and that life was quite simply cheaper there than almost anywhere else. He described the destruction of the tribal lifestyle driving village men down to the city, where they couldn't get work and so had to steal to live. We were not to go outside our hotel under any circumstances without an escort; once we flew up to the Highlands, the escort would be a team of men, all heavily armed.

We spent the afternoon with a group of teenage peer educators, hand-picked by church leaders to take the safe-sex message back to the young people of their villages. This was not easy in a population that was both deeply religious and chronically misogynistic. In PNG, rape and rough sex were common, and these are the practices that most easily spread HIV. The Papuans had more than eight hundred languages among them; often the entire language, not just the dialect, was different from town to town – this made it almost impossible to spread a coherent HIV/AIDS prevention message.

The Holiday Inn was an absolute dump, the four of us concluded when we were finally able to check in. Little did we know we'd be pining for its luxuries by the end of the following day. It had a proper restaurant and a pool with a bar. Around the perimeter, though, there were five-metre-high chain-link fences topped with curls of razor wire, and at the front gates, four armed guards.

There was no road connecting Port Moresby to Mount Hagen in the Highlands, so we flew there the next day. As we walked out of the airport at our destination, there was a rush of bodies towards the wire fence that kept non-passengers out. Among a crowd of more than a hundred, no one said anything; they just watched us in complete silence.

Our UNICEF regional host was Mike, a Scotsman with a dry sense of humour. Noreen found our security detail: five local guys with guns in a ute marked 'Mad Dog Security'. They smiled shyly with eyes averted as we shook their hands – *Is that the thing to do here? Am I offending them?* – then made themselves our shadows for the next two days.

The hotel was just plain scary. As soon as I dumped my bag on the bed, I found the ranch-sliders in my room didn't fully close. I had to make a decision: *Do I act all brave? Or do I insist that the four of us arm ourselves and bunk down in one room for the night with someone on watch?* I chose the first option, and so did the others, but the nerves led us to drink quite a lot of wine at dinner.

In the morning Mike picked us up in his van. We set off into the jungle, heading for the Maria Kwin centre, an AIDS facility a couple of hours away. It was run by a 75-year-old Catholic nun, Sister Rose Bernard, who was from Ohio but had come to PNG in 1964 as a missionary and never left. She had carved a garden out of the jungle – lawns, shade trees, flowerbeds and vegetable patches – as well as a piggery. She was simply the most lovely and inspirational person I'd ever met.

The HIV/AIDS patients, mainly women and children, who came to Sister Rose were allowed to stay for one week a month, regain their strength, and get whatever respite they could from the wrath of their families and fellow villagers. AIDS had all the stigma of witchcraft in PNG, and those who had it almost always died, as no one wanted to get tested. If they did test positive, they would often not be allowed back into their villages, and if they were, they would be shunned. You can imagine how much these patients loved coming with their children to Sister Rose. She and the other nuns taught them animal husbandry, and to grow vegetables, and to cook, nutrition being an important and accessible form of treatment for AIDS up there.

Word had spread that we were coming, and a group of Sister Rose's regular patients had gathered to talk to us. They seemed genuinely amazed that a bunch of foreigners had come all the way from New Zealand to meet them. Everyone was nervous and awkward as we sat cross-legged in a group on the lawn.

To break the ice, I passed around a glossy magazine – I was on the cover, in a pink sundress, all airbrushed and perfect. The women laughed so hard I was worried they'd wet themselves; they pointed from me to the magazine as if they couldn't believe it was the same person. It did the trick: they talked about their experiences, what was left of their families, how most of them had been blamed for a disease that men had brought into the village and that had claimed life after life.

The kids were crawling with headlice and some had ulcerating sores on their limbs. When I smiled down at them, I could see in most cases their baby teeth had rotted away to stumps – and strangely, that's what got to me most. My own children were around the same age and had never needed a filling.

When we left, Mike said he wanted to take us on a half-hour detour to a health centre in a nearby village. This centre was a shack with a doctor and two nurses, and at least fifty people were waiting patiently on the grass to be seen, most of them pregnant women. The building was clean but bare-bones basic, and oddly it had ten iron bedframes but no mattresses. A nurse told me the beds had been sent from Port Moresby as an aid package, but the mattresses had mysteriously disappeared en route. *For god's sake!* Suddenly I was very, very angry. I told Georgina I wanted to buy mattresses myself, and she said something sarcastic like, 'Okay, let's pop down to Harvey Norman now, shall we?' Which was deflating, but true.

There were other difficult experiences to come in the next day or so, but nothing haunted me like those stolen mattresses – and what that theft meant for the women who came down from the hills to give birth at the health centre.

In the end, did our trip to meet HIV/AIDS sufferers make a difference? Down the line, it did: an article I wrote was published in *The Australian Women's Weekly,* and the UNICEF Christmas Appeal was dedicated to the efforts in PNG: that raised an extra hundred grand. People care – well, some people do – and that's what makes the difference.

* * *

The trip to PNG, while hardly a holiday, had been a brief but welcome distraction from the tension at home. That same year I insisted to Simon that we try couples counselling. It failed after two excruciating sessions. Perhaps if we'd thought to do it years before, it might have worked.

In moments when I could think logically, I knew our kids deserved to see their parents in happy, loving relationships. Although we kept up a decent pretence for their sake – never fought in front of them and barely fought at all, as neither of us could bear to raise our voices if the kids might hear – those words no longer described ours.

That might have been enough to convince me to end it, but I knew there would be another penalty for the failure of this relationship: a public one. I hated myself for my cowardice, but I couldn't face it. So, once I'd kept my promise to Mum and done everything I could, I stayed and did nothing.

In 2009, the decision was made for me, and I had to accept that my husband was in love with someone else.

We sat the children down on the 'good' couches in the big lounge room to tell them the news as gently as we could, and it was awful, but at least that bit was real. The next task was to make an appointment to see our boss and tell him his high-profile newsreader couple would not be a couple anymore. He then had to brief TVNZ's board of directors.

I wish I could tell you that this was the most bizarre thing that happened in the following weeks, but that would be untrue. The efficient TVNZ publicity department swung into action, helping us draft a short statement that was released within a day. It had all the usual, desperate, sincere-but-useless pleas for privacy for our children's sake.

Making the kids dinner in the kitchen that night, I listened to National Radio broadcast my words, describing my life's failure as the lead story on its 5 pm news bulletin.

Within a day or so, as expected, it became clear that privacy was not a gift we'd be getting any time soon. Across the street from the roller-gate of the TVNZ carpark, the paparazzi's cars idled in wait. Conveniently for them, there was no need to guess when we'd be coming or going – our schedules were available in the TV guide at any corner dairy.

Management quickly realised this could be dangerous, especially as I was still in the family home and trying to keep things on a regular schedule for the children. I was called back to the boss's office, where he introduced me to someone. 'Ali, this is Tim. He's from [a private security firm]. With your permission, we've asked him to show you how to drive defensively and some tactics you might use to … uh … get the paps off your tail.'

I accepted gratefully and sat down with Tim, who taught me how to spot a following car in traffic and how to plot circuitous routes from work to home. I would be taking a different motorway exit every time, looping into hospital and supermarket carparks, and exploiting my knowledge of suburban streets to lose the tail.

Every outing was like a movie car chase but at fifty kilometres an hour. It worked for a while and made me feel a little less helpless – but then the photographers began parking on the road outside the house instead.

The TVNZ publicity department called me and Simon into another meeting. 'We think you should consider a public meet-up, which we will, uh, signal to the magazines beforehand. Let them get their picture of you together, and then it'll be over.'

A set-up, then. I'd heard of this kind of secret deal being made in Hollywood, but it felt ridiculous to try it in Auckland – and besides, it would be a blatant lie. Call me old-fashioned, but if we were going to say or do anything publicly, wasn't it our job to tell the truth? Simon and I refused, but the publicists insisted it was the only way. The disruption to the kids' daily lives had to stop, so maybe it was, I thought.

But there was another issue to be wrestled with, murkier but likely to surface nonetheless: hypocrisy. For fifteen years, Simon and I had occasionally agreed off our own bat to appear on the covers of those same magazines. This had also been part of our contracts with TVNZ, and the publicity department had pushed repeatedly for those stories as they were great for promotional purposes. Sometimes they were about our personal as well as our work lives – a four-page wedding spread is a hard one to miss! After leaning on our brand as a couple in the past, did we really have the right to refuse now?

Feeling we had little choice, in the end we did agree. A day later, we sat outside a Ponsonby cafe on a breezy day, forcing smiles in the knowledge a bloke across the street with a long lens was snapping merrily away.

It was one of the more bizarre things I've ever done, and it's a decision I still feel shame for making. But the media minders were ultimately right: it did work.

16.

It started with a basket of baking.

My daughter bounced in, dropped off home by a friend's mum after her first ever hip-hop lesson.

'How did it go?' I asked.

'Good. I can't dance yet.' She frowned, our little perfectionist. Then, more brightly, 'I did some cartwheels instead. And! K says we can bring her cookies next time if we want.'

I laughed. That sounded intriguing, and it was doable. I hadn't met K – short for Karleen – yet, but it's always a good idea to impress the teacher.

The following week, I took Paris to class with a wicker basket of chocolate chip cookies, tied up with a red bow. Karleen ripped them open right there on the spot and crunched into one with gusto, making the kids laugh. Then she tied the red bow in her ponytail.

I had no knowledge of the dance world, save for those Saturday mornings I'd spent in my teens sitting cross-legged at the back of my friend Katie's ballet school class. Karleen – a pioneer of hip-hop dance in Australasia and beyond – had no knowledge of the world of television. We were unlikely friends, and aside from the early win with the cookies, our relationship didn't start well.

Soon after that first meeting, I checked my email inbox at the kitchen bench and groaned. 'Oh my god, Paris,' I said. 'There's an email from your dance teacher saying you have to spend all of Saturday morning – from 8 am! – rehearsing for a competition. In costume! You already have hockey, and there's Joel's rugby as well. As if we have time!'

Paris gave me a pleading look, expecting trouble, as I wrote a snippy reply.

Dear Karleen,
Thank you for the wonderful job you're doing with Paris's dance class. However, I think you'll find that Saturday mornings are already very tightly scheduled for parents of school-aged children. Perhaps you could find a more suitable time for the rehearsal?
   Kind regards, Ali

What a biggity cow. Plus, I'd underestimated K's years of experience handling uppity eastern-suburbs mothers, and her return email left me in no doubt who was in charge here. It made me laugh out loud; there weren't too many people prepared to put me in my place so firmly. I was both chastened and a little bit impressed. On the Saturday morning, we were at the St Heliers School hall for rehearsal at eight on the dot.

For the rest of the year, I took note of the ways K went above and beyond for her students, giving just as much encouragement and time to the strugglers as she did to the stars. She was tough as nails and demanding, but for some reason none of the students seemed to resent or push back again the high standards they were held to: their efforts were in lockstep with their teacher's expectations. There is something quite magical about a truly gifted teacher of children, and K had it in spades. The kids adored her, competing constantly for her attention and approval.

By the time the end-of-year show came around, I found myself doing the same. I signed up as a backstage helper and made sure K was properly fed in the long hours she spent at the theatre.

It was months before I learned about her business background. She'd built several successful companies from scratch, and now she travelled Australia and Asia visiting dozens of dance schools that used her hip-hop syllabus.

As we chatted by the front desk after class one afternoon, she asked me what I intended to do next.

I frowned, not understanding. 'Next?'

'You can't be a telly presenter forever, surely. Have you thought about how you could use your skills to make something for yourself? You know, be your own boss.'

That touched a nerve. K's point was that I should seize control of my career trajectory, but underneath that lay an uncomfortable truth. In the artificially youthful realm of television presenting, I was already in my dotage. Decrepitude was just a cancelled contract away, and no amount of Botox would ward that off when the execs on level seven decided it was time for me to go. I'd had vague thoughts of setting something up – a training business, perhaps? But I had no clue how to wrangle thirty years of television knowledge into a saleable form. I wouldn't have known where to start.

'You need to write a curriculum,' said K. 'Put everything you know into a teachable system with modules that cover all the essential skills. I can help you.'

And so she did. For nine months, we worked together a couple of afternoons a week; in the moments I lost faith, she would insist I keep going. At the end, I had a plan for a coaching business – and, more importantly, the belief that I could make it work. This was a revelation; I was good at one thing and one thing only, or so I'd thought. Karleen made me look over the horizon, beyond the only work I'd known for three decades, to other possibilities. All I had to do was believe in myself.

**

There's no other way to say it, and she will hate it when she reads this, but K is simply one of life's magnetic personalities. You don't have to take my word for it – everybody who meets her feels the same. Once, early in our relationship, we went out for a casual dinner with a group that included a household-name celebrity who sat mostly in silence, trying hard not to stare at K throughout. After the dinner, the celebrity told our mutual friend she'd been mesmerised by K and wanted to be like her. 'Join the queue,' I replied with a laugh.

It's charisma, not just a physical thing, although I'd be lying if I said there wasn't that, too. I recall a maitre d' asking me who my dinner companion was so he could take me to the right table and then saying, 'Oh yes, I know who you mean, the *eyes*!'

It was impossible, even as a straight woman – which is what I believed myself to be at the time – to ignore K's physicality. Shuffling Paris into class one afternoon, I joined the knot of dance mums watching through the studio windows. There were three of them, neatly dressed, wearing gold watches and fob necklaces, with expensively highlighted hair much like my own. They were married, wealthy white women – ostensibly – who were there to watch their kids dance.

After about ten minutes, one of them broke the silence with a theatrical, throaty moan. 'God. She's amaaaazing, isn't she?' The woman pulled the vowel out like she was stretching taffy at a country fair.

It was true, K most certainly was amazing, but the comment didn't seem to invite my input. The women were still staring straight at K as she took the children through a routine, and I stayed silent.

The speaker then turned to face me, with a sly narrowing of her eyes. 'You know she's gay, don't you?'

I was struck by the way this was delivered – half-threat, half-challenge, daring me to react. No way was I going to fall into her little trap. I shrugged. 'No, I didn't … So?'

Another woman cut in before the first could answer, never taking her eyes off the studio. She sighed. 'We'd *all* turn gay for Karleen.'

You don't, I hope, get to your mid-forties without understanding that looks are not the be-all and end-all. K is also a kind and moral person. I hesitate to use that last adjective, as it has different connotations for everyone; what I mean is, she has an inviolable sense of right and wrong, and she'll go to incredible lengths to support the people she cares about. True kindness, the sort that does not seek any benefit for self, is sadly a rarity.

After my marriage fell apart, K was the one dropping trays of homemade lasagne or roast chicken at the door to make sure we all ate, often pushing the bell and then hopping back in her car to get to work. She cared for me and the kids, without intruding on my grief.

* * *

'Let's run it again.' K re-cued the iPod and motioned me to join her in front of the mirror in the dance studio. Once again she talked me through the opening steps, counting me in, slowing down the beat until the utter confusion on my face was replaced by (partial!) understanding, and we began.

I'd had such envy for dancers ever since Katie had gone to ballet school. I'd envied their total freedom and their mastery over their bodies – being a natural klutz all your life will do that to a person. And I'd moaned on enough about it to K that one day she'd called me on it: 'If you really want to learn, I'll give you lessons.'

The steps were easy, or would have been for someone with a single skerrick of rhythm, coordination or musicality. I looked like a stick insect attempting to breakdance. Lucky for me, the studio was empty. I tripped over my feet for the umpteenth time.

'It's okay,' she said. 'Again.'

She was wearing khaki combat pants, Nike high tops and a black NYC baseball cap, and her ankles seemed made of rubber. Her entire body was fluid as flowing water. The music was loud, and I kept my eyes glued to her reflection.

Just before the bridge, mid-step-touch, I felt something unexpected inside me: a jolt of pure energy like a lightning strike. And a flush rose right from my toes, creeping upward, until every cell of my body felt suffused by … what? What on earth was this?

'Ah, I'm really not getting this,' I said. 'Could you run it again for me? I'll just, ah, sit back here for a minute.' I could feel my face turning red as I scuttled to the back of the studio like a cockroach chased with a can of Mortein, then I scooched down the wall until I was cross-legged on the floor.

A lie – I knew the dance move. But I had a sudden piercing need to watch *her* do it.

She re-cued Flo Rida and ran the dance through, twice. My heart was pounding painfully in my chest. What the hell was this?

After the lesson, I left carrying my secret delicately, like a featherless baby bird cupped in my hands. A completely new feeling. A thought that had never, ever entered my head before this moment … But that wasn't entirely true.

* * *

Back in October 2008, my younger sister had called me from Melbourne. 'I'm going to New York,' Sam told me. 'I want to move there, I've always wanted to move there, and I need to check it out. Would you come with me?'

'When?'

'I leave in a couple of days, but I've got a week in Hawaii first, so – ten days from now?'

I laughed. I had two little kids and a job on the telly – heck no, I could not go to New York in ten days' time.

'Please? I need my big sister with me. Just think about it …?'

'I'll have a think about it,' I said, before hanging up and climbing the stairs to tuck the kids into bed. In her pretty gabled room, Paris was reading. I turned the lamp off and gave her a hug, sitting on the edge of her bed. Seized by a force of I-don't-know-what, I told her what her aunty Sam had asked, adding a little dismissive chuckle at the end. 'As if!'

Paris was not buying it. 'Mum, you should. When will you ever get another chance to go on a holiday to New York with your sister?'

Such wisdom from a ten year old. I went back downstairs, told Simon my plans and booked my flight.

Two weeks later, Sam and I settled into our plush red seats in the Ambassador Theatre on West 49th Street in Manhattan. This was a bucket-list moment for me: a Broadway show, and not just any show, mind – *Chicago*, my favourite musical of all time. I started to cry from pure joy.

'Stop it!' Sam laughed. 'You're embarrassing!'

'Sorry, sorry, I'm just so happy!' I dabbed at my eyes with the single crumpled tissue in the bottom of my bag, thinking I should have come better prepared.

Then the lights dimmed, and I was mesmerised. By the show, yes; by John Kander's incredible score that I'd loved since I was a child, yes; by Bob Fosse's choreography, yes. But also. Also. In the third number, 'Cell Block Tango', the merry murderesses wound themselves around bentwood chairs and sang of their feckless dead husbands, and there was one – tall, black, with a beautiful voice and an even more beautiful body – who made me sit up straight in my seat.

My eyes followed her across the stage as if she was the only performer. A ridiculous thought played through my head: *What if I go to the stage door and ask her to come for a drink?* It arrived unbidden and from nowhere, and was gone almost before I realised I'd had it. I blushed suddenly, crimson in the darkened theatre. *What the hell was that?*

***

Like most humans, I am a creature of habit, and as a journalist, my habit is research. So, I researched. After that day in the dance studio, where my perception of myself was turned on its head, I read scholarly theories on sexual fluidity, learning it was quite common for women to experience a first same-sex attraction in their middle years, a stage in life where we begin to assess what we really want in life. I was among the women who'd grown up without any mention of queerness in our education, in a culture that held the belief that only heterosexuality was 'normal'. For some of my generation, it was downright dangerous to be queer. That resonated with me, and I realised with shame that these were things I'd never bothered to seek out or understand in all the years I'd considered myself an ally of the rainbow community. I thought a lot, until late every night, about what – even if *nothing ever happened* – I was learning about myself. Posed hypotheticals: *Ali, if you saw a complete stranger in a Ponsonby bar* – a situation of almost zero probability, since I almost never went out – *and that stranger was attractive and happened to be a woman, would you …?* I couldn't even finish the question. But I did have an answer and that was, *No, I don't think so.*

In the evening hours after the kids were in bed, I gave that baby bird the nurturing it needed until it grew rainbow plumes and was ready to fly. I did this not in a panic but in vibrant curiosity. If Karleen had been any random woman, I wondered, would I have felt the same? *No, I don't think so.* I gradually understood that for me, this was about a person, and the gender of that person was immaterial.

All of this was fine when it was held in the confines of my head. I considered locking it in there forever and barricading the door with the heavy furniture of fear, because the only other option was to tell her, and that was the scary bit. I knew she liked me, and we had a lovely friendship – but did she like me in *that* way? I'd never had much trouble telling when men were, you know, *interested* … did it work the same way for women? Would there be clues when we hung out together, in our calls or texts? She was such a vibrant, generous character, both interesting and interested, so how the bloody hell would I know for sure?

I thought a lot about touching her – perhaps taking her hand and grazing my thumb across her palm. How would that feel? My imagination would take me no further. Later, several friends teased me about my naivete: 'Ali, surely you must have experimented with women when you were younger, at uni? In your twenties?' Ah, nope. That had never been in my grab bag of coming-of-age experiences, not once.

I started to read things into our conversations, and eventually I was pretty sure (as sure as I was going to get) that we had a flirtation maybe, just maybe, strong enough for me to act on. As the Greeks like to say, I'd joined the dancing, now I must dance.

* * *

We were in her apartment, sharing a bottle of champagne she'd bought duty free, catching up over dinner on her travels, chatting lightly about this and that. My heart had been pounding with terror and anticipation well before I'd knocked on the door – later K would tell me she had assumed, from the stricken look on my face, that I was there to tell her we couldn't be friends anymore for some unspoken reason. I can't blame her: I was awkward as hell, trying and failing several times to tell her how I felt.

She didn't seem to be catching any of my hints, and there was one awful moment when I thought, *If I have this arse-about, if I've grabbed* entirely the wrong end of the stick, *the humiliation will be too much, I'll have to just bolt out of here and never see her again.*

I asked her questions about her interest in women, and she could have told me to fuck right off and mind my own business. But because she is a kind person, she ignored my stupidity and answered with a light laugh. And then – with risible formality – I asked whether she might be interested in *me*.

She looked at me for a long moment, evaluating. 'You're not just one of those straight women who want to try it out, are you?'

If the floor had opened up at that moment, I would have willingly dived into the void. 'Nononononono!' I was babbling, but I would not take it back. I made it crystal clear, then, what it was I wanted. The invitation lay in front of us both, and then it was accepted. And from that moment, in the way that lesbians tend to joke about, we were inseparable.

17.

It was an ordinary cafe on a corner in an ordinary East Auckland suburb on an ordinary Sunday morning. Patrons were enjoying a break over croissants and coffee, their little dogs tied to a lamppost or the legs of the red Property Press bin on the pavement. Nothing to see here – apart from me, lurking by the counter, lit up with terror like a wicker man.

I was wearing dark glasses inside, an affectation I don't like but was about to become close chums with. I heard every page of the complimentary Sunday papers turn like a roar rather than a rustle. *Don't look up, don't look up,* I willed these strangers as they skipped from the front page – with its banner headline 'ALI MAU'S LADY LOVE. Exclusive pictures: TV star's dancer girlfriend' – to the back, where the juicy details were promised. There were images of both of us, taken by a hidden man with a long lens. One diner did look up, her gaze floating across the unremarkable scene in Scorsese slo-mo, stopping on my face for a second …? Perhaps just my imagination. She turned back to the gossip column. I got out of there as soon as the barista pressed the takeaway cup into my shaking hand.

The call the day before had come from a well-connected media mate. 'Ah. Hiiii.' He drew the word out like a sigh. 'I'm sorry, hon. Don't ask me how I know, but they've got the story. It'll be in the paper tomorrow. I'm so sorry.'

It was kind of him to warn us about the coming storm. And I knew the winds of scuttlebutt had been picking up already; a couple of days before, a fellow news presenter had dragged me into a corner of the makeup room and, blushing right to the roots of her backcombed hair, whispered what was being said around the dinner-party tables of the well-heeled. I had smiled and thanked her warmly, and walked away.

Over the phone, my media mate and I discussed my next steps. What would my response be? Did I need to make one? Was silence the best option? As we talked, I stepped outside my body and watched – with detached curiosity – the other Ali, the one calmly discussing what strategy she might employ to protect her kids, her new and treasured relationship. We even had a little giggle at the absurdity of it all.

When I hung up, Karleen was beside me, those extraordinary eyes steady on my face. She reached for my hand. 'Bastards.'

They'll be expecting a response, I thought. *They do not deserve a window into our private lives, but a response is the dignified thing to offer.*

I gave them what they asked for, and it appeared in the paper the next day, sitting among the gossip columnist's stock-in-trade phrases like 'understood to be' and 'believed to be', and a bunch of facts ripped from Karleen's business website.

I am aware that there's been a lot of speculation in recent weeks about my personal life; these rumours don't bother me [not entirely untrue – it wasn't the rumours but the vomiting of them over the front pages that bothered me]. *I said in June last year that my children were my most important priority and to protect them I would not discuss our private lives in a public forum.*

My position on this has not changed. I'd like to hope that the New Zealand media will be responsible and continue to protect my children's right to privacy despite my reasonably high-profile career. I'd also like to reassure people that I am happy, my children are happy and for my family that's the most important thing.

These few simple sentences had taken me several hours to draft, pushing down the bile that rose because our most private details were being picked over just to sell copies of a newspaper for a few bucks apiece. I don't think I can do an adequate job of describing the feeling, even now, fifteen years on. But I'll have a go.

It was certainly rage – for my kids, who felt nothing but love and joy at home but who would sense the eyes of the school-gate mothers on them come Monday and feel that prickle of unease; and for my love, who'd been blissfully unaware of the media's sharp teeth until now; who could be quietly rueing the day she'd fallen for me as I had for her, but who still took my hand and called them bastards. And if I'm honest, for myself.

It was revulsion – for the men who made their money slumped in the front seats of cars, poking their lenses at us all as we'd gone about our lives.

It was pity – for the person who'd scattered the details of my private life like seeds and then confirmed them to the editors who published them.

I felt all that, but there was no time to wallow.

The night before the news was released, I picked up the phone and worked through my contact list, dialling the people who didn't already know but probably needed to before the next day dawned. I explained to them one by one what they were likely to see in print, and that some of it would be true but none of it anybody's bloody business. As the ringtone bleated, before each call was answered, I took a big, deep and unsteady breath. I readied myself to say, over and over: 'Just thought you should be prepared in case anyone brings it up.'

People surprise you in these moments. My former mother-and-sisters-in-law were solid and supportive and quietly furious with the gossip hounds. A friend seemed completely thrown and started to babble, refusing to believe I could be in a same-sex relationship and making me spell it out. Another laughed as she congratulated me, saying, 'Oh my god, yay! Good for you. I'd always had you pegged as the most heterosexual person I ever met!' Whatever that was supposed to mean – and she wasn't the only one.

Coming out is stressful. It can be a political act and in some countries a dangerous one. The first step, or so the accepted psychology goes, is coming out to yourself. I'd had to do that in a hurry, but it had caused me no angst – I'd felt, instead, simple curiosity as I sat on the deck of my former marital home, in the late hours when the kids were tucked up in bed, looking up at the stars and feeling wonder about falling in love so completely with a person, not a gender. For me, gender has nothing at all to do with anything. There are plenty of others in the LGBTQIA+ community who will disagree, but with the utmost respect for their experiences, this is the truth of mine.

The next step in coming out is telling the people you trust. You choose those people carefully, because they must keep it private lest you lose control over the rest of your process. Like so many others, I had been taking it slowly. My relationship with K was so new, so precious, that I'd been gathering courage in small but important fragments, telling those who mattered most as the opportunity arose. My parents, under the bleaching fluorescent lights of a suburban Thai restaurant in Melbourne, and who both – even though in their seventies – reacted with genuine joy at my happiness. The Sisters and my closest friends: ditto.

It took me months to properly understand I deserved the same as any other person who was grappling with their sexuality – I deserved some control over the process. I deserved – as anyone does – the right to choose.

What I did not feel, not even for a second, was shame. Not even the tiniest bit. But I did feel cold fury at the intrusion into my family's lives.

* * *

Things got weird very quickly once the story was out there. For the following days and weeks, our lives were like a mishandled suitcase, the private contents like lacy undies spilling out all over an airport carousel.

Out of sheer stubbornness, I refused to take time off work – I would not allow myself to be publicly cowed. But the logistics were simple anyway: my garage to TVNZ's underground carpark was a relatively easy and protected journey, and I remembered the defensive-driving training I'd been given the year before.

Outside of work it was a different story. I dreaded going anyplace I would have to get out of the car – to the school gates to pick up the kids, to the supermarket; it felt like emerging from a foxhole into the line of fire, making it easy for the paparazzi, and that was the last thing I wanted to do.

I felt torn by conflicting feelings. I had nothing to be ashamed of, and they would not make me feel ashamed – I was clear on that. On a logical level, buried below the fight/flight/freeze and the constant pumping cortisol, I also knew the motivation of the photographers, the journalists and the editors was not to shame us: they just wanted a racy story to boost their sales numbers. It was the *effect* of those stories that made me claw the walls in frustration – the knowledge that we (even my children!) were being spied on, and the real or imagined sense that everyone was gossiping about us, judging us. These twin perspectives jostled for primacy in my head minute to minute, and I flip-flopped between them.

The immediate concern was the photographers, but at least they didn't know which house we lived in, I consoled myself. Silly me. Sweeping out leaves from the garage one midweek afternoon, I saw a man with a large camera and a long lens wander down the right-of-way we shared with several neighbours. He was peering over hedges and fences. Stepping back into the shadows, I pressed the close button on the garage door. *Yes! He hasn't seen me!* I gave myself a mental high five.

Moments later, the photographer knocked on a neighbour's door and asked which house was ours. He must have left out the crucial bit – that he was from the newspaper – so the neighbour assumed he was from a real estate firm and helpfully pointed us out. That neighbour texted me an apology later, full of horror at his mistake. But the damage was done.

The next day I was backing out of the garage, on our way to dance class, when I almost ran over the *Herald*'s crack scandal journalist in the driveway. She came up to the open window, shouting questions at me as the kids goggled in fright from the back seat.

'Carolyne, *please*, I have the children in the car!' I begged. I didn't wait for a reply, gunning the car backwards with a squeal of tyres.

By this stage there was no hiding our situation from the kids, although I was very careful to only let the tears fall when I was alone. And anyway, I had to wrestle with my pledge to them: honesty above all.

Joel, who was eight, came home from school keen to tell me about his ingenious thinking. 'Mum! So, my friend Andrew and I have a plan for when a photographer jumps out of the bushes.' His dark eyebrows knitted together in excitement and pride. 'We know what to do! Andrew's going to shout at them, and I will have time to run away.'

I drew his little body into a hug, resting my chin on his wiry black hair for a moment. Then I congratulated him on this cleverness and sent him off to play. Once he'd left the room, I cried and cried.

* * *

'Oh, hi, Alison, it's [redacted]. I'm calling to get your comment on Dom Harvey's rap song …?'

The caller, a journalist, sounded shocked that I'd answered my phone. Fair, since I'd ignored several of his calls already that morning.

Hold on. 'The *what* song?'

'Are you saying you haven't heard it?' he asked.

'I don't have a clue what you're talking about.'

This was plainly not the answer my caller had hoped for, because it meant he now had to explain. 'Uh. On The Edge … his radio show … he, uh … sang a song about you …'

'How nice.' I suspected it wasn't, in fact, nice. 'What are the lyrics?'

'Um. Well, it talks about rug-munching. And strap-on dildos. It's to the tune of "Single Ladies (Put a Ring on It)".'

Nice choice of tune, at least, I thought.

'Can you read the lyrics out to me?' I asked. I realised this would increase the poor man's already escalating discomfort level by a factor of thousands, but I had a rule I rarely broke: don't give a comment until you know the *exact* details of what is being alleged.

He did as requested, stumbling over the worst bits. Then he asked, 'Are you angry?'

I said I was, and I suppose that was true, but it stung only for a few days. It was a small detail in light of everything else, and the shock-jock Dom Harvey was a small annoyance of a man. There were much bigger things on the way to worry about.

The *Herald On Sunday* must have copped a bit of public ire over their 'scoop', because the next Sunday – my birthday, coincidentally – it doubled down, running a feature-length justification of its original article. I read that story through, thinking – as I had years ago at Channel 9 – about the public interest test: that media intrusion must be justified if public interest is the shield. Who will suffer, and who will benefit? And will wider society benefit? The answers seemed pretty clear; there's a big difference between 'in the public interest' and 'what the public might be interested to read'. I was a journalist with thirty years in the industry under my belt, and I could see the difference.

That article was simply a second hit at the body already prone on the floor. There was a third when the gossip mag *Woman's Day* hit the newsstands a day later.

That day, a Monday, I had an important meeting to attend – and despite all the drama, I was not going to bail. It's not easy to pick a date that suits the lawyers, the parties to the action *and* a qualified mediator, so I felt it was worth getting on with the marital property settlement agreement while the stars and everyone's calendars aligned. Yes, there was a *lot* going on in my life, and most of it was slinging me like a hockey puck from tears to defiance and back again every few hours. But I'd decided to keep working and not let the bastards get me down, so there didn't seem to be any real reason to cancel the mediation.

I was proud of that meeting. What could have been a face-off filled with spite or vitriol was handled, by all, with dignity. And it felt good to concentrate on dry but important stuff for a few hours.

***

TVNZ asked me to fill in for Paul Henry on *Breakfast* that week, which meant I'd be cohosting the show with Pippa Wetzell. Rather ironically, we'd be the first women to do this.

I got out of bed at 3 am and drove through the dark streets to TVNZ's city studios, superstitiously avoiding glances at dairies as if that would make *Woman's Day* and its posters – with our faces under shouty block-letter headlines – disappear. In the makeup room, the team put my 45-year-old face, puffy from tears and lack of sleep, back together. I swear those women could take a pair of eyeballs marinated for a year in rotgut liquor and make them look like Audrey Hepburn's.

It was Tuesday – and Tuesday, coincidentally, was the day of *Breakfast*'s regular 'what's in the magazines' segment. I'd had an idea, which I took first thing that morning to my executive producer. He agreed it fit within the context of the segment, and we worked on the script together, my EP suggesting a few changes and removing some of the more emotional language. I briefed Pippa to make sure she was comfortable, and the script was duly typed into the autocue.

A couple of hours later, I delivered to our nationwide *Breakfast* audience my three-minute response to the agony my family was being put through. Holding the magazine cover up to the camera, I demanded, 'When is this kind of thing going to stop? Just give me an idea, maybe, when the dogs are going to be called off, and me and my friends and my family can go about our business without having a creepy guy in a Corolla station wagon following us around?'

I felt for Pippa, who had to look at me with concern all the way through (three minutes is a *very* long time in television), but when we cut to the commercial break directly afterwards, I was shaking with a combination of fear and exhilaration. I had fought back, in the only way I could, and I was content with that – even a tiny bit proud of myself.

Murmurs of support, disembodied, floated from the control-room crew into my earpiece.

My executive producer appeared from the gloom behind the cameras and stood in the pool of intense light. We looked at each other for a moment, and I didn't trust my voice, so I waited for him to speak. 'Well done,' he said. 'That can't have been easy.'

I nodded, giving him a grateful smile.

From the media, there was an immediate and, I suppose, predictable uproar. Many commenters – who as 'media experts' ought to have known better – appeared to believe I'd hijacked *Breakfast* and delivered a stream-of-consciousness rant. That made me laugh – have you ever tried to ad-lib on live television for three long minutes? They could not have been more wrong; it was planned and executed with great care, my only way of regaining control of my story. And it worked – the paparazzi cars disappeared.

I found myself fascinated by how the various players chose to defend their actions. The CEO of *Woman's Day* claimed the photos had been taken 'over a 24-hour period' and added that '[W]e know there are boundaries when researching stories and we would never intentionally step over them.' There was little point continuing the argument with him in public. Explaining is losing, or so the saying goes.

He continued to gaslight me over the years. In 2014, when I wrote an op-ed criticising *Woman's Day* for printing paparazzi pictures, taken with a long lens, of seventeen-year-old Lorde in a bikini, he responded like this: 'Frankly, why would we be concerned about what someone like Ali Mau thinks?' It was a neat way of dismissing me – I was that annoying woman to him.

* * *

Ten years later, in 2020, I was asked if I would talk about being publicly outed for a panel discussion at a queer writer's festival. I'd never discussed it publicly at any length, so this required some thought, and I didn't immediately say yes. But one question the festival's convenor asked me struck a chord: 'Would the same thing happen today, a decade on?'

'Hmm, great question,' I replied. 'Why don't I see if I can find out?'

I made some calls. The journalist who had written the *Sunday Herald*'s follow-up story apologised profusely and said he'd been uncomfortable but had felt pressured to do it.

I then phoned the man who had been the editor at the time and who had commissioned the story, catching him on the sidelines at his kid's sports day. 'Oh my god, no,' he told me, 'we would never do that these days.' I had a friendly, constructive conversation with him about why that might be and how time had changed his views.

I pressed him on some issues and was content with his response in the end. As we wrapped up the call, he gave me a fulsome apology, which I was happy to accept.

And, naively, I did think times had changed – until the forced outing of actor Rebel Wilson by a *Sydney Morning Herald* gossip columnist in 2022. *Holy heck*, I thought, *can this be happening? More than a decade on, more of the same ...?*

My phone began to ring: several New Zealand news outlets – including *Stuff*, my own employer – asking for my comment on what that must feel like. I wanted to help, but I knew that if I agreed, the story would go live with my response as the hook. I would comment, I told them, if they were prepared to speak to the editors and journalists who had pursued me and my family in 2010. 'The readers should know how they feel about this now,' I said – *then* and only then would there be a story that could have any hope of properly examining the issue.

By 2022, I'd seen time and time again in my years of reporting on sexual harassment that it's too easy to go to the survivor, drag up their painful experience for a clickable headline and leave it at that. Reviving those memories can be retraumatising, and the knowledge that they'll again be in the news can cause the survivor real anxiety – that's why I always made every effort to contact them when a follow-up to their story was likely to run, if I knew about it. I would explain their options and make sure they were comfortable. Anything less is just lazy reporting.

I waited in an anxious sweat but heard nothing from anyone other than the TVNZ reporter, and I'm grateful for the care he took. After four days, I called the others to ask what they'd heard and when the story might run. The journalists at *Stuff* and *The Spinoff* seemed surprised to hear from me; for whatever reason, they'd moved on and had not thought about letting me know.

Rebel Wilson did get some vindication after the *Sydney Morning Herald*'s 'grubby behaviour' (her words). The Australian Press Council ruled the paper had sought to publish on a personal matter 'which had no apparent connection to her public activities [and] intruded on her reasonable expectation of privacy'. There was not enough public interest to justify the intrusion, it said. And after doubling down and criticising Wilson for gazumping his story, the gossip columnist apologised in print, writing: 'The *Herald* and I will approach things differently from now on to make sure we always take into consideration the extra layer of complexities people face when it comes to their sexuality.'

* * *

'Are you sure?' Bimbo blinked her fluffy black eyelashes at me, shifting from foot to foot on enormous platform stilettos. She exchanged a concerned glance with Buffy.

The celebrated drag duo were moments from striding onstage in front of a packed audience at the Aotea Centre, and I'd just dropped a bombshell.

'Yes, I'm sure. There's no audience more supportive than this one, is there?' I gave them a nervous grin.

I'd known Jonathan Smith (Bimbo) and Kevin Baker (Buffy) since the early 90s, through the New Zealand AIDS Foundation and its incredible work for people living with HIV/AIDS. I'd been a judge at their gala fundraiser show, *Queen of the Whole Universe*, for half a decade and had risen that year to the honoured position of chief judge. It was November 2010, nine months on from the public outing, and now I felt ready to speak – or, rather, compelled by some greater force to do so.

This felt important – crucial, actually – not just for myself but for Karleen too. Through everything, she had been an absolute rock; had not put a single foot wrong in word or deed as I flailed around in self-absorbed agony in those early days; had wordlessly taken over every task I was too distressed to manage. If she was upset for her own shattered privacy, she never once showed it to me or to the kids. Although she does not like public attention, she agreed with perfect grace to my plan for that night.

'Well, you mustn't feel any pressure at all to say anything.' Bimbo laid a bejewelled hand on my arm. 'But they'll love it if you do.'

And so a few minutes later, standing on that huge stage and shaking with nerves, I made a short, off-the-cuff speech acknowledging the queer community – and particularly Karleen, who was sitting a few rows from the front. I told them how happy I was, how much I loved her and how much all of their support meant to me.

Two thousand people roared and stamped their approval. I could not stop smiling.

18.

'Hello, is anyone in there?' I asked, knocking lightly on the door of the campervan. My words sounded unnaturally loud, and it took me a few seconds to place the reason: there were no other sounds. No birdsong. No droning of insects. No noise from any living thing, apart from the mud-muffled paw-pads of a neighbourhood dog in the street and the sound of our breathing.

The flimsy tin door of the van was flung open, and a white-haired man popped his head out, a woman appearing over his shoulder. They took in our small, gumbooted team standing in the ruins of their driveway, and their faces split with wide grins – not the usual reaction from someone opening the door to a *Fair Go* camera crew.

'You're the first people we've seen since the quake.' There was a tremor in his voice on that last word. He swept a hand towards his house, a brick and tile bungalow, formerly neat and well kept. I could tell by the rosebushes, the tops of which were peeking above the mounds of grey silt, that the couple were keen gardeners. But now the house was split in two by a crack like a lightning bolt, each crumbled half slumped into the earth. My eyes went automatically to the roof, where a red-brick chimney teetered in the breeze, loosed from its mortar like a diseased tooth. One of thousands of broken chimneys.

'Uh, we're from *Fair Go*,' I said. 'Is this where you're living? Has anyone come to help you?'

'No, not a soul. We're lucky we're got the van.' He patted its side like a proud dad. 'We moved into it after the house …' He shot a despairing look at the mess.

It had been four days since the February 2011 earthquake, and in this stretch of the eastern suburbs, thousands of residents had yet to be offered anything at all.

'We don't have power, but we have a gas stove. We've been coping okay.' Once again his voice trembled, and the woman (his wife, I assumed) placed a reassuring hand on his shoulder. At her touch, he seemed to rally. 'We could use a shower and some water.'

'Oh, we can definitely help with that.' I looked around for our director, but she was already squelching through the mud to the rental car and rummaging in the boot. A moment later, she hauled a wrapped brick of bottled water back to the van.

We made plans with the couple to take them to my motel room near the airport to shower, then passed them a flyer with information about evacuation centres and Red Cross help, and moved along to the next house.

* * *

I hadn't exactly been flushed with enthusiasm when, at the close of 2008, the boss had asked me if I'd like to move to work on *Fair Go*. I'm ashamed to say I hadn't been a regular viewer – the show had already been a venerable elder of the telly scene when I'd arrived in New Zealand fifteen years before, and I guess I'd dismissed it as a slightly hokey relic, buttressed by loyal fans. How wrong I was.

I was also reluctant to let go of one of the great conceits of my profession: that advocacy had no place in journalism. It'd been drummed into me since I was a small child. 'Never let the facts interfere with a good story' may have been a favourite saying of Dad's, but it was meant as a joke. I'd had many conversations with him over the years, some tipping into arguments, about his belief in a Walter Lippmann-like 'detachment' as the boundary never to be crossed, rigid as a chalk outline on asphalt. This doctrine went beyond the usual tenets of balance and fairness, and even as a D-grade newspaper reporter on the *Herald*'s social issues round, I had struggled with it, uncomfortable as a penitent in a hair shirt.

'Perfect objectivity is a myth!' I would argue. 'How can I write about the homeless, or the AIDS crisis, without taking some kind of viewpoint? There is no *on the other hand* when people are dying.'

Under his pitying gaze I felt every bit the rookie reporter. 'Tough shit, it's your job,' he would say, pious as a pastor – ironic, considering his loathing of all things holy.

As much as I would poke and prod at his reasoning, looking for the threads I might pull to unravel it, the legacy of his work and his father's before him always won the day. I was my father's daughter, and his beliefs – when it came to the craft, anyhow – had become mine.

And so – 'Uh … I'll think about it …?' was all I'd said to my TVNZ boss in 2008, prevaricating until I could gather some intel.

I set off to find people who could give me a steer on what it was like to work on the show and, importantly, on its impact. I tried to keep an open mind, expecting to strike as many scoffers as fans. What I found, from those who knew enough to be counted as reliable sources, was unanimity: 'Do it. You won't regret it.'

They were right. The *Fair Go* team were devoted to some of the most rigorous journalism in television, although you had to look under the bonnet for it. Stories about insurance payouts, dodgy car dealers, or whiteware warranties were not easy stories to tell. These were not murders, or political scandals, or gold-medal tales of sporting triumph – those kinds of stories largely told themselves. *Fair Go* stories, while in some cases every bit as life-changing, dramatic and tear-jerking, required a particular creativity in the telling, if the audience was to stay glued to TV One without reaching for the remote. If you can make a seven-minute yarn about washing powder worth sticking with, you have something to be proud of! Then there was the ever-present threat of legal action. Defamation law in New Zealand is strict; if you plan to stand with cameras rolling in a muddy field/building site/corporate HQ reception area and argue for an explanation of apparent embezzlement/betrayal/corruption, you'd better be sure of your facts.

And it wasn't just a good professional move, I realised after I said yes to the job and joined *Fair Go* in a hybrid host/reporter role in early 2009. For the first time since London, I found a real work family. These people, and the *Sunday* programme reporters we shared desk space with, helped carry me through the ruins of my marriage break-up – never prying, but always there. One minute, they'd be challenging my draft story edit in the pre-show review meeting (as a unique chance to improve, this was my favourite couple of hours in any week), and the next, offering quiet emotional support. I was brittle and secretive at work in those early days, post break-up, and I'm sure it was difficult for my workmates; the other half of this front-page story worked just one floor below us, after all. I bet I pushed them away as often as I accepted their comfort. But they did not falter, and I came to love them for that.

So, by 2011, I was well aware of the power of this beloved show. But even I couldn't work out, when our phones began to ping like stretched rubber bands on 22 February, what role *Fair Go* might have in a national emergency. TVNZ reporters would be relaying the facts of buildings collapsed, suburbs buried in liquefaction, and then the grim work of Urban Search and Rescue teams. What could a consumer affairs programme possibly contribute?

As dozens of our news colleagues jumped in taxis and headed to Auckland Airport, we gathered to brainstorm in our executive producer's office.

'What do our people want from us, when it really comes down to it?' the EP asked the room.

'Help. They want our help.' I think it was Gordon Harcourt who said this – that's what I'd like to think anyway, as Gordon is a legend.

'Yep,' said the EP. 'So, what's the best way to help them?'

We came up with a plan: to find a street in a badly hit suburb and, with the residents' permission, tackle their problems one by one. If they were willing to tell us their needs, we would try to fulfil them. The director and the camera operator were handed the most difficult task: flying to Christchurch ahead of the rest of the team to scope out probable contenders. This meant driving into the red zone, donning gumboots and walking the silt-caked roads, talking to whoever they could find in the wasteland. Eventually, they found a cul-de-sac where, for whatever reason, the locals had decided to stay put in their wrecked homes.

It was difficult for our team to stay detached. Walking to the end of a street rent by deep fissures and barren as a desert, we'd find a trestle table piled high with cooked dinners in plastic dishes, dropped there by anonymous people from a neighbouring postcode that had (miraculously, inconceivably) escaped the quake's damage altogether. These corner tables were springing up like moss between paving stones, stocked by people who didn't mind being filmed but wouldn't give their names, needed no thanks, and would be back again later the same day with more. Streets that had been deathly quiet for days began finally to fill with the ring of spades on concrete and with chatter, as Student Volunteer Army members piled out of beaten-up cars. I looked with wonder at those young people and their boundless energy, so usefully hitched to a need to help.

But how were *we* helping? We were there to make television – and the making of episodic television can be a long, repetitive and sometimes rather tedious process, even in perfect conditions. In this post-quake silt desert, the slightest breeze made filming almost impossible. The retakes and back-cuts took hours, and as those hours passed, I felt mounting frustration. Amid such pain and loss, it all seemed so trivial.

We met a woman and her two kids at one of the road-end tables, picking up a donated mac and cheese to take back to her broken house. She told us how, when the awful shaking stopped, she'd run, lungs bursting, without stopping to the daycare centre, praying all the way that she would find her babies alive and unhurt. The memories of panic surfaced and played across her face, flickering like old film stock. I thought of my own children, and when the interview was done, I thanked her, then turned back to the car before the tears came.

Our director told me later that she'd watched my reporter's hard shell crack and reform, as I morphed between journalist and human being in those few days. In the aftermath, a new set of beliefs about my craft and its potential for good had formed where my father's edicts had been before.

It's 2019. A year has passed since Lisa's phone call, the one that brought our father's crimes into plain view, and she has been meeting regularly with a specialised counsellor, taking the first steps to confront the agony of the past. Lisa tells me on the phone how hard this has been, how deep she has to dig for courage in every session – and how much she cries! We are all criers, so that's expected. But she says it's helping.

We have become closer again, as sisters, since this monster rose from the backlog of years. That's been a positive. On The Sisters' WhatsApp thread, we talk with Sam (who, thankfully, mercifully, was unharmed by Dad) about what might happen next.

Benny has taken a different path. After some counselling, he began to watch painting videos on YouTube. As his creative voice developed, so the art became his therapy. This is not surprising: he studied graphic design and has always been a creative soul. It makes me intensely happy that such beauty can be born from great pain.

When it comes to Dad, we are still keeping all options open. This is sensible, but at the same time it feels dangerous, like swinging out over a murky rock pool on a rope. Who knows what lies under that unbroken surface, or when the rope might break?

The main thing holding us back from any formal action is Mum. I don't mean she's made any plea for mercy for the man she's spent sixty years with, just the opposite: she doesn't know. Or maybe she does? Maybe she always has …? It's so much easier to know how to feel about our father, although even those feelings often swing back and forth from disgust, to rage, to pity. But Mum? We feel protective of her, to different degrees, and depending on what we each suspect she knows, or does not know. Unfortunately, it might be too late for us to ever be sure.

'I'm going to write Leigh a letter,' Lisa tells me. 'I'm going to put everything in it. I want him to know what he's done. And I want him to know we know.' She stopped calling him Dad a while ago and now uses his first name, or his initials, LM. 'I've talked a lot to my counsellor about it,' she adds, 'and we've agreed it's the best way forward for me. I might never send it. I haven't decided.'

I agree this is a good idea – not that she needs my affirmation – and we talk about the possible consequences, particularly for Mum. I think if not for Mum, we would almost certainly go to the police. There are three of us, and there is strength and safety in numbers in a criminal case.

I don't feel any pleasure at the thought of my father spending his twilight years in jail. It would be valid if I did: accountability can be such a crucial step towards healing. But I don't feel any particular way about it, which is strange, this detachment. I know he has committed unspeakable criminal acts. I know he has done that without thinking about the consequences he has visited upon his own flesh and blood. This tracks with what I know about how my dad has lived his whole adult life: he is a creative, garrulous, sometimes brilliant but always selfish character who has done exactly what he has thought best for himself at any point, and damn the torpedoes.

I think a lot about this, why I am angry but not consumed by that anger. I wonder why I have not followed Lisa into therapy and explored techniques like CBT or EMDR, which sound so useful. I check myself – am I avoiding it, refusing to let my mind explore what has happened to me?

I don't think so, but I seek out the literature anyway, spending hours outside in the yard as I build compost heaps from old pallets and listen to audiobooks like Bessel van der Kolk's *The Body Keeps the Score*. I learn that you can't outrun trauma like this, but you can calm the body's response to the memories. The research had its own soothing effect: the more I learned about trauma, the better I felt about my own.

19.

It was 2012, and *Fair Go*'s executive producer, Briar, was perched on the corner of her desk, looking at me with genuine worry. 'I don't know if you should do this,' she said. 'Is it safe?'

This threw me for a second: stupidly, I hadn't even considered there might be danger in the act of speaking up. I hadn't, in fact, given much thought to the email from the *Close Up* producer one floor below, asking whether I'd come on the show to debate marriage equality. Journalists did not generally interview journalists – that level of inbred navel-gazing was still frowned upon in media circles – so the request was unusual enough for me to handball it off to the higher-ups, right away: 'Ask the boss, and if she says it's okay, I'll do it,' I'd replied – and then forgotten all about it.

Now I was having to evaluate something I hadn't considered. In the middle of a heated public debate on the right or otherwise of same-sex couples to marry, was it a bad idea to stick my head above the parapet?

'What's the worst that could happen?' I tried to laugh it off. 'I already get daily emails calling me a lesbo and a dyke, and it's not the insult they think it is. Hey, I'm used it! Water off a duck's back.'

I could see Briar was not convinced. 'Who are they putting you up against?'

'Um? A Baptist theologian, I believe.'

I thought about the letters that arrived on my desk via the mailroom, two or three times a week, from devout Christians (or so they claimed). It had been two years since the outing, and still these letters came, regular as clockwork. In small, neat, cursive handwriting on blue-lined notepaper, or in greyscale type clattered from a home laser printer, they all began conventionally, genially even –

Dear Alison,

I have enjoyed watching you on television for many years …

Often the narrative remained friendly for a couple of paragraphs before the mask came off and words like 'unnatural', 'wicked', 'immoral', 'ungodly' and 'repent' or the expression 'burn in flames eternally!' jumped from the page like goblins.

My desk mates, bless them, became attuned to these moments and would sit in silent solidarity, glancing at me now and then in case I needed support. I'd carefully slide my finger under the flap of the envelope, which was no longer stuck down – by this point all my mail was being opened before it was delivered, to ensure the worst of the threats were caught early. I'd then scan the contents with my heart beating fast.

Many of the letter-writers told me in detail their lurid – and false – assumptions about the causes of my marriage breakdown. They wanted me to know how much they disapproved of actions that weren't mine. For Paris, Joel and Karleen's sakes, I had not once spoken publicly about my divorce – so that, at least, could be written off as plain ol' ignorance.

I made myself a hard and fast rule: if I read far enough for the eternal hellfire to make an appearance, the letter went straight into the wastepaper bin in a wadded-up ball.

I was left with a lingering question: what motivated all these people to pick up a pen, buy a stamp and stop by a postbox – and then to send those words, calculated to humiliate? To me, that seemed more ungodly than a same-sex relationship. But some Kiwis appeared to fear marriage equality as they would the Four Horsemen of the Apocalypse: conquest, war, famine, and two-gays-in-matching-boutonnieres pledging their love – a sign of the end of the world, to be sure!

The issue had been pushed into the spotlight the year before by the Legalise Love public campaign, led by a determined group of Kiwis who thought our country was lagging behind not just on marriage rights for LGBTQIA+ people, but on adoption rights as well. They were bang on, I thought. Aotearoa was internationally renowned for setting an example on human rights, whether this was true or not – and yet, fifteen other countries had already legalised same-sex marriage. The Labour MP Louisa Wall's private member's bill had been drawn from Parliament's ballot that very week, soon after being submitted; although I am not at all superstitious, I couldn't help seeing *that* as a sign.

But there was plenty of opposition to marriage equality in New Zealand, and it was playing fierce and dirty. The sponsors of a petition signed by fifty thousand people claimed the bill would open the door for polygamy, incestuous relationships and worse. And while I might be able to dismiss all of that as risible nonsense, I knew there were people in the rainbow community who'd be cut to the quick by it. I didn't only receive letters from purse-lipped hellfire-and-damnation writers; there were others who wrote in quiet support, thanking me for standing strong and wishing they could do the same.

One letter in particular I have never forgotten. Writing anonymously, a woman in her thirties told me she felt so trapped by convention in her conservative corporate job that she could never even consider coming out to her workmates or managers. *I can't do it*, she told me, *but I'm so glad you have.*

I left Briar's office thinking not just about whether or not the TV debate would be safe but about something more abstruse: was I even qualified to say yes to this? I had been part of the LGBTQIA+ community for all of what, five minutes? There were determined people – heroes, come to that – who had been fighting for equality for decades before this Janey-come-lately popped up waving the rainbow flag. What right did I have to assume I could represent them, even in a fleeting television appearance? And yet. I was both passionate about the cause and at home in a television studio – an environment that turned most folks into puddles of nerves. On a stunning summer's morning a few months before, I had asked the great love of my life to marry me, so I was smack-bang in the right demographic.

And if I said no, didn't that carry its own commentary? What would that say about my convictions? The campaign for change needed as many voices as it could gather; there was an opportunity here, if I managed to deliver my message effectively.

The next day I caught Briar in the corridor. 'I want to do it.' A mental squaring of my shoulders.

She smiled and gave one of them a squeeze.

* * *

Studio three was the largest of the TVNZ studios, a cavernous space where all the flagship news and current affairs shows were beamed to the public from six in the morning until after the late news wrapped close to midnight. I knew every centimetre of this space; I'd sat there almost every working day of my life for years. No call for nerves, surely. And yet I trembled like Hans Christian Andersen's little match seller in the snow.

The Baptist theologian in the next chair was a gentle, genuine man. Just moments earlier, we'd had a great chat in the green room as if we'd decided there would be *no hard feelings*, but I knew the next few minutes would be crucial.

The *Close Up* host Mark Sainsbury gave us both a crinkle-eyed nod of support as the seconds ticked towards the intro music.

Don't get angry. Don't get upset. Be reasonable, stick to the facts – the prep cycled through my head as the introductions were made. When it was my turn to speak, I did my best to present the logic for change: it did not make sense for New Zealanders to be divided by outdated ideas that excluded people who simply wanted to love and be loved, and show it to the world.

I'd been educated in a Baptist school, so I knew how dearly the Church's beliefs were held, I said. But in the end, the tide was against them.

And the Baptist theologian, however reluctantly, agreed with me.

* * *

We were vindicated, in the end. By April 2013, I'd changed jobs and was cohosting *Seven Sharp*, the new (and widely loathed) replacement for *Close Up*, which had been kicked to the kerb in September. By the close of the year, I'd be out of television altogether and relieved about it; it was a year I'd much rather forget. Apart from one very special night.

On 17 April, as torrential rain lashed Christchurch, I hosted *Seven Sharp* from the Pegasus Arms Tavern, where singer-songwriter Anika Moa was headlining a celebration concert. Gripping Karleen's hand in a crowd full of wide smiles, I watched the screens in awe as the *Marriage (Definition of Marriage) Amendment Act* was passed, seventy-seven votes to forty-four.

As the opponents of marriage equality filed quietly out of Parliament's public gallery, the rest of the House spontaneously broke into 'Pōkarekare Ana': a beautiful waiata to mark a seismic change in New Zealand history. I felt so incredibly privileged to have witnessed it.

20.

'Mum!' I cried. '*Nooooooooooo!*' As I teetered on the edge of the kerb at Lafayette and Bond, I realised I'd literally wet my pants – just a little bit – in blood-thumping terror at the proximity of speeding yellow cab to petite white-haired woman.

It wasn't the first time Mum had put herself in harm's way in New York traffic, and this time it almost ended in disaster: the taxi missed her by millimetres. Sam and I had mugs like Munch's *The Scream* as we waited for the crosswalk lights, and then all three sisters gave Mum the kind of telling-off a toddler gets when they've tried to pull a bubbling pot off a hot stove. Poor Mum – it wasn't her fault. At five foot three, she has always struggled to keep up with her Amazonian daughters on foot; so when Lisa had caught the light, she'd dashed across the road to keep up.

The trip to New York, in the steamy summer of 2014, had been Sam's idea. She'd been living in Manhattan for five years, and neither of our parents had visited to date; she wanted Mum to see her thriving in her new life. This had always been a *thing* with Mum – she needed to *see* us in place. She'd long ago accepted (with ever-so-slightly bad grace) that two of her daughters would live away from Australia and there wasn't a damn thing she could do about it.

'It's karma,' she would tell me. 'It's God paying me back for leaving my parents all those years ago.'

She must have said that dozens of times in the years since I'd left home, always with that stoic endurance, that oh-well-it-can't-be-helped acceptance. I knew that was both her nature *and* a front, for the deep pain of the decades she'd lost, so far away from her family in Somerset. I would wrap my arms around her, feeling guilt for my own absence, and we would sit silently for a beat, in the faint echo of the loneliness of her early years in Australia.

She would be the one to push away first, straightening her shoulders, any trace of wistfulness banished. 'But if I can picture you, in your place … if I can see where you are in my mind's eye, well. Then I'm alright.' And that would be the firm end of any wallowing.

So, Lisa agreed to bring Mum from Melbourne, and I flew from Auckland, and we met up at Sam's NoHo apartment.

I couldn't remember the Mau women ever having a holiday together before, just us. There were the hunting trips when we girls were really young, where women and kids were tag-alongs. I know Mum hated the heat, the flies, the utterly foreign landscapes. Having to doss down in shearing sheds. The year Nanny and Grandad came from England (the year of Lofty and *next door*), our Kingswood pulled up for the first time at a real house on one of those trips: a tiny white-painted cottage where the freezing wind whistled through gaps in the floorboards. But it had beds, and although they were cast-iron relics and more hammock than innerspring, we were giddy with the luxury of it. I suspect this came from Mum's pleadings for a scrap of civility with her parents in tow – a blow struck, at last, for her needs.

Once Lisa and I were into our teens, our family had a summer holiday each year on the Mornington Peninsula. We stayed in a series of modest rented houses a few blocks back from the beach. These were halcyon days where we'd oil ourselves like barbecue chickens and lie for hours on the baking sand, and in the late afternoons we'd walk to the Rye carnival, where there was fairyfloss to eat and boys to flirt with. I don't know what Mum got up to during those holidays, when she wasn't cooking and cleaning as usual, and Sam was just a kid – we were too self-absorbed as fifteen and seventeen year olds to notice or care.

So, this trip to New York was the first time that Mum had been on holiday with her three daughters and no one else. That she was a wisp of a 78-year-old lady didn't matter at all – she was with her precious girls and having the time of her life.

Lisa, Mum and I slept together in Sam's lounge room each night, and in the mornings we planned our adventures. We visited the Frick Collection and MoMA to marvel at old masters and contemporary wonders, then we had dinner underground at La Esquina, where Mum got tipsy on their excellent margaritas. The next day, riding in the sunshine on a double-decker bus, she expressed deep and childlike delight at the architecture of buildings that dated back hundreds of years – nothing like them in Australia.

'This is extraordinary!' she exclaimed. 'I'd believed New York was all faceless glass skyscrapers.'

'You're thinking of Midtown,' I said.

We sisters smiled indulgently and never took our eyes off the joy on her beautiful face.

It was wreathed in smiles again when we sat down for brunch in SoHo at Balthazar, where the room, with its foxed mirrors and yellow walls, reminded her of her trip to Europe in the 1950s. She ordered French onion soup gratinee and, with delight, claimed it was just like the one she'd tasted with her best friend in Paris – two English roses in circle skirts and headscarves, looking not unlike Grace Kelly.

Mum walked and walked around Manhattan like a trooper. We took turns hanging back with her, linking an arm through hers and adjusting our long gait to her shorter one, while the other two strode ahead.

There's a selfie taken of all of us, squished together on the couch, Mum closest to the camera and lower than her giant daughters. Our big grins are so similar and yet subtly different. When I look at that photo now, complex feelings muscle their way to the front of my mind. Perhaps they're sorrow and betrayal, loyalty and suspicion and devotion all at once – I don't know for sure, because I don't let them come close enough. I stuff them back and concentrate instead on our smiles, the remembered feeling of our cheeks against each other's cheeks. I think that's the last time we were together, just the four of us, in the same place.

* * *

'Ali, please,' Mum said, 'will you just stop and sit down?' A year after the New York trip, I was home in Melbourne visiting, and things weren't quite so rosy.

'Yep, sure, I will in a minute – I'll just finish the fridge. Then I'll make us a brandy and dry.' I stretched my mouth into what I hoped was a convincing smile, shamelessly distracting her with the plan for our little evening ritual, the treat we had shared every time we'd been under the same roof since I was in my early twenties. A 6 pm brandy, that had always been our thing. I could see I'd coaxed the tiniest of smiles to her face.

I was cloaked to the elbows with rubber gloves, and I was not intending to sit down anytime soon. Recently my visits had a routine, starting with the fridge and a big plastic rubbish bag. I would throw out everything months past its use-by date: into the bag went chutney, lumps of cheese, long-curdled cream, half-loaves of bread with fuzzy white coatings of mould. The bag filled up, I would scrub the fridge and the pantry, and head to the supermarket to restock. Then I would scrub, in order, the hobs, the benches, the sink, under the sink (disgusting), and move on to the bathrooms, scouring on my knees with a toothbrush.

I spent at least two days cleaning each time, with Mum following me around the house, pleading for me to stop. But I couldn't stop – it was my obsessive response to the obvious, if natural, decline of my parents. Their cleaner came every fortnight, but as far as I could tell, she only mopped the floors. Each time I raised it, Mum would tell me they liked their cleaner and were happy with the job she did. 'So butt out, will you?' That was unspoken, of course; my mum would never say something so crass.

The problem wasn't with Mum but with me, and I knew it. The problem was not that the house wasn't clean but that it was not as clean as it used to be, which meant my parents weren't as capable as they used to be. The problem was not the present, or the past, but the murky depths of an inevitable future – one I didn't want to peer into, even though I knew what was lurking there. I could see my mother deteriorating in more ways than her ability to keep house. She could no longer cope with her former routines, or perhaps even recall what they were.

I asked myself: *Is it that she's tired and just doesn't care as much? Why should she? She's worked like a navy conscript all her life in the service of her family! She can down tools if she wants, who am I to argue?* But for some reason, I couldn't stop the scrubbing and sit down. I mentioned that Mum might go and see her GP for a check-up …? She rejected the idea outright. 'Alison. I'm *fine*.' She was cross, wounded that I would even ask.

Mum had always been a puzzler, and not just of the plain ol' crossword – she did the cryptic in the paper every morning. Said it was her daily mental tune-up. I'd begun to notice she didn't seem so interested in puzzles; more than that, she'd started to forget things. This was concerning – my mother had run her house, as well as other people's businesses, with military precision for many years. She'd worked as an office manager for a hoity-toity English gentlemen's clothing importer for four decades and knew that business inside and out. When we sisters were children we would visit her occasionally, in the school holidays, on the first floor of a building at the 'Paris End' of Collins Street. I was always struck by that other version of my mum; at home she was softer but still brisk, whereas at work she was a mite intimidating. She wasn't so keen to have us under her feet, poking around, and would put us on a tram home as soon as practicable, the better to 'get on with things'.

At seventy, she felt devastated when she was let go. She got a job as a receptionist at a doctor's surgery for a time, but she hated it. I couldn't get her to explain why; all she would say was, 'They treat me like I'm an idiot.' This was bad news; if there was one thing I knew about my mother, it was that she needed – at her very core – to be useful. That supersized Presbyterian work ethic had to have an outlet, or she'd go completely la-la. At seventy-one, though, she'd have been pushing shit uphill to find many employment alternatives.

By my next visit, in 2006, I thought I might have cracked it. 'Come on, you're getting in the car, and I'm taking you to Box Hill Hospital to sign you up as a volunteer.'

She looked at me doubtfully, raising her chin an inch. 'Volunteer? Why would they want me? What could I offer a hospital?'

'Just get in the car,' I said firmly, hoping for an end-of-story kind of authority.

For the next dozen years, Mum spent three days a week at the hospital, organising fundraisers, helming the baked goods stall in the foyer, and helping lost people find their loved ones in the wards. She loved it, would describe the hospital as 'hers', and with her volunteer mates raised tens of thousands for new equipment. I was quietly chuffed I'd managed to solve that gnarly problem for her.

Now, a decade later, she seemed to be loosening her grip on the day-to-day stuff. At first, the signs were so subtle I dismissed them – I didn't want to admit, even to myself, that Mum might be losing it. But I knew my mum, and that person was slipping away, her mind eroded a little more every time I visited. I pushed, as gently as I could, for a couple of years, and eventually she did go to her GP, reporting back with alacrity that it was 'normal age-related stuff'.

Within five years, her short-term memory would be gone altogether.

* * *

'It's great to get these things sorted. We want to make sure you're both in the best possible position to enjoy the rest of your lives.' The words sounded overly formal coming out of my mouth, but they seemed to fit the occasion.

It was a few days later, and I'd put down the cleaning tools for the day, because this was no usual family gathering. Sam was back from New York for a visit, making it the first time The Sisters had all been in the family home at once, in quite a while. This coming together spoke of the urgency of the task at hand: after several years of urging, Mum and Dad had agreed to sit down with us and talk about their future. They were in their late seventies, and the house they had built in the early 2000s (on the same site as the one we grew up in) wasn't going to work for much longer, with its steep concrete steps and slippery tiles – the potential for harm was hair-raising.

My sisters and I had been trying to introduce the idea of them moving. We knew Mum would love the social life at one of the bougie retirement villages in the area. But now, sitting around the table where we'd eaten every family meal since we were children, I felt like I was play-acting, a little girl trying to tell my parents what to do.

We worked through the documents they'd gathered for us, and it was mostly boring stuff like insurance and Medicare details. There were some surprises too. A bank document we'd never seen proved that, years before, Mum and Dad had pledged 60 percent of the value of the house to the bank in a reverse mortgage. I looked at Lisa and Sam with raised eyebrows, but we weren't upset with our parents – it was their life and their choices. I felt a flush of shame, like I was peeking into something I wasn't supposed to see.

Lisa had done the homework: she had brought brochures from several retirement villages and had visited them to make sure they were suitable, comfortable, beautiful even.

Dad leafed through a few brochures, eyeing the modern kitchens, neatly trimmed pathways, indoor swimming pools.

'Some of them have gardens!' I said feebly, knowing full well our parents had given up gardening years ago, hence the jungle outside the window. Every few months, one of The Sisters hired a landscape company to chainsaw the whole thing into submission.

I watched Dad's face carefully, expecting him to toss the lot aside. He put them back in a neat pile. 'Well, yes, I suppose we could go and have a look.'

Lisa and Sam's eyes widened with surprise, just as mine did. I looked closely at him again, but he wasn't having us on. He seemed relaxed and genuine. At first I was flooded with relief – we had assumed we'd have a mighty battle on our hands, but they both seemed willing to listen. Docile, even.

I couldn't put my finger on why, but that in itself made me uneasy. Since when had my parents, fiercely independent to the point of secrecy, been willing to bend to anyone's suggestions? Even – especially? – their children's.

There was a small pause, and I shifted in my seat, assessing. Then I thought, *Don't be paranoid, for god's sake. We're making progress. Take the win.*

But the next time the idea of visits to retirement villages was raised – I think it was around six months later – Dad changed his tune. The genial and reasonable man had gone, and in his place was the gruff cartoon giant we'd always known. 'You'll be carrying me out of this house in a box. Now stop yakking – the footy's about to start.'

21.

Our interview was over, and in the commercial break Tracey Spicer and I had a few minutes to talk, off the record. 'Ali,' she said, 'you have to do something just like this in New Zealand.'

The interview with Spicer on my drive-time RadioLive show had been my idea. Weeks earlier, the world had been rocked by the revelations of women who'd suffered decades of harassment and abuse at the hands of Hollywood mogul Harvey Weinstein. The fallout had been immediate and immense, and as #MeToo swept social media, I'd read about Spicer's plans for an investigation into similar allegations in the Australian media and entertainment world. Across the ditch, a revolution was brewing.

Although we hadn't spoken in more than twenty-five years, Spicer and I had a bond that way too many working women share. She'd been alongside me in that newsroom at Channel 9 in the early 1990s – subjected, as I was, to John Sorell's disgusting tyranny. Since then, she'd built a powerful career as one of Australia's top broadcasters – and she'd laid Sorell's depravities bare in a memoir that chronicled decades of sexism in the media. It was a bestseller.

Spicer's idea intrigued me. It was unconventional – media outlets did not generally announce an investigation before there was actually something to publish – but the concept made sense. The #MeToo movement was proving that millions of women wanted their stories told, but there was no organised way for them to do that. Spicer's passion for the fight was obvious, and I had no doubt her intentions were legitimate.

'This behaviour is everywhere,' she said down the line from Sydney. 'It won't be any different in New Zealand.'

I knew in my gut she was right, but it seemed a big ask. Sexual harassment stories in the media were rare, for completely understandable reasons. Survivors suspected they wouldn't be believed if they came forward, and they feared they'd lose their jobs if they rocked the boat – worse, if they didn't do what their harasser wanted and with a smile on their face, too. And they were, too often, dead right about those fears. In many cases, they weren't even so sure about what they had endured; it's easy to begin to doubt yourself when all you hear are things like 'You're overreacting' and 'Can't you take a joke?' Those people rarely reported it to anyone, let alone a journalist. Who would *choose* to have their most private agony – something they often felt (entirely unwarranted) shame and self-blame about – splashed in technicolour detail on the homepage, unless it was their only choice left?

And yet. I couldn't shake the feeling that there must also be thousands of New Zealanders who would want their story heard if handled with both precision and care, did want to be believed by someone willing to listen with empathy, and did crave the chance to reach for some kind of accountability, however unlikely. The idea bounced around in my brain, nagging at me for weeks, as I waited for local #MeToo stories to appear in the media. But the summer wore on, and none did. As the days passed, I became more and more afraid this worldwide window of opportunity, where women could finally speak about what they regularly had to endure, would pass us by altogether. And I knew where this sense of urgency was flowing from.

Three months earlier, I'd been overcome with fury at the treatment of Rachel MacGregor by the politician Colin Craig, her one-time boss. I'd worked with MacGregor at TVNZ a decade before, and now she was embroiled in the most notorious sexual harassment and defamation case the country had ever seen. With a group of like-minded women, I'd formed a trust to help raise legal funds for the fight MacGregor had ahead of her: one ordinary woman up against a multimillionaire. Sexually harassed for years, then called a liar, and without the means to defend herself. It seemed so brutally unfair – but not, I knew in my bones, unusual.

* * *

Two determinative events took place that summer. One of them came dressed in masquerade, and one arrived bare-faced and screaming bloody murder.

The first took place in the most banal of settings: the supermarket wine aisle, two working days before Christmas. I had that end-of-year stare, tired from a year of change and of broken promises.

I could see that RadioLive was being poorly run, was losing money and listeners, and I was not the only one frustrated by this – but I loved the work, the intimacy of radio, too much to make a break of my own accord. Silly me.

'Kia ora, Ali speaking.' I was juggling a too-full shopping basket and eyeing the chardonnay, and I had not seen the boss's caller ID.

'Oh, Ali, have you got a minute?'

'Uh, sure! Just buying wine, ha-ha, Christmas and all. What can I do for you?'

'I'm calling to inform you we're not renewing your contract.' And there it was, spilled unvarnished onto the supermarket lino, naked as a newborn. He did not appear to have anything further to add.

The second event, three months later, was when the dam finally broke over New Zealand's cosy #MeToo complacency. As I sipped my first coffee on 13 February 2018, a news alert popped up on my phone – 'The Summer Interns and the Law Firm', the *Newsroom* headline read. I tapped to open it. Read it carefully. Was struck most not by the depressing details of entitled older men using their power to sexually manipulate young women, or the obvious comparison drawn between the Russell McVeagh complaints and international cases that had 'propelled the global #Metoo movement', but by something that resonated more than any lurid details could. Five of the ten university students who had taken summer clerk positions – all of them women – had declined offers of permanent jobs at the firm. I stared at the screen. What were the odds that all of them, law students fighting for job opportunities in a fiercely competitive cohort, would turn down guaranteed positions at one of the country's most prestigious firms? It did not make sense – unless the allegations were true. 'A highly unusual outcome,' the *Newsroom* article noted. Likely an understatement.

It was my final spur to action on the itch that had been vexing me all summer. I was handed my opportunity not long after, when I looked up to see the CEO of Stuff, Sinead Boucher, hovering with a smile in the doorway of the meeting room where her editorial director, Mark Stevens, was politely listening to my (doomed) pitch for a new video project.

'Kia ora,' Sinead said. 'I'm just on the way to the airport back to Wellington, and I wanted to pop my head in and say hi.'

My final week at RadioLive was about to end, and that meant no more pay packet. I'm not ashamed to say things were looking pretty desperate. But running into Sinead struck me as exquisite timing, the kind of opportunity you're only offered when fortune has turned its wide smile specifically at you.

It's now or literally never, I thought. *Get your arse up and say your piece, Ali.* I shot to my feet, the wheeled boardroom chair scooting backwards towards the wall. 'May I pitch an idea to you, Sinead? It'll only take a couple of minutes!' *It'd better*, I thought. *The lady looks keen to get out of here.*

Trying not to babble, I poured out my plan for a wide-ranging investigation into sexual harassment in the country's workplaces. Not just the flashy stuff like media industries: stories from every sector would be welcome. We would build a team who worked in a trauma-informed way, supporting our sources to find the help they needed as they worked with us on bringing their experiences to light. The reporting would be as detailed and careful as any long-form investigative reporting in the country, but without rape-myth language or victim-blaming headlines. We would prove that #MeToo stories could be told with nuance, context and as much journalistic rigour as any other investigation.

After a minute or so, I ran out of big words and high concepts, and there was a short silence. Was it awkward? Perhaps only for me.

Sinead looked briefly at Mark, then back at me, and said, 'Yes. Come and work here, and let's do that. I'll leave you with Mark to figure out the details.' And then she was gone.

Not so long afterwards, I looked around the table at the newly formed #MeTooNZ team, nervous at the prospect of leading a group of my peers – not something I'd ever tried to do before now. Our editor watched on as four journalists, three women and one man, all nodded at me encouragingly.

'Thank you for putting your hands up to be part of this,' I said. 'I'm especially grateful to you for volunteering to take this on, because I think we all understand the kind of abuse we're likely to be facing once we begin publishing these stories.'

This time, only three heads nodded. The young male reporter looked baffled and slowly raised his hand. 'Uh, abuse? What do you mean?'

'Well, I guess I mean on your socials and maybe your email – you know, from people who don't want this kind of thing brought to light.'

He still looked confused.

I stifled a nervous laugh and tried again. 'Well, I guess ... as female reporters we're pretty used to it, eh.' More vigorous nodding from the women. 'But hopefully it won't be death threats ...'

The male reporter lowered his hand and said no more; the next day he told the boss he'd changed his mind and would rather not be involved. I tried my best not to judge – we would be hit by, soon enough, the volley of bullets he'd dodged.

* * *

There I was, in the newspaper, on a broomstick, in a conical black hat. Or I guessed it was supposed to be me, long crooked nose, broken teeth and all. My inky witch-robe had *RUMOUR* slashed across it in white capitals. The speech bubble coming out of witch-me's mouth read – I could hear the cackly, high-pitched scream – *I'm going on a witch-hunt after men!* Other witches streaked across the page, close behind me; their robes had capital letters spelling things like *INNUENDO* and *GOSSIP*.

Infuriated, I clicked out of *The Press*'s website, pouting at Karleen. 'Don't these people understand what a witch-hunt is?' I grumbled. 'Witch-hunts were sixteenth-century persecution campaigns against *women*, not men.'

I knew pedantry was not going to help, but even in modern usage, a witch-hunt was not a fit description for our project. The repeated suggestion of this was making me ornery.

I clicked on another tab. 'According to this definition, a witch-hunt is undertaken against someone who holds views that are a threat to society. I'm trying to bring stories of serial sexual predators to light. How is reporting about harassment a threat to society? How am I the one on the broomstick? Make it make sense!'

Being the sensible one, Karleen gently suggested I try to ignore the scribblings of an old white man with 1950s ideas and remember what I was there to do.

I wasn't entirely naive. I had suspected there'd be some pushback – isn't there always for a woman trying do something new? But the plan was a good one. I knew I had the backing of Stuff management right to the very top, along with the belief of a team of the best investigative reporters. Given the chance, we could clearly explain why the project was needed, what the response rate was likely to be, how we would protect people and why this was no witch-hunt. Still, there'd been a knot in my stomach when we had launched the project a week earlier, on 28 February 2018.

To call it a launch is an overstatement – there was no flash video campaign, no marketing agency, just a short clip filmed in my lounge room on my iPhone and released on Twitter. I gave a couple of interviews explaining the plan.

And then the backlash started. 'It's about hearsay, rumour, innuendo, scuttlebutt – sleaze and gossip,' a right-wing radio host ranted. 'It's about alleged pinched bums, wolf whistles, and tacky one-liners. Not that any of those things is remotely acceptable – but they're not crimes and they're not front-page news.'

'Maybe read the legislation, Mike,' I muttered under my breath as I opened another email. 'Unwanted sexual contact is against the law.'

Honestly, I had no problem with explaining why I thought there was a need for this work, and I might have done a decent job of that if there'd been any coherent, informed concerns. But it was like a game of whack-a-mole: one minute we were told that offering support to survivors was somehow unbecoming (as if journalists don't regularly do that) and the next that it wouldn't be enough support. New Zealand wasn't like the US, so harassment wasn't a problem here. Everybody knew it was a problem already, so why talk about it more? The investigation was McCarthyism. This was not the role of a journalist – to do what, exactly, to break news stories?

It did cross my mind that some of the criticism – yes, even from women – came from misogyny. An article in *The Spinoff*, helpfully, said that bit out loud:

I doubt if the team investigating the topic was comprised entirely of men that we would be having the same discussion. In fact, they would probably have been praised for their bravery.

Taken together, the backlash shared the stink of one underlying fallacy: that the stories of Kiwis whose working lives were made miserable and unsafe had no place on our websites or in our news bulletins. And despite the sting of the criticisms, that is where I dug in my toes. I just did not, *could not* accept that. I knew off-colour jokes and pinched bottoms were never likely to be the focus of our reporting, but if they made up a part of the stories, so be it.

And as for the need for this investigation – well, the emails were pouring in. Seventy arrived in my inbox in the first twenty-four hours. However cross it was making me, exposing the logic gaps in the musings of the Janets, Tims and Mikes of the media was just a distraction. Having set the thing in motion, I had work to do.

It was no surprise to find most of the emails were upsetting to read. Some ran to four or five pages, every detail of their author's sometimes violent, sometimes humiliating experiences poured out in a torrent. They usually included an unneeded apology towards the end: *I'm so sorry but once I started writing I just couldn't stop.* Or the email would be short and chilling: *Something really terrible happened to me thirty years ago. I've never told a soul before today.* Some knew they were victims of a serial predator: *There are others – I have the documents and screenshots ready to go.* And some wanted no action at all: *It's way too late for me, but I did just want to say, good on you and your team.*

As the team and I got on with the work, trying to ignore the sniping of the naysayers, I carried a precious talisman with me. It was a screenshot of a Snapchat message sent to my daughter, at university in Australia, from one of her school friends. *Please tell your mum thanks for doing something about #MeToo here in Aotearoa*, it read. *She's such a Boss Bitch.* I can't even describe how many dark days that little Gen Z endorsement pulled me through. One day I'm going to immortalise that message in cross-stich, frame it and hang it on my dang wall.

* * *

There were so many emails to triage in those first days post-launch, I almost let our first big story slip right through my fingers. Fortunately for me, it was caught by two of the team: the investigative reporters Michelle Duff and Amanda Saxton. I may well owe my reputation to those incredible journalists.

The story they broke – about bullying and abuse of power by the charity founder Craig Koning – took three months to research and piece together. Koning had set up the Floating Foundation in 2014, a charity delivering medical aid to remote Tongan island villages. By 2018, a number of former workers and volunteers were ready to speak out, alleging predatory sexual behaviour and severe bullying by Koning, often towards young and vulnerable women. It was an important story for many reasons, but crucially it explored the nuance, the 'grey areas' in sexual conduct that the global #MeToo conversation had exposed. It showed how – just as in the *New York Times*' reporting on Harvey Weinstein – actions that may or may not be criminal but can still ruin lives could be normalised and dismissed by those who witness them but do not act.

When I opened the newspaper on that June Sunday, I could not have been more grateful for the group of women who'd shown such bravery, some agreeing to use their real names and images, and for Michelle and Amanda's careful and detailed work. But I had no idea, on that morning, of the other powerful and ongoing consequences that story would have.

The email from Amy Coronakes came in that same night. A Kiwi living with her husband and daughter in Queensland, Australia, she had a regular habit of reading the *Stuff* website just before lights out to catch up on news at home. What she read that night sent her straight to her laptop: *I saw the story on Craig,* she wrote, *and I couldn't believe my eyes. That's the man who raped me fourteen years ago.*

I phoned Amy the next day, as soon as the time difference allowed, and we spoke for an hour about what had happened to her, the feelings the story had raised for her, and what she wanted to do next. She'd been Koning's girlfriend when he attacked her in 2004, chasing her down and raping her twice in his Auckland apartment after she'd shown up unexpectedly with a dish of lasagne for his dinner. Such a banal set of circumstances for such a brutal act – her description sent spikes of horror through me. Sexual assault is a crime that mostly takes place behind closed doors. There are rarely witnesses.

The next day, Koning threatened to kill himself if Amy told a soul about what had taken place that night. She became pregnant from the rape and had to seek an abortion. She was just eighteen years old; the emotional burden was too much at the time, she told me. She knew no one would believe her – it would be his word against hers.

But the fear that she was not the only one nagged at the back of her mind for years. In 2012, after talking to a therapist, she sent a Facebook private message to Koning. *If I ever hear you've hurt someone else*, she wrote, *I will go straight to the police.*

And then, six years later, she'd read our article.

'I'm ready – I'm going to do it,' she told me by phone a few days later. 'Queensland police say I'll have to report it directly to the police in Auckland, so I'm going to fly in next month.'

We stayed in close touch as the case progressed, police agreed to file charges and court dates were set, with the trial to commence in November 2020. It all took a teeth-grindingly long time, as these cases mostly do.

* * *

While the emails and messages flooded in – and there were hundreds – patterns emerged. Those patterns would in time unfold like a hidden map showing the breadth and ugliness of the sexual harassment perpetrated every day in New Zealand. But at first, the lack of research available was frustrating. There didn't seem to be anything in officialdom that told the macro story, that documented the size of the thing. No doubt this was part of the reason our attackers found it so easy to deny there was a problem – evil does love plausible deniability, after all. We needed that macro story to give the wider context to the personal stories our survivors were telling.

Notably, at least one industry had done the work. A survey of the screen industry found 66 percent of workers said they'd been harassed in ways that ranged from grubby, unwelcome comments to assault. But that survey was one small chink of light in a barrier as impenetrable as Hadrian's Wall. The Ministry of Business, Innovation and Employment – the workers' ministry – did not collect those figures and never had. It was odd: in a developed country with a healthy public service, you generally have statistics up the wazoo. We could find an eighteen-year-old review of case law under the *Employment Relations Act* and a government promise that a national register would start in July. Meanwhile, as the weeks passed, we had plenty of evidence from the raw and personal stories of our readership.

It was those readers, the survivors themselves, who set us on the right path. Over and over again, we heard that their complaints, so bravely made, were dismissed or minimised by the employers they trusted. Promises would be made of 'thorough' investigations that never took place, were botched, or petered out without result. Many survivors who were vindicated, their experiences proven, were legally gagged – pressed to sign non-disclosure agreements. Some prevented the survivors from telling their parents, their friends, even their therapists. It wasn't that sexual harassment wasn't happening; it was that it was deliberately being hidden.

'I came out worse for wear for complaining than if I had said nothing' was a thing I heard too many times. The executive-level hypocrisy of it all was what stuck in my craw the most. These same organisations traded publicly on banner promises of 'zero tolerance' and 'robust policies' – policies that sat proudly on their websites but, as far as my team and I could tell, were essentially worthless. It made me quietly furious, and rage (as I've noted) is a powerful engine for a woman who has no more fucks to give.

It was clear we would have to find the truth ourselves. One of the #MeTooNZ team, the fine journalist John Anthony – yes, we finally had a male reporter volunteer! – decided to go after the information that *was* available to us. He made a huge, all-encompassing *Official Information Act* request to almost three thousand public sector organisations. The results of that pulled back some of the curtain that had kept the issue shrouded.

Three years later, a nationwide study commissioned by the Human Rights Commission would show close to 30 percent of New Zealanders had been sexually harassed at work in the past five years alone. Later research has shown that this costs Kiwi businesses more than $1.3 billion a year.

The critics can no longer claim this is a non-issue. And while I'm proud of the work we did, the main credit must go to the survivors who agreed to tell their excruciatingly personal stories to us. Many of them came to us in desperation; a journalist was the very last person they would have chosen to talk to if they'd had a fair go in the first place. But come they did, and they are the ones who made the real difference.

Email from Lisa to Sam and Ali, 20 May 2021

Hi sistas

After 18 months I have decided to type out that letter to Leigh. I have attached it for you so that you both have a copy. I will sit on it for a couple of days, just to settle and make sure it's clear enough. If you want me to take out any references to you both please tell me. That's ok.

He's lived with the knowledge that he's gotten away with this for too long. It's time.

Email from Leigh to Ali, 27 May 2021

Alison,

Will you talk to me? I haven't told Mum yet but I will have to. We have a completely different and constructive relationship now since her dementia has begun to emerge and neither of us have very long to go. I'm so terribly frightened . . . I had no idea at the time what the consequences could be. I woke up (too late) 17 years ago. It never should have happened. I will die with my foolishness and stupidity and selfishness as my final thoughts. along with my love for you all. I will, of course, comply with Lisa's wishes as to contact (or absence of it.)

[He talks a bit about waiting for Mum's health issues to be sorted before he tells her.]

> *Let me know by email whether or not you wish ever to speak to me again. It is difficult for me to talk as I would want with Maureen nearby.*
> *Leigh.*

I call Lisa and (carefully!) explain Dad has been in touch. I tell her she does not have to read his email, but she insists on seeing it. We consult with Sam and agree that I will become the point of contact for Dad. Lisa is adamant she will not see or speak to him again, but she will have an ongoing relationship with Mum. This will take careful management, but it's doable.

It dawns on me that it is my work as a reporter which allows me to say yes to this. I can shoulder this responsibility – keeping in contact with my abuser – because of the people who have come to me for help. I've spoken to so many people whose lives have been marked by violence they did nothing to invite. I spent months talking to them while working through their investigations, and at some point, in almost every case, they said something like, 'I feel ashamed/I feel as though it must have been my fault somehow/I don't want people to think less of me.'

Each time I thought, *Why is it the survivor who carries the shame?* Each time I told them, *This is not your fault. It was never your fault.* I realise I have said that – and meant it – so many times, and therefore it must apply to me, too.

22.

'Come and sit by the fire with me.' Karleen waved her wineglass invitingly, a tiny note of pleading in her voice.

'I've just got to finish this one story and file it ...' Typing at speed, I didn't even look up from the keyboard. My phone rang then, and I spent the next hour talking to someone I'd never met, about allegations of awful doings.

I don't know how much time passed before Karleen placed the fire screen in front of the dying embers and went to bed. Neither of us said goodnight.

It was June 2020, and the picturesque log cabin overlooking the Waiau River was our second stop on a week-long driving tour of the South Island. The trip was to celebrate Karleen's birthday – and god knows, we both needed a break. We'd had a romantic dinner at our favourite Queenstown restaurant, Rātā, and driven south to Te Anau that morning, where Karleen had booked the cabin specifically because the place offered horse-riding. Such a sweet gesture, and I hadn't ridden for years.

But despite the beautiful scenery and feeling that familiar ease as soon as I planted my bottom in the saddle, I couldn't completely relax. A couple of weeks before we'd left Auckland, an investigation I'd been working on for months had been published: an exposé of years of sexual harassment by a world-renowned academic towards a younger Australian researcher. The story had made waves across the Tasman, appearing on the home pages of Australian media outlets, and more allegations were coming in every day; all in all, I would end up with more than forty sources for this one. And it had a real impact: an investigation into the culture at Auckland University of Technology, led by a QC, had already been announced. I felt a huge responsibility to pull the follow-up stories together, one after the other, and get them out as fast as possible. I knew I should stop, just for a few days, but my focus on work had slipped into a kind of mania – and I couldn't admit it, even to myself.

The first months of the pandemic had also been a hugely tough time for K, who worked for a charity focused on child poverty. COVID-19 had thrown business-as-usual into the air like a pack of cards; her workload had doubled, then tripled, as the lockdowns rolled through the first half of 2020. But she, at least, had recognised we needed a holiday. A week was not too much to ask – but I couldn't admit that, either.

Our friends had noticed signs of tension between us, which surprised them; for nine years we had been the 'golden' couple everyone laughed at for being so ridiculously in love, glued to each other's sides at dinners and parties, always touching, never arguing. It made the cracks even more obvious.

Eventually we couldn't deny it and couldn't seem to fix it either. By the time we had both woken up to the spiral of emotional and physical burnout we'd fallen into and sought help, it was too late. We separated quietly in late 2020, telling almost no one.

* * *

I threw myself even deeper into the work. In November 2020, the trial of Craig Koning on charges of rape took place in the Auckland District Court over two weeks. Unlike the neo-Gothic grandeur and leafy surrounds of the High Court, the District Court occupies a serviceable but anonymous office building in the centre of the CBD, an unlikely setting for the dramatic scenes that often play out inside.

I spent every day there for the duration of Koning's trial, watching Amy on a screen as she gave testimony from a featureless room in a court facility in Queensland. She laid bare the horrific details of what Koning had done, how he had thrown the lasagne dish to the floor and chased her in a rage to the bathroom and then the bedroom. How she'd begged him to stop. And how she'd then been betrayed by others who had sought to protect him.

The video showed only her head and torso, arms tucked at her sides and hands folded tightly on the desk in front of her. The lack of any other features in that windowless annexe thousands of kilometres away drew focus to her face, a pale oval in the centre of the screen. Her eyes were trained on the corresponding screen in front of her, where she would see the mirror image, the Auckland courtroom, the judge and the lawyers in their black gowns at the benches, like Alice through the looking glass. Amy's voice, a blend of Trans-Tasman accents honouring both her home country and her new home, was unwavering throughout the prosecution questioning and then broke a little at times under the long, relentless defence cross-examination.

Pop culture might lead you to believe that a reporter will feel nothing as they bear public witness to a trial like this one, but that's not the truth as I know it. I'm proud to call some of the most experienced court reporters in the country my friends, and I know, as fact, they are deeply affected by what they hear and see at work. They do not become automatons as soon as the court doors swing open at 10 am, no matter how pervasive the myth of perfect objectivity would have it. What matters is they leave all that at the door on their way out, before they open their laptops to play their part in the principle of open justice.

Amy's time in front of the court was the bravest thing I've ever seen anyone do. As I listened to her words, I could not forget for a moment how high the stakes were. A trial like this one always feels like it rests on a knife edge; it was her word against his – who would the jury believe? It was not so many years ago that a rape complainant's testimony wasn't even seen as evidence – had we come far enough from that time for Amy to be considered credible?

We waited overnight for the verdict. The wait was made excruciating by the jury's admission, on the Monday afternoon, that they couldn't reach a unanimous decision. The judge said a majority verdict would suffice and told them to retire for the night.

Most of Tuesday passed without word. Then, after lunch, there was a knock on the courtroom door.

The jury filed back to their seats. The foreperson answered 'yes' to the question of whether they'd reached a verdict, and suddenly it was over.

For a long moment, I struggled to move or speak. I sent Amy a text message – *guilty on both counts* – from outside the courtroom, and I introduced myself to her mother, whose face was glowing with pride for her daughter. Then I packed away my emotions, tucked myself into the corner of an unused courtroom lobby, and wrote the story.

Later, Koning would be sentenced to five years in jail. Amy then requested that her automatic name suppression be lifted, a rare move by a rape survivor.

I asked her why she'd decided to do that.

'I didn't do anything wrong,' she said. 'If I'm not ashamed to be named, that's showing other women and other survivors there is nothing to be ashamed of.'

That. Right there. That's what all this is for, I thought.

* * *

I hadn't imagined selling my house and moving, but I ended up as one of those Covid refugees you heard so much about during the pandemic, the crazy ones who threw their settled urban life to the four winds and got outta Dodge. As the pandemic spread in 2021, I was still hard at work, mostly at home, but I no longer had any reason to stay in the city suburbs.

My kids, grown up now, had flown home from work and university in Australia in March 2020, beating the border closure by a day. Between us all, we decided one would stay with each parent, and so in the lockdowns Karleen and I had Paris at our house, and – although he was with Simon just a few kilometres away – only saw Joel on FaceTime. They both stayed for the better part of a year, and that was the sweetest of gifts in a terrible era: having them home and safe with their family. Then they went back to Australia around the time my world was utterly changed. I was reeling from the loss of a relationship I'd thought would last forever, although I was still connected to Karleen as a close friend. This was news to me, that you could build a new and different dynamic with an 'ex'; I'd never experienced that before.

I was living on my own for the first time in more than thirty years. I found that concept quite scary. But the thought of it was scarier than the reality, it turned out. And I was proud of myself for coping so well, for being content with my own company! Although I'll admit having Frankie the spaniel helped a lot.

On a whim, I made the decision to go for a dream I'd had for fifty years, since that first riding lesson on a shaggy brown Shetland pony. I'd sell up and swap the city for the sticks. Live and work on my own land, with horses in a paddock I could see from my kitchen window. If I could make that fifty-year dream come true, anything was possible.

The house I found, on Auckland's west coast, was small but perfect. From the highest point in the valley, the swathe of green swept steeply downwards, ponga and cordyline at the lowest point like a frilled hemline on the brocade of the kauri forest behind. That view felt like it might have the power to heal me. I moved in the morning after a big storm, the sky washed pale blue and fresh to form the canvas of a new life.

The third and longest Covid lockdown was announced three weeks later, and in the way the universe has of sorting your life when you least expect it, Karleen and I have that to thank for bringing us back together, albeit slowly.

We were by then both living alone: she was in the central city, and I was on that hill. We decided a bubble of two would at least mean we'd have company each week; this seemed a natural and sensible arrangement – and looking back I can see it was more than mere convenience. The love, although bruised by burnout and misunderstanding, was still there.

Over more than a year, and well after the lockdowns were gone, we spent increasing amounts of time together. There was a slow but sure rebuilding of our trust, a strengthening of our connection. This was a new kind of relationship, with a depth neither of us had experienced before. Love can take you entirely by surprise sometimes, no matter how old you've grown nor how familiar you think your lover is. It's a gift I'll never take for granted.

* * *

'I think you're going to win it.' My colleague Kirsty Johnston – one of the country's most respected journalists – tossed out the comment almost casually as the makeup artist added another sweep of mascara to her lashes.

It was a Friday night in early June 2021, and my kitchen-lounge resembled a salon. Half a dozen of us from Stuff's Auckland newsroom were taking turns being transformed at the hands of two hair-and-makeup geniuses, ahead of the national journalism awards. Excited chatter and the clink of glasses rose above the roar of hairdryers.

My forced laugh, reaching for lightly dismissive and oh-who-cares-really, teetered just on the edge of hysteria instead. '*Crikey*, don't say that! Anyway, we don't want to jinx it, do we? Who wants a top-up?' I waved the champagne bottle as a distraction, but there was no fooling Kirsty, who watched me with narrowed eyes. I was absolutely shitting bricks, and she knew it. I had never, in all of my career, won anything, let alone something as serious as Reporter of the Year in the Voyager Awards. There had been 'best presenter' nominations way back in the 1990s and early 2000s, but nothing like this.

Journalism awards nights have a long history of concurrent but competing vibes. Onstage, dignified speeches of thanks are given and trophies humbly received, while in the audience (and the bar) colleagues – who don't get time in their furious schedule to catch up much – get liquored up and, often, loud. That is to say, those nights are like any industry awards night. But I was more used to being the one at the microphone, steering the evening as an emcee, than sitting nervously waiting to see if I'd triumph or fail.

People will tell you awards don't matter, but that's only true if you lose. If you win – for that brief moment, anyway – they're the best thing that ever happened. I was still having trouble believing I'd been nominated for one of the year's top honours.

When the sponsor company's CEO opened the envelope and spoke my name, he mispronounced it, which threw me for that long second where time slows down and you think, *Okay, was that really my name or did I mishear? Because if I get on my feet and it wasn't my name, I will need the floor to open up and shoot me straight to hell* right now.

Despite the hundreds of stages I have walked in ballgowns over the years, this felt completely new. I prayed I wouldn't trip on my heels or do something awkward, but alas, to no avail. My first words on the mic were, 'Oh my god look, it's a trophy!' which was stupid enough to garner a laugh from the audience.

Once back in my seat and surrounded by delighted colleagues, I took out my phone and snapped a selfie with the large, rather ugly Reporter of the Year cup. It had my name engraved on the side, I noted, and that tiny detail, inexplicably, brought the tears welling.

I sent the picture to Paris, Joel and Karleen with no caption – it didn't need one. As everyone's attention moved back to the stage, and the awards ceremony swept on, I had a sudden vision of the person I would *not* be calling, fizzing with excitement, at the dinner break. I could see Dad's face as if he was sitting there with me, could see his eyes crinkle with pride. It was so vivid I had to shake my head to make it dissipate. For more than forty years, it had been his opinion that mattered; from the start, my career had been shaped in subtle and not-so-subtle ways by his legacy. For a few long seconds, I did something I hadn't done much until then: I allowed the sadness to wash through me, rinsing out unseen pockets of shame and anger.

I should have been able to celebrate with the one person in my life who had understood most what it was that we, as journalists, do and why we do it. That I could not seemed like a true tragedy in that moment. But you reap what you sow. I put the cup gently down on the table and excused myself to get another drink.

* * *

A month later, I flew to Melbourne to see my daughter perform onstage in her first lead role. I'd organised a surprise for her: her two besties from Auckland had flown over in secret to see the show too, and her brother Joel and his partner Georgia had come down from Brisbane.

But within an hour of their arrival, reports filtered through on mainstream media: the spread of the Delta variant meant both Melbourne and Sydney would lock down for five days. We met back up at an inner-suburban bar, all gripped by a strange rush of exhilaration.

As we clinked our margarita glasses, Joel bent forward and locked eyes with me. 'Mum, I wanted to take Georgia to Grandy and Poppa Leigh's place – they've never met.'

I tried not to flinch. I was well aware that Georgia, who had been his love for three years, had never met my parents. I had not exactly kept them away, but I hadn't encouraged it, either, and I knew that might be confusing for Joel and Georgia. It often played on my mind.

'It doesn't look like we'll be able to visit on this trip anyway, but ...' He trailed off, uncertain, took a big breath and squared his shoulders – broad now, a man's shoulders. A little piece of my heart broke off. 'I can't help feeling there's something ... wrong.' He could see by my face he was right.

I grabbed his hand and stood. Honesty first – the one rule I'd had as a parent since they were little. *If they ask, tell them the truth.* 'Come outside for a minute.'

A soft but soaking rain was falling in the dusk, the beer garden glowing sulphur under the streetlight. We sat on a damp bench while I explained, as gently as I could, why my family had broken apart so catastrophically.

I had told his sister during the lockdown in Auckland a year before, and just as she had then, Joel listened without interrupting and then put his arms tight around me. We sat wordlessly for a moment.

'Thank you for telling me, Mum. I'm so sorry you went through that, and I hope you know it's not your fault. You're the strongest person I know. I'm proud of you.' He was so serious, twenty years old and so grown up. Yes, of course I had a little cry at that.

23.

It was March 2022. I'd spent the past seven days in isolation, watching movies and having indoor picnics with Paris and her flatmate Maddie, who had tested positive for Covid the day I arrived from Auckland. The lockdowns may have been over, but there were still strict isolation rules for households.

I had been planning to visit Mum and Dad on my second day in Melbourne; instead, I'd been phoning every day. No one had answered, which had pushed my anxiety levels sky-high. The second I was able to leave isolation, I drove over to the house in Surrey Hills. Soon I was standing just inside the front door, feeling confused.

'Where's Mum?' I asked.

Dad was there, and the dog, but Mum was nowhere to be seen. This felt wrong on a cellular level: Mum was always there. Lately she was positively glued to her husband's side – he was her North Star. The house felt different without her, with an altered energy, and an empty one, and a dangerous one.

I scoffed at myself internally. Of course my father was no danger to me anymore, but this feeling was a callback to when Mum would take Sam to England and leave me and Lisa behind with Dad. How precarious life felt while Mum was away. And there was no one to intervene, should anything bad happen. No one at all.

Thanks to Covid and border closures, it had been two years since I'd seen Dad in person, and I was shocked at his decline. He had a walking frame and looked every minute of his eighty-four years.

'Mum …?' He made it a question, as though he was trying to remember an acquaintance – a little bit of theatre. 'Oh yes. She's in hospital.' He waved a hand and explained she'd had another bowel blockage, the same issue she had in 2017, which had led to surgery and the removal of a thirty-centimetre section of her bowel. He said this matter-of-factly, as though it hadn't occurred to him that her daughters might like to know.

I picked up my bag.

'Where are you going?' he asked.

'To the hospital *to see my mother*,' I replied through clenched teeth.

'Alison. Please stay a minute. I need to talk to you. About …'

I knew what he wanted to talk about. I hesitated on the doorstep, eager to get out, but something stopped me.

'Five minutes, then I'm leaving,' I told him.

He motioned for me to sit next to him on the couch, then he began to talk. Within seconds I realised what this would be. I reached into my bag without looking inside and fished around among the tissues and lip balm for my phone, turned on the voice recorder app and placed the phone on top of my bag. If he noticed me doing this, he didn't react.

As he spoke, my heart started to hammer, but I was absolutely still and cold as if I'd been turned to stone.

He said he was scared, hadn't been sleeping. 'It just preys on my mind. I know I was wrong to do it. All the way through.'

I asked him more questions. His answers chilled me, and I sat bolt upright, clenching my fists and digging my nails into my palms. While I listened intently, another part of my brain was working independently, thinking, *Who is this version of myself, able to sit and hear this?* I had clicked somehow into professional mode, asking questions, listening to his monstrous answers, as the voice recorder silently sucked in the words. *I have him now*, I thought, but vowed to myself I would never, ever allow Lisa to listen to this callousness or tell her what the recording contained.

After a few minutes, I couldn't sit there anymore. I said, 'I think that's enough for now,' stood on shaky legs and forced the conversation on to Mum's needs: 'Does she have a nightie? Her phone?' When I listened back to the recording later, I even heard myself laugh when he told me how she'd come through the surgery like a trooper. There was no mirth in the sound.

I went to leave, but he hadn't finished with me. 'Hang on, darling. There's something else I want to say. One of the things I've lost out of this is the feeling that we can love ... [he was rambling now] ... I think there's going to be a fairly sad future ... I just hope I can achieve some forgiveness.'

There was a long intake of breath from me as I processed his words. One of the things *he'd* lost. *His* sad future.

I stood a little taller. 'Instead of thinking about yourself, you need to think about the trauma you've visited on others and what their future looks like. That is the only path for you.'

Part of me – the child part – was marvelling at the boldness of those words as soon as they dropped, hung with icicles, from my mouth. *Get you! What a little scrapper you are, sassing your father like that! That sort of cheek would have gotten you a belting once upon a time!* The other part – the wordsmith my father had so carefully curated all those years ago – was assessing. Was this what I wanted to convey, no matter how freaked out I was, and had it landed? What did I want to leave him with, in this moment?

Two things, I decided. Most importantly, he needed to know my priority was now my mother. And behind that – close behind – he needed to know that the rules had changed. They weren't set by him anymore, and I knew full well what pain that would bring him, but I didn't rush to soften the impact as I would have years ago, when I'd been a good girl and done what he told me to do.

I resisted the temptation to say anything else and walked to the door, the little dog yapping at my heels. Even walking out felt like a statement.

As soon as the flyscreen door had clanged shut behind me, I pulled my phone out, hands shaking, and automatically checked the recording had saved. I walked up the driveway to the car. Then I phoned Lisa and told her about Mum.

'Oh fuck,' she said, 'I'll be right there.'

***

We met at the hospital and found Mum's room. She was awake but groggy, so we sat with her and talked cheerful nonsense, taking turns to hold her hands. They were a collection of little bones lying in our large paws, ballooning into large, lumpy wrists from her years of arthritis. It hurt to look at her; she'd lost a dramatic amount of weight, and her beautiful face was near-skeletal, a bobble head on a long, thin neck. Always tiny, she now looked as though she'd blow away if someone opened a window.

I wondered, furious, how long she'd been without food. When had she stopped eating because of the pain? How long had she been like this before she was rushed to hospital? I suspected I wouldn't get any answers from Dad.

Mum drifted to sleep, and Lisa and I made plans. We thought this might be a watershed moment – there was no way she could go home this time, not with Dad's mobility issues. She was the one who had always looked after him, making every meal and doing all the housework, busy every minute of their sixty years together, in service of him.

After her 2017 surgery, I'd stayed with them and explained to Dad he'd have to pick up his share of the chores. I had specifically told him he would have to do the washing. On her second day home, I'd caught Mum at the clothesline, risking her stitches secretly hanging out wet towels. Five years on, Lisa and I thought there was no way either of them would cope.

The Sisters were soon busy working things out. I was gaming the time difference, devoting my after-work hours – while the Aussie bureaucracy were still behind their desks – to getting our parents registered with aged-care authorities and getting them help. Lisa was doing the same. Sam was in charge of finding Mum and Dad's wee dog a new home in case they had to leave theirs. The system was slow and clunky – at the start of the process, we were told it might be almost a year before a needs assessment could be scheduled.

Mum spent a few days in rehab as we scrambled to find them a place. Dad swore he'd accepted the inevitable: that Mum would have to go into care, and he would follow. They were plainly desperate to stay together. When Lisa was at her bedside, with me and Sam on the phone, Mum fretted constantly about her husband. 'Is Dad okay? Where is he?'

My heart twisted, but we honoured her wishes – it was all she wanted. We swore to her we'd keep them together, wherever that was. We only discovered when he'd already taken her from the hospital that they'd released her into his care.

He swore black and blue it was just for a week. 'I just want to have her enjoy the home environment for one last time before outside placement.'

We believed him.

Two weeks later, another email announced he'd had a solicitor sign off his request for full medical and financial power of attorney: 'This PoA now replaces any pre-existing such authority and is the ONLY authority in existence. The bank will be compelled to comply with my directions on Maureen's behalf. She is totally in agreement with my actions.'

I marvelled at the formality of the words in a supposedly friendly email updating his daughters. What must he have been thinking to have typed it, forefinger by forefinger, in that exact way. My father is not careless with words – entirely the opposite. He would have chosen them carefully, backspaced and replaced any inadequate ones with words that more exactly expressed his present thought. That exactness was bred into me; it comes entirely from him and has been my professional talisman for more than thirty years.

The air left my lungs in a big whoosh and was then sucked back in and held. I had no doubt he was right: Mum would have agreed with anything he told her – she was determined to be with him till the end.

* * *

In early 2023, my boss's name popped up on my phone screen. I was working at home, and I grabbed it by the third ring.

I liked him a lot – he was one of the managers who'd shown enormous faith in my work over the past five years, always checking in with congratulations and praise when I'd got an investigation over the line, most often to prominence on the front page of the Sunday paper. Those stories often took months to produce, and the legal risks in publishing them meant my editors had to have great faith in the reporting – along with nerves of steel.

I answered with a cheery hello.

He did not sound nearly so upbeat. 'Ali. We need you to come in for a meeting tomorrow. I've booked a room – I'll send you the invitation now. You can bring a support person if you like.'

Ah. I'd heard that before. My next words were out of my mouth before I could stop them. 'Am I being made redundant?'

There was a process to follow when an employer proposed to let someone go. Employment legislation demanded a path be followed, which included consultation and feedback and consideration of other possibilities. But I'd been there so many times before. I was a veteran of this particular battle, and I knew.

When I hung up the phone, I didn't cry, or yell, or head straight for the tequila (as I may or may not have done in previous identical circumstances). I simply blew out a sigh and said, 'Bloody hell,' with no more emotion than if I'd been opening a parking fine notice.

My daughter, who was staying with me, poked her head out from the bathroom door. 'What's up, Mum?'

'I think I've lost my job.' I barked a short, exasperated laugh. 'That makes five times!'

The emotions were as complicated and overwhelming as they'd always been. I felt betrayal, and anger, and sadness and fear and anxiety in a muddled mix that came and went in waves. I found myself begging for my job in an eight-page Word doc of 'proposal feedback'. Some days I woke feeling hopeful, and some days I wanted to pull the duvet over my head (on those days I wished I could trade places with my dog – what a lovely life they have).

It took a minute, but after the grief subsided I understood I'd reached one of life's crossroads. I had a choice, and not an easy one: I could stay in the craft I'd devoted my working life to, if I could find another job as a journalist – and that was a pretty big *if*. But to do that, I'd have to let go of what had become a speciality, one in which I'd built up many, many contacts and a certain amount of mana, too. I'd seen the appetite for #MeToo reporting wane over the past year, as budgets tightened and the media landscape shrank. Long-form investigations that held predators to account were expensive. They took time. They were legally risky, and specialist advice to ensure we did not get sued for defamation did not come cheap. Likely, I'd have to park the enormous amount of knowledge I'd amassed over my five years at Stuff and go back to general reporting.

I'd been a journalist since my eighteenth birthday. Forty years! Not something to throw away lightly – how do you toss aside the thing that has defined you for most of your life?

In the end I realised there was something more important I could do than filling space on a news website homepage each day. I had the opportunity to make a difference, given the right project. And that project would soon fall right into my lap.

For the moment, though, my focus returned to my family.

* * *

Three months later, Lisa called me. Mum had fallen in the kitchen and broken her hip. My stomach plummeted. I googled 'survival rates for hip fractures in the elderly', then snapped the laptop closed in fright.

A year had passed since Mum's last hospitalisation. Miraculously, she and Dad had coped until now. But a hip replacement? After that, how would this frail eighty-six year old, who now had no recall of events from just a few minutes ago, look after an almost immobile husband?

The rehab would be much longer this time, as she learned to walk on her new titanium hip, but on the third day she phoned me to say the rehabilitation centre was releasing her.

I snorted in disbelief.

'There's nothing wrong with me!' she exclaimed, but of course it was fantasy. The doctors were worried about her – she was frail and underweight.

They mentioned something about a history with alcohol, Lisa said on the WhatsApp thread. *Has Mum been drinking heavily?*

What, wrote Sam, *you mean like everyone?*

The post-pandemic gallows humour made me snort-laugh.

Incredibly, Mum passed a cognitive test after three weeks at the rehab centre, and they let her go home. But we'd had something of a breakthrough, at least with support care: she would get an $18,000 budget for services every year.

Maybe them staying at home is the best idea, if there's enough wraparound care? Lisa messaged.

It went unspoken, but I understood what it took for her to suggest this. I thought, *Wow, that's a feat of human forbearance, right there.* It was also part of a letting-go. When Mum had insisted on going home this time, Lisa had needed to make a choice, on the spot at the hospital bedside. She had to tell her mother – her own mother! – that she would probably never see her again. And she had to tell her exactly why. She had to tell Mum what her adored husband had done. Lisa cried like the Algea all the way through that one-sided conversation. The fact that Mum would not remember it beyond a stretch of a few minutes must have made it easier and harder all at the same time.

Our parents were already getting meals delivered, and we made a care plan, scheduling shopping, gardening, cleaning, and a care worker to shower Mum every second day. We had an hour-long video call with the service manager, Kylie. She was kind and experienced, clearly used to dealing with people like us: children who were pretending – acting all brisk, focused on schedules and cleaning personnel, when inside their hearts were disintegrating.

Kylie mentioned one thing that sent me into an internal rage. In the assessment report, there was a note from the assessor about family. Mum had been asked whether she had children who could visit regularly, and she'd responded that Lisa lived locally but 'oh, they have their own lives now'. This was so far from the truth about why Lisa could no longer bear to enter the house, that I was certain it had come from Dad. To me, this seemed both deeply and casually cruel – and obviously done to protect himself from being exposed. I also understood that in Dad's mind, he'd arranged the truth in his own way and would believe he'd done that to protect Mum. My head spun with the effort.

But when I talked to Lisa afterwards, she was calm. 'My counsellor told me ages ago I'd have to work on grieving the loss of our parents before they die,' she said simply. 'So that's what I've done.'

The Sisters agreed we were on top of the crucial arrangements. Although it had taken months, Mum and Dad would have what they needed and be where they wanted to be.

But a day after the first worker arrived, a gardener, the contract was mysteriously cancelled. Kylie wanted to know if one of us was behind that. Lisa and I were stunned. Perhaps there had been a glitch in the system, Kylie soothed.

She called back within the hour and told us Dad had cancelled the care package. From what she could see in the system, he may have made arrangements with another provider; she couldn't access that information so had no way of telling. Dad was certainly not telling.

I felt chilled right to my bones as Kylie spoke. I did not tell her that just a day earlier, Dad had cancelled a doctor's visit for Mum, painstakingly scheduled by Lisa so she could pick Mum up, drive her to the doctor and take her out for lunch.

My gut clenched. 'I'll deal with it,' I told Kylie and Lisa.

After ending the call, I walked from the house into the sunshine, to the horse paddock, where I hoisted myself onto the fence, hooking the toes of my boots under the rail. I looked out at the hill behind me, where dawn appeared every morning, took a long, deep breath and pressed Dad's number. He answered, and suddenly I couldn't help myself. I felt myself unspooling, losing my grip on … what, civility? Did he deserve that?

Theo the thoroughbred ambled over and pushed his velvety grey muzzle into my hand, looking for treats in his labrador-like way. I cupped his nose gently, and my hand became the obverse of my head. My hand was soft. My mind was exploding.

Until that moment I had been (yes, actually) civil, and it had cost me. Although I'd never been a shouter, had been an avoider of personal conflict all my life, a good girl, lately I'd wanted to shout at Dad each and every time I had heard his voice. But there had been arrangements, so many of them, to make, and I was the only liaison – and so I'd contained the rage by dividing my brain into two emotional parts: the umbrage sat in one virtual hemisphere, and the reasonable in the other. Now they were blending.

I deliberated over each word, which made my sentences feel stiff and formal. 'Dad, when you change arrangements like this ...' I paused, at a momentary loss. Every word falling from my mouth felt crucial, but an effort, like another step towards a distant mountain peak. I trudged on. 'You have to understand there's an emotional factor for us girls. We're trying to make sure you both have the support you need, not to stifle or control you but to let you both live as you've made it plain you want to, in your own home. Given you already have power of attorney, both medical and financial – it ... it makes us feel cut off from our mother.'

'I can assure you,' Dad said in his ponderously formal and haughty way, 'that everything I do is entirely for the care of your mother and in her best interests.'

That was it. Enough. I snapped. 'That may be, but given the circumstances, forgive me if I have some scepticism about that.'

Mum was having none of it. 'Alison, I won't have you talking about your father in that way! He looks after me!'

I shrank on the fence as I realised how deeply I'd upset her. 'I'm so sorry, Mum, I really am.' How to explain?

Theo had wandered off to find a patch of fresh grass, and I missed his sun-warmed solidarity. I panicked for a moment. It had been four years, and not once had I breathed a single word of any of it to Mum; I had visited and called and had the same breezy conversation with her over and over. She always sounded happy to hear from her daughters (genuine) and always knew exactly which sister she was talking to (also genuine), but as her dementia had progressed and her short-term memory had melted away, she had developed a script for herself: the same words each time, in the same order. My online research told me this was called looping; she was reaching for comfort and security. For a committed stoic like my mum, loss of control of the dialogue inside her head would be catastrophic, so she was clinging to what she could control.

On those visits and calls, I always chatted brightly as I brought up a sweet or funny memory from the deep past – 'Hey, I was just thinking about that time you picked me up from the Year 7 school trip. You were the most glamorous mum in the bunch with those big sunglasses and that auburn Purdey haircut you loved …' – and we'd laugh together. I told her in lots of detail about goings-on in New Zealand, but I didn't ask her much about her day or week anymore, as that would bring a note of doubt to her voice and she'd falter, confused. Pretending had become the way I showed her my love.

The system only fell apart when she insisted on handing the phone to Dad, so I could repeat it all to him. Although I remained the only point of contact for Dad, we had few words for each other on the phone. When we did speak, our voices were tight with tension. The 'business' of our relationship was almost entirely done via email, and those emails lurked with malice in a folder named 'Family' and were only opened after I'd poured a stiff drink.

'I wish it could be different,' I said to them now. 'None of us take any pleasure in this. We wish it could be different, we truly do. But it is what it is, and it can't be changed.' As I spoke the words, I knew Mum didn't know what 'this' even was – she didn't remember.

'What do you mean?' she asked.

My heart broke a little more.

'Lisa did tell you, back when you were in hospital.' I floundered.

'Did she?' Mum was understandably confused.

Dad interjected. 'I know what she means.'

I hadn't expected this response from him – and oddly, considering everything, it struck me as brave. Close to tears, I searched for a reply. 'Perhaps you should tell her, then.'

I immediately wished I could bite back the words, thinking, *No, that was the wrong call.* He should tell her – it was his responsibility, his crimes, his shame to carry; the bearing of this burden should not fall to The Sisters. But what would be the point? It was futile. I believed he wouldn't, no matter what he promised, and it wouldn't make a difference if he did. Mum was unlikely to remember for more than a minute or two. It struck me this was both the worst and the best of outcomes.

I pulled back and said simply, 'I love you, Mum. I love you so much.'

Her voice softened. 'I love you too, darling.'

'Let's talk again in a few days. We'll sort all the details for the doctor's visit then.'

Dad's voice was softer too, compliant – perhaps a bit relieved. 'Do that. That would be good.'

I hung up, drained, and called Lisa.

One day later, Kylie from the care agency sent an email to Lisa and me. She said we had options, and there was a link to a government service called the Adult Safeguarding Unit, for vulnerable adults. I opened the link and read the information but did not act upon it; I knew by now what my mother wanted for the end stages of her life. She'd made that perfectly clear, and I had to honour her wishes.

Epilogue

You could miss the house if you didn't know it was there. All that can be seen from the street is a cheap green Bunnings letterbox at the head of a long driveway. I tell Paris to stay in the car. I gave her the option of skipping this visit altogether, but she insisted. 'Nope, I'm coming for moral support. I want to. And I want to see Grandy.'

I relented, but now I won't let her come down the driveway. I was okay when we were on the freeway, chatting away in her little blue Suzuki Swift, but my heart rate began to rack up when we crossed a major intersection into Surrey Hills. By the time we swept round the small roundabout at the bottom of our street, I'd fallen silent.

Shouldering my bag, I close the car door and focus on the laces of my white leather Nikes, right-left-right. A swell of anger roils in my stomach – this is so unfair. I once walked this path to my family home eagerly, knowing those who loved me were inside. That was decades ago, before they pulled the old place down, before I knew what I know now. I hate that I now walk, right-left-right, down the driveway not with lightness and anticipation but with dread. I hate my father for bringing us all to this.

I take a very deep breath as I knock on the door.

Mum answers, and she is dressed and ready for an outing. I called an hour ago with a gentle reminder – 'We're coming to take you out to morning tea, Mum, me and Paris. We'll see you soon.' – and she's remembered. I feel a stab of hope. Maybe we'll get out quickly.

'Okay!' I declare, too loud and too breezily. 'Grab your bag, Mumma, and I'll take you up to the car.'

Winter sun streams through the tall windows. Dad is sitting in the chair facing the TV, where an Olympic athletics highlights package is playing. He's wearing huge black sunglasses, like Arnie in *The Terminator*. For a moment I think he's gone blind.

'Why the glasses?' I ask, looking at Mum for an answer.

'Oh, the sunlight gets too bright for him. Take your glasses off, Leigh!'

He does, and I see his lower lids are drooping open, revealing a larger expanse of red-webbed eyeballs than normal. The inside of the lids are bright crimson. *He looks exactly like an elderly basset hound*, I think, before he draws breath and speaks. 'Alison. Sit down. I want to talk to you.' His voice carries an echo from years ago, the faintest ring of a long-lost authority.

I hover, reluctant, but he says it again, and I don't know why, but my body obeys. I perch on the arm of the green vinyl couch opposite him in compromise, with my bag clutched in my lap like a shield.

'I want to ...' He adds a small note of drama, a slight quiver of emotion in his already quavery voice. '... to achieve some kind of reconciliation. I want things to go back to how they were ... as much as we can ...'

I'm hunched over the bag now, with a perfect C-curve spine my pilates teacher would be proud of. I can see he's genuine – that's beyond doubt. But he does not mention me, or Lisa, or Benny. It remains, after all these decades, about him.

I shake my head to clear the fog, wait another beat, and then my voice pushes like a thumb on a bruise. 'That's what *you* want, is it?'

He does not miss the inflection ... Even half deaf and, if I'm to be truthful, with at least five of ten toes in the grave, words have precise meanings to my dad. And he is the last person who would miss that meaning. He switches tack. 'Well, I know that what I want is perhaps secondary these days, but I realised a long time ago what I did was wrong ...'

He looks at Mum, who is standing behind me, the navy Kate Spade handbag I bought her ten years ago dangling from her arm.

'Maureen knows what I'm talking about,' Dad declares. 'I tell her every day!'

If true, this is major news. I twist around to face Mum. I wonder what that must be like for her, each day hearing about her husband's monstrous appetites, and how he wasn't content with affairs with other women but used his children and then his grandchild. And each day blissfully forgetting, only to be told again the next day, and again, and again.

'Do you know?' I ask her. I don't know whether I really want the answer, but it's too late now; we are in the flow of a discourse I could never have imagined and cannot stop.

She dips her head towards me, confiding. 'Not really, darling.'

Dad will not be stopped. 'You know, that I had a sexual relationship. With Ben.'

A *relationship*. The gall of it, that he chooses that framing.

There's a vice tightening around my skull as I track Mum's shuffling steps around the end of the couch, around the coffee table, until she settles herself with effort next to her husband and reaches for his hand. Bile rises in my throat, but I do not glance back at Dad – I have been waiting half my life for this moment, and now it's here I want time to slow down, thank you very much, and give me a minute to catch up. This is the big reveal, and I'm not ready.

Mum only speaks a handful of dismissive words. But they are the end of everything. 'Oh, well yes, but that was years ago!'

And that is it. The last inch of the rope of history and emotion linking me to my parents pulls free.

'That's enough,' I say. 'I'm going to take my mum to morning tea now.' I stand up and move to her elbow, steering her into the hallway and through the front door.

As the screen door bangs behind us, I hear Dad's plaintive call. He sounds nothing like the man I've known all my life. 'Come back to me, Maureen.' I know he thinks I'm kidnapping her.

Paris takes over when we get her, step by slow step, to the car. Then my daughter chats brightly to her grandy and does not stop throughout the brunch – pancakes and fruit toast and poached eggs – we have at the cafe that was once Mum's favourite. I'm grateful for this, as I can't really speak. I'm stunned, stars circling as though I'm a cartoon character struck with a giant mallet. Paris gets it and takes over completely.

The cafe is busy and noisy, and along with Paris's chatter, that gives me some cover as I surreptitiously watch the woman I've loved all of my life. Even leaving aside the shock of her words – *oh, well yes, but that was years ago* – I can tell there is little left of her former self. The remnants are confused and scared, and within half an hour, she wants out.

We take her home, and I leave her there with Dad as he babbles about me coming back for another talk tomorrow.

I wonder whether I will ever see them again.

* * *

An hour later, I take Paris's car and drive north towards the Dandenong Ranges, along Melbourne's eastern fringes, to visit Lisa in hospital. She is spending a full week lying down with physician-sanctioned ketamine dripping into her veins through a catheter, a progressive treatment for chronic pain. As I sit on the end of her hospital bed, we giggle a lot about this – she's rather high (no surprises), and I find it hilarious to see her high under these very official circumstances. We hold hands and laugh, and it breaks the tension that has been wrapped around me since I left Surrey Hills.

We talk about the pain she's lived with for years, in her back, her hip – all the original injuries that have long healed but left in their wake this agony. Sometimes, she says, the pain in her hip is a nine out of ten and keeps her awake all night. Her doctors are baffled – hence the experimental drug treatment – but after so many years, it's dawning on her that there may be another cause. 'If this doesn't work,' she says, 'I'm definitely going back to my counsellor to see if it might be from trauma, a coping mechanism maybe …? I can't think what else it could be.'

I suggest she should get Bessel van der Kolk's *The Body Keeps the Score*, a book full of wisdom about the mind–body connection and how abuse in childhood can manifest in physical ways – but I don't tell her she should *read* it. Reading was not something we ever had in common when we were children. Once upon a time, Dad and I would have teased Lisa about that, but I know better now. I look for another option: something that will suit her, not make her feel derided. 'Get it as an audiobook, maybe. Then you can listen while you paint or do the gardening.' She promises she will.

I tell her about the scene at Mum and Dad's just hours before. Although I am shaking as I speak, she is calm and unsurprised, which helps to settle my churning emotions. I have only confirmed what she has long suspected and has had to learn to let go of.

We hug and stay locked like that, without tension or awkwardness, for a long time, looking out of the hospital room window, over green hills and the patchwork of suburbs. I make a joke about the drugs, but I know she has felt it too, the peace of sisterhood.

I leave the hospital and drive further out, into the hills, which are green and lush this wintry day. I'm going to an art gallery. At the crunch of tyres on gravel, Benny appears at the door. In 2020, he and Lisa opened this gallery, and within a few years his stunning pieces were selling for thousands. He will be a father soon, for the first time: his partner is seven months pregnant with a little girl.

At dinner the night before, he told me he is in a good place, a safe place, more so than ever in his life, and I'm so, so happy for him. We both know that today I am here about the past, not the future, but he takes me on my regular tour of the gallery, and we talk about art for a beautiful half-hour. I stare for a long time at a large work of his, *Existential II*, part of a series he's created exploring his mental health. A hundred gold marks march across a canvas layered in extraordinary depth of colour, each representing the days of endurance – and then, in the middle, there is a single slash of turquoise. The same size as the other marks, it is different only in colour, but it draws your eye immediately. It says, *Look at me, I'm a good day. I'm worth noticing. I'm worth celebrating.*

Then we sit by the glowing wood burner and share details neither of us has heard before. I am tentative at first; I do not want to upset him or take him into a past he wants nothing to do with, but he tells me not to be scared: I can ask him anything, and he will answer me honestly. As he talks I begin to realise that Lisa and I were a kind of experiment for my father, a tentative peeling back of the seal that held depravity at bay. By the time his gaze turned to Benny, he had left any hesitation behind. We were not raped. Benny was.

'Just so you know, it was hundreds of times.' Benny's face is calm, belying the enormity of it.

I feel an intense bond between us as we talk, our words dropping gently into the woodsmoke air. If not for him, would I ever have spoken a word, to a single soul, of what my father had done? If Benny hadn't, in his fourth decade of life, gathered the courage to tell his mum, risk breaking her heart, would I have gathered the courage in my sixth?

Lisa has told me that she made revelations to partners over the years, and yet the two of us had never spoken of it to each other. This was part of the deal we had made as children on our father's instruction: 'Don't tell anyone. This is our secret.' I marvel at how strong the hold of that promise had been down the years. Why it had taken until recently to say, 'Fuck you,' and, 'No, I won't be silent.' But I know it wasn't just the child's vow that kept me so: I did not know what would happen when I let those words pass my lips, how it would feel, who would judge, what form the shame would take when it was exposed to the air.

I wish I had known that holding the shadow inside me for so long only served to keep it alive. Shame can't survive the light. I'm filled with gratitude for Benny, and for Lisa, because they lent me that courage and let us pool it between us like the most precious resource.

When I get up to leave, I hug Benny tightly, standing on tiptoes because he is so tall, and promise I will be back soon to meet his baby.

**

At the Airbnb, Paris becomes her mother's mother for a night, ordering Uber Eats and choosing a Tom Holland movie, nurturing me as we sit together under a blanket on the couch.

The next day I fly to the Gold Coast, where newlyweds Joel and Georgia pick up the reins, absorbing me with love and without effort into their busy, vibrant lives for a few days.

At home in Auckland, Karleen is at the airport, keen to whisk me back to our nest on top of the windy West Coast hill.

I realise that from the moment I walked back up the driveway at Surrey Hills, I have been passed gently between the embraces of the people who matter most. The remnants of my family draw gently around me like a feather cloak, and while I feel the loss of the illusionary happy family of my childhood, they're all I need.

* * *

By the time all of this takes place, I am more than a year into a post-journalism life, and that still feels a little strange. Journalism has been baked into my sense of identity since I was a small girl. News and storytelling have been what I have worked at, what I have thought about, for every one of the past forty years.

Now I'm using what I'd learnt in another way. A year in, the project I'm working on with the barrister Zoë Lawton is gathering steam – a new NGO, a first of its kind, which will use technology and free legal advice to pave a less lonely path to justice and accountability for survivors of sexual harm in all its forms. We've called this project Tika, which means 'justice' or 'fairness' in te reo Māori – a beautiful, memorable kupu; we are proud to have permission to use it. With Tika, Zoë and I – and the allies we are gathering every day – have an opportunity to make real change.

The thought wakes me early every morning, full of excitement for the possibilities.

There are plenty of people who just don't get this, who think I'm on some unhinged crusade. One of the most common questions I've been asked in interviews over recent years is, 'What drives you to do this work?' This comes, invariably, from a journalist, and it's a very journalist thing to ask – a member of the public never would, although perhaps they would wonder about it.

I've always answered with a laugh, because the answer is too intense for the asker and for me without the sprinkle of humour as leavening. 'Rage, of course! Rage drives me.' And I give them my biggest television smile.

If it isn't made into a joke, a woman's rage is too uncomfortable for most people to handle. Never mind that we women are angry for good cause – angry at employers who pay us less than they pay men, and for women of colour, less than everyone; angry at the men who hurt and kill the women they are supposed to love and protect, in the places where they ought to be safest. Angry because as children we should have been safe, and the monsters of our night terrors should have existed only in our imaginations; angry because when they turn out to be real, we are scutinised, minimised, called liars, expected to be the perfect victim and to move on, get over it, forgive.

Yes, boys are the targets of ordinary monsters, too – personally and professionally I know this better than most – but boys and men are permitted their anger. As women, we must be A Good Girl.

There are some people who, through lack of imagination, will hear my joke and nod knowingly. 'Ah yes, of course, I suspected it all along,' they will say. 'She does it because she was hurt. It all makes sense now.' The abused child is seeking her own salvation – or maybe her revenge – by making bloody sure the topic of sexual violence never leaves the headlines, that her own story is echoed over and over again in the stories of others, a never-ending refrain. What a neatly tied bow that would be.

And they are right, in a way, but it is not the burn they imagine it is. Outside of my work I'm a Pollyanna: ever-hopeful, largely cheerful – a little bit ditsy even, my partner and my kids would tell you if you asked. But it's true my past impels me, like a jockey taking the whip to his mount in the final furlong. As much as I can, in the time I have left, I do want to help a group of people society would prefer not to hear from: a large group of us – almost a million New Zealanders, police have estimated – who are most often silenced, blamed and dismissed.

There is nothing exceptional about this desire of mine. Almost every survivor I have spoken to in the past six years – and there have been thousands – has the same desire. Sometimes they were abused in childhood and are just, like me, speaking of it for the first time. Some were harmed by a recent or current partner, a friend, their boss, a Tinder date. Some want accountability, some feel that the time for that has passed for them and their situation. For some the pain is raw, and others are many steps along the path to their healing.

But when you ask, they all say the same thing, in almost exactly the same words: 'I just don't want this to happen to anyone else.'

* * *

In the years since our family's secret was first spoken out loud, I have thought a lot about consequences. Whenever I have considered, often with Lisa and Benny, what we might do with what we know, what justice and accountability mean to each of us, and what Mum and Dad deserve or do not deserve, I have made sure to leave space for that. Had things been different – had we been able to give our mum another path, had she wanted to seek that path then, Dad might have faced a more traditional kind of justice.

The truth came too late for that, and Mum resolutely pushed us away, clinging to the only choice her splintering mind would allow. My father remained free only because of her, and they've been granted freedom to live out their last years in exactly the way they so fiercely want. They are there, in their house, and it looks a lot like the thing they want. Only, it's not. Not *exactly*.

My mother wants to be close to her daughters in the way she was until not too many years ago. My father, who put such little effort into winning our love but had it anyway, wants things to go back to the way they were – not before he preyed upon us (that, after all, is way too far back) but to before we called him on it. Before we spoke the truth aloud. Those are his consequences, and although he can pretend he lives as he chooses in his final years, he can't have what he really wants: love, respect, the regard of his family.

I will die with my foolishness and stupidity and selfishness as my final thoughts, his email to me read. Those are consequences not to be lightly dismissed, and even if I wanted to, I could not change them now.

* * *

On The Sisters WhatsApp thread, Sam has suggested we catch up for cocktails. The time zones over three continents are tricky, so while Sam nurses a gin and tonic, and the fairy lights gleam in the dusk of her Manhattan apartment, Lisa and I sip cups of tea in the bright light of day in Melbourne and Auckland. Our three faces in their on-screen squares are so similar and so different all at once, our voices subtly echoing each other, all with the Australian accent underlaid no matter how long we've spent living away.

For once, we don't talk much about Mum and Dad, keeping the chat to lighter topics, filling each other in on the small, ordinary details of our lives, as any sisters might. As we talk, I think about the message Sam, in a pensive moment, sent me about two years back. *I thought I knew what my childhood was*, she wrote. *I don't know how to feel about my family anymore.*

As we finish our drinks and promise to do this again soon, I tell my sisters what I told her then: 'We get to choose, and I choose you both. We are our family now.'

Acknowledgements

This book would never have been written if not for the bond of sisterhood. To Lisa and Sam, for holding me up and never once wavering, I love you both to bits. Until the end of my days I will be in debt to my darling Benny, whose bravery broke through decades of shame and allowed all of us to climb into the light. He is the proof that, from trauma, sometimes, comes extreme beauty; his led him to art, and now his luminous pieces grace the walls of homes across Victoria and beyond (including mine). Whenever I think of that part of his story, I cannot stop myself from grinning with delight.

I'm so fortunate to have landed with the incredible team at HarperCollins. To Holly Hunter, who fixed me with a steely gaze when I told her that writing about myself 'gives me the ick' and told me no male author had ever said such a thing to her. That sorted me out. I'm grateful for her careful stewardship, in tandem with the wonderful Margaret Sinclair and Shannon Kelly. To Kate Goldsworthy, for her sharp eye and firm focus on the reader, as it should be – you were a joy to work with. Thank you, Eva Chan, for your skill in the proofread, and to Michelle Zaiter and Fiona Luke for the beautiful design. And to Sandra Noakes and Holly Hart Jenkins for making the marketing of this project so comfortable – and a little bit exciting!

To Katie, for your enthusiasm and patience, for being my longest-lasting friend, and for sending me all those teenage memories you cleverly saved. And to Gillian for answering questions from that random stranger who invaded her Top End home for the summer holidays all those years ago. Thanks to Peter, for seeing the makings of a television presenter where none existed before, and setting me on the path to a twenty-year television career.

My former journalist colleagues and editorial leaders at *Stuff*, who grasped the importance of survivors' stories when no-one else seemed to, thank you for understanding the stakes and giving your hearts and skills to that project, and to Tracey Spicer for the inspiration. To Jono Milne, Craig Hoyle and Tracy Watkins, for publishing whatever was in my head or heart on a weekly basis.

My deepest thanks to every survivor who came to me with their stories (and still do); even if we weren't able to publish, the trust you showed me has changed me forever. And Zoë Lawton, the person who all along has understood why I do what I do – thank you for trusting me with your vision – Tika will be a game-changer.

Thanks to my TTS crew, Raina and Nikki, for being my bubble of safety and positivity, and not ever getting tired of hearing about this bloody book.

To Paris and Joel, twin lights of my life, what incredible support you've always been. I'm so grateful for you both.

And finally, to Karleen, my greatest love. Simply could not have done it without you.